Subjectivity in ʿAṭṭār, Persian Sufism, and European Mysticism

Comparative Cultural Studies
Ari Ofengenden, Series Editor

The Purdue University Press monograph series of Books in Comparative Cultural Studies publishes single-authored and thematic collected volumes of new scholarship. Manuscripts are invited for publication in the series in fields of the study of culture, literature, the arts, media studies, communication studies, the history of ideas, etc., and related disciplines of the humanities and social sciences to the series editor via e-mail at <clcweb@purdue.edu>. Comparative cultural studies is a contextual approach in the study of culture in a global and intercultural context and work with a plurality of methods and approaches; the theoretical and methodological framework of comparative cultural studies is built on tenets borrowed from the disciplines of cultural studies and comparative literature and from a range of thought including literary and culture theory, (radical) constructivism, communication theories, and systems theories; in comparative cultural studies focus is on theory and method as well as application. For a detailed description of the aims and scope of the series including the style guide of the series link to <http://docs.lib.purdue.edu/clcweblibrary/seriespurdueccs>. Manuscripts submitted to the series are peer reviewed followed by the usual standards of editing, copy editing, marketing, and distribution. The series is affiliated with *CLCWeb: Comparative Literature and Culture* (ISSN 1481-4374), the peer-reviewed, full-text, and open-access quarterly published by Purdue University Press at <http://docs.lib.purdue.edu/clcweb>.

Volumes in the Purdue series of Books in Comparative Cultural Studies include <http://www.thepress.purdue.edu/series/comparative-cultural-studies>

Claudia Yaghoobi, *Subjectivity in ʿAṭṭār, Persian Sufism, and European Mysticism*
Lorna Fitzsimmons, ed. *Faust Adaptations from Marlowe to Aboudoma and Markland*
Regina R. Félix and Scott D. Juall, eds., *Cultural Exchanges between Brazil and France*
James Patrick Wilper, *Reconsidering the Emergence of the Gay Novel in English and German*
Li Guo, *Women's* Tanci *Fiction in Late Imperial and Early Twentieth-Century China*
Arianna Dagnino, *Transcultural Writers and Novels in the Age of Global Mobility*
Elke Sturm-Trigonakis, *Comparative Cultural Studies and the New* Weltliteratur
Lauren Rule Maxwell, *Romantic Revisions in Novels from the Americas*
Liisa Steinby, *Kundera and Modernity*
Text and Image in Modern European Culture, ed. Natasha Grigorian, Thomas Baldwin, and Margaret Rigaud-Drayton
Sheng-mei Ma, *Asian Diaspora and East-West Modernity*
Irene Marques, *Transnational Discourses on Class, Gender, and Cultural Identity*
Comparative Hungarian Cultural Studies, ed. Steven Tötösy de Zepetnek and Louise O. Vasvári
Hui Zou, *A Jesuit Garden in Beijing and Early Modern Chinese Culture*
Yi Zheng, *From Burke and Wordsworth to the Modern Sublime in Chinese Literature*
Agata Anna Lisiak, *Urban Cultures in (Post)Colonial Central Europe*
Representing Humanity in an Age of Terror, ed. Sophia A. McClennen and Henry James Morello
Michael Goddard, *Gombrowicz, Polish Modernism, and the Subversion of Form*
Shakespeare in Hollywood, Asia, and Cyberspace, ed. Alexander C.Y. Huang and Charles S. Ross
Gustav Shpet's Contribution to Philosophy and Cultural Theory, ed. Galin Tihanov
Comparative Central European Holocaust Studies, ed. Louise O. Vasvári and Steven Tötösy de Zepetnek
Marko Juvan, *History and Poetics of Intertextuality*

Subjectivity in ʿAṭṭār, Persian Sufism, and European Mysticism

Claudia Yaghoobi

Purdue University Press
West Lafayette, Indiana

Copyright 2017 by Purdue University. All rights reserved.

Printed in the United States of America.

Cataloging-in-Publication Data on file at the Library of Congress.

Paper ISBN: 9781557537836
ePDF ISBN: 9781612495002
ePUB ISBN: 9781612495019

Cover image: The miniature "Sheikh Ṣan'ān and the Christian Maiden," from 'Aṭṭār's *Conference of the Birds*, inv. no. 34/2006. Photograph by Pernille Klemp. Courtesy of The David Collection, Copenhagen.

To my parents Parkooei Nazari and Avak Yaghoobi,
who always encourage me to venture out and go on adventures,
especially this one

بعد از این وادی عشق آید پدید
غرق آتش شد کسی کانجا رسید
کس درین وادی بجز آتش مباد
وانک آتش نیست عیشش خوش مباد
عاشق آن باشد که چون آتش بود
گرم رو سوزنده و سرکش بود
عاقبت اندیش نبود یک زمان
در کشد خوش خوش بر آتش صد جهان

—عطار، منطق الطیر "بیان وادی عشق"

Love's valley is the next, and here desire
Will plunge the pilgrim into seas of fire,
Until his very being is enflamed
And those whom fire rejects turn back ashamed.
The lover is a man who flares and burns,
Whose face is fevered, who in frenzy yearns,
Who knows no prudence, who will gladly send
A hundred worlds toward their blazing end . . .

—ʿAṭṭār, *Manṭiq al-ṭayr* (*Conference of the Birds*), "The Valley of Love"

Contents

Acknowledgments ix

Note on Transliteration, Dates, and Translation xi

Introduction 1

Chapter 1
Sufism, ʿAṭṭār, and His Works 15

Chapter 2
Modern Theory, Michel Foucault, and His Predecessors 31

Chapter 3
Rābiʿa al-ʿAdawiyya and Margery Kempe 45

Chapter 4
Maḥmūd and Ayāz, Sufi Homoeroticism, and European Same-Sex Relationships 71

Chapter 5
Majnūn and Lailā, and Lancelot and Guinevere 95

Chapter 6
Shaykh Ṣanʿān and the Christian Girl, and Abelard and Heloise 123

Conclusion
Human Diversity and Inclusiveness 151

Works Cited 161

Author's Profile 185

Index 187

Acknowledgments

This book would not have been possible without the comments, feedback, guidance, and help of several individuals who in one way or another extended their valuable assistance in the preparation and completion of this study. First and foremost, I am heartily thankful to Dwight Reynolds for his breadth of knowledge and unfailing support. His remarkable comments have no doubt led to a better text than I could have ever produced on my own. I would like to express my deepest gratitude to Janet Afary, whose encouragement, guidance, and support from the initial to the final stages of this project enabled me to develop a thorough understanding of the subject in its historical context. Thanks are also due to Aranye Fradenburg for her guidance and valuable insights. Without her suggestions on European literature and literary theory, this book would not have the nuanced aspects it embodies now. A special word of gratitude is due to Nasrin Rahimieh, whose suggestions and recommendations regarding literary analysis and Persian literature have been invaluable for the project. Special thanks should be given to Sara Lindheim, Susan Derwin, and Catherin Nesci, Mireille Miller-Young, Elisabeth Weber, Barbara Tomlinson, and Heather Blurton. I would also like to thank my colleagues and friends, Rolando Longoria, Morteza Lak, Maryam Moqaddam, Matthew Thomas Miller, and Amir Khadem, who carefully read chapters of my work and provided insight and expertise. I offer my regards to the Purdue University Press director, editorial board, external reviewers, and administrative staff. Finally, words alone cannot express the thanks I owe to my family for their never-ending encouragement and moral support. This is how the project was born out of love.

I would like to thank the University of North Carolina for the University Research Council Publication Grant, which covered copyediting, indexing, and copyright expenses for this book. My early research on this topic was funded by a Regents Internship-Fellowship for Research (2012) through the Comparative Literature program at the University of California at Santa Barbara. My gratitude is due to the Iranian Studies Initiative at the University of California at Santa Barbara for a generous funding from a Mellichamp Research Fellowship in 2010.

In this book, I read ʿAṭṭār's works, European literature, and modern theory alongside each other; that is, I undertake a contrapuntal reading of works that are modern and medieval, literature and theory, and Middle Eastern and European. In that sense, this book is based on an interdisciplinary approach to literature, and benefits from a comparative cross-cultural, cross-historical, and cross-disciplinary perspective. Throughout, I illustrate the interdependence of literature and theory from different times and places in regard to our understanding of the concepts of transgression and the limit, and how crossing boundaries can lead to the construction of subjectivity.

Earlier parts of this book have been published. Excerpts from the book titled, "Against the Current: Farīd al-Dīn ʿAṭṭār's Diverse Voices," have been published in *Persian Literary Studies Journal* and awarded The Jafar and Shokoh Farzaneh Paper Prize in Persian Literature and Culture. The same article, under the title, "Hamzisti dar Asar-e ʿAṭṭār" (Co-existence in 'Attar's Works), has also been translated into Persian in *Rahavard Persian/English Journal of Iranian Studies*. Excerpts from chapter 3 have also been published in *Persian Literary Studies Journal* under the title, "Sexual Trauma and Spiritual Experience: Rābiʿa al-ʿAdawiyya and Margery Kempe." Excerpts from chapter 5 in the form of an article titled, "Subjectivity in ʿAṭṭār's Shaykh Ṣanʿān Story in *The Conference of the Birds*," have been published online on *CLCWeb: Comparative Literature and Culture*.

Note on Transliteration, Dates, and Translation

The *International Journal of Middle East Studies* (*IJMES*) pronunciation-based Persian and Arabic transliteration system has been used. The following is a guide to the *IJMES* transliteration system. For Persian proper names and words which have been adopted in European languages, I have used the most commonly used transcription rather than the *IJMES* transliteration. Most Arabic and Persian names from the classical period have been transliterated, but contemporary ones have not. All citations are indicated in the text by the edited work followed by the translation into English. All translations, summaries, and paraphrases of the Persian secondary sources and ʿAṭṭār's *Muṣībat-nāma* are the author's. Dates are based on the Gregorian calendar. Book and article titles have been transliterated for consistency, but original titles are used in the bibliography.

IJMES Transliteration System for Arabic and Persian

Consonants

A = Arabic, P = Persian

	A	P		A	P		A	P
ء	ʾ	ʾ	ز	z	z	ک	k	k or g
ب	b	b	ژ	---	zh	گ	---	g
پ	---	p	س	s	s	ل	l	l
ت	t	t	ش	sh	sh	م	m	m
ث	th	s̱	ص	ṣ	ṣ	ن	n	n
ج	j	j	ض	ḍ	ż	ه	h	h
چ	---	ch	ط	ṭ	ṭ	و	w	v or u
ح	ḥ	ḥ	ظ	ẓ	ẓ	ی	y	y
خ	kh	kh	ع	ʿ	ʿ	ة	a*	
د	d	d	غ	gh	gh	ال	**	
ذ	dh	ẕ	ف	f	f			
ر	r	r	ق	q	q			

*In construct state: at. **For the article, al- and –l-.

Vowels

Long	ا or ىا	ā
	و	ū
	ي	ī
Doubled	ِيّ	iyy (final form ī)
	ُوّ	uww (final form ū)
Diphthongs	َو	au *or* aw
	َى	ai *or* ay
Short	َ	a
	ُ	u
	ِ	i

Introduction

In the wake of modern discourses about human diversity, exclusion and inclusion, self and the other, scholars of medieval Middle Eastern studies, such as myself, tend to think of racial, sexual, religious, social, and other minorities in the medieval period, and ponder whether medieval minority populations, including transgressors and deviators, were embraced and integrated fully in their societies or communities. When we think of transgression, the first things that come to mind are a movement towards and beyond the limit and an individual who is pushed towards that limit, after which new limits unfold. Transgression allows individuals to push the boundaries and transcend the framework of their limited minds, and in doing so, they are enabled to undo the structures that have produced constraining binaries, such as exclusion and inclusion, and the self and the other, in their minds. The rewriting of such established binary narratives in turn leads to a multitude of alternatives and possibilities of human forms, lifestyles, and ways of loving.

In the postmodern theoretical discourses, the concepts of transgression and the limit have been central to the works of Friedrich Nietzsche, the Marquis de Sade, Georges Bataille, and Michel Foucault, to name a few. In their works, which portray a secular world, sexuality has become the site for the construction of knowledge and power, and transgression and the limit have replaced the traditional sacred and profane binary. Although the centrality of sexuality in the construction of power and knowledge might have been new in the post-Enlightenment era, the concept of transgression itself was not new; its roots can be traced back to the biblical story of Adam and his transgression of the sacred limit, which led to Adam's acquisition of knowledge. As a medievalist who constantly engages with these modern theoretical concepts, too, I propose that we can detect similar or at times even more subversive acts, leading to inclusiveness, in the works of the medieval Persian Sufi poet Farīd al-Dīn ʿAṭṭār Nishāpūrī (1145/46-1221). In the meantime, I would like to suggest that the medieval period itself was a more egalitarian one than the era we live in. Thus, in this book, I also draw on European literature to present a further nuanced and comparative look into the medieval period. Then, I create a bridge between the medieval and the modern, literature and theory, and Middle Eastern and European literatures and cultures. In his "Sufi Symbolism in the Persian Hermeneutic

Tradition: Reconstructing the Pagoda of ʿAṭṭār's Esoteric Poetics," Leonard Lewisohn aptly remarks that "ʿAṭṭār is distinguished in the Persian-speaking Muslim world for his radical and subversive theology of love, expressed in poetic aphorisms often cited independently of their poems and read as maxims in their own right" (255). As Lewisohn points out, ʿAṭṭār's works are precious for his "subversive theology of love." What this indicates is that ʿAṭṭār's spirituality is of course radical, but it is the element of unconventional love which makes it even more subversive. ʿAṭṭār's radical spirituality, his love of the divine, and love of God's creations allow him to integrate elements of subversion in his works. ʿAṭṭār creates characters with liminal experiences, which can hardly be found in modern works. These are thought-provoking concepts, given the time in which he was writing. His use of the theme of transgressive love and his inclusion of marginalized members of society, social pariahs, and transgressors as earthly manifestations of divine love and beauty, which will be examined in this book, is particularly noteworthy in regard to their construction of subjectivity, also central to European literature and modern theory.

While ʿAṭṭār calls into question the issues of transgression and the limit, self and the other, human diversity, and inclusiveness of minorities within one nation in the medieval period, we still witness similar (or worse) treatment of minorities in our modern world. Centuries after ʿAṭṭār advocated inclusiveness through breaking the law and transcending the constructed boundaries of one's mind in his poetry, scholars still find that there is a need to question the assumptions that shape our thinking and challenge the binaries of the self and the other. We should realize that these worldly set boundaries and paradigms are artificial and based on our misguided perception, whereby the self defines whatever is alien as other. Of course, this is not to say that we should erase the differences between the self and the other, but to encourage acceptance of the differences. This is what medieval poets such as ʿAṭṭār ventured to do long ago, and our modern theorists continue to foster. It would therefore be interesting to read ʿAṭṭār's poetry contrapuntally with modern theory and European literature to see whether medieval literature can shed further light on these modern concepts, and whether modern theory can help us better understand medieval subjectivities.

In this type of reading, I have in mind Edward Said's well-known suggestion of the contrapuntal reading of exilic poetry and exiled subjects by taking into consideration both the colonized and the colonizer. By looking at ʿAṭṭār's poetry contrapuntally with medieval European literature and modern theory, I intend to trace the intertwined histories and perspectives. In this way, I attempt to take into account the different perspectives, cultures, and histories simultaneously, and map out the ways ʿAṭṭār's poetry interacts with itself within the Persian cultural and historical framework as well as with medieval European culture and modern Western theoretical perspectives in regard to the concepts of transgression and the breaking of taboos, and the construction of subjectivity. Since what has not been said is as important as what has been voiced, this contrapuntal reading necessitates a vision in which literature and theory, medieval and modern, Western and Middle Eastern cultures are viewed simultaneously. The research on ʿAṭṭār's understanding of the violation of the worldly constructed laws, the construction of liminality, and the embracement of human diversity, although not entirely neglected, has been limited in some respects. The reasons for ʿAṭṭār's incorporation of unconventional love narratives and marginalized members of society, while briefly mentioned in a handful of studies, have yet to be examined in a book-length project. What is even more crucial to look at is ʿAṭṭār's use of the concepts of transgression and the limit for the construction of subjectivity. Positioning ʿAṭṭār in the medieval world makes it essential to read him alongside medieval European authors. It is therefore important to initiate a conversation between ʿAṭṭār (and his ideology), the medieval European writers, and modern theorists such as Foucault, regarding these concepts to address some of the following questions in this book: Why does ʿAṭṭār choose such unconventional love stories to portray divine love and beauty? What does ʿAṭṭār's attention to societal outcasts tell us about him, his spirituality, and his writings? What does he try to do with these outcasts, some of whom are familiar character types in Persian literature? What is he trying to achieve through these familiar lawbreakers? How does ʿAṭṭār's integration of such profane love narratives and liminal experiences contribute to a better understanding both of contemporaneous literature and of Sufism and medieval Persian culture in general? What would ʿAṭṭār's characters tell us if we looked at them alongside medieval European literature and modern theory? Is modern theory relevant to medieval culture? Can exploration of subjectivity in medieval literature shed light on our understanding of subjectivity in the modern world and vice versa? This book is an attempt to answer these questions.

However, while asking these questions and trying to answer them in the suggested way, I do not intend to fall into the trap of what H. Porter Abbott calls "reductionism." Abbott argues that when "[humanists] make arguments, of whatever analytic or interpretive stripe," they stereotype and reduce people to categories. He rationalizes this argument, saying, "Our brains aren't big enough to do otherwise" (216). On the other hand, Abbott also writes:

> In our efforts to understand the world and to communicate that understanding, we are fated by our neuronal equipment to endless approximation. Therefore, plurality and diversity abet our constant efforts to approach the world with this imperfect equipment and to tell ourselves what we have found. On the other hand the behavior that flows in the wake of these novel understandings has a chance, at least, of being adaptive. Multiple constructions open up multiple possibilities for action. So here we have a general cognitive and evolutionary explanatory framework to account for novelty both in art and the interpretation of it—that is, forms of thinking, communication, and conduct that are necessarily unpredictable and potentially infinite. (209)

Although, in Abbott's words, humanists tend to stereotype and approximate people and characters, it is always possible to adapt diverse interpretations resulting from reduction and approximation so as to attain a novel understanding of art, which must also be applicable to literature. My interest here lies in reaching a novel understanding of ʿAṭṭār's works and proposing various possible ways of interpreting them. Although "controlling the interpretation of literature is a mode of cultural replication that goes on in academic research all the time," we as literary scholars face "novelties that we never expected to find in our interactions with texts" (Abbott 214). In my interaction with ʿAṭṭār's works, I encountered these kinds of unexpected novelties. It is within this context, novel to the previous scholarship, that I contribute my study of ʿAṭṭār's tendency of pushing the limits and being inclusive in order to aid the construction of subjectivity. I introduce a new approach by reading modern theory, medieval Persian works, and European works alongside one another, and encouraging explorations of new possibilities which can dismantle established narratives of our present experience and (mis)perceptions not only about infringement of the law, human diversity, and integration of minorities, but also about our understanding of medieval subjectivities as well as modern theory.

My research on ʿAṭṭār's works owes tremendously to the previous scholarship that has investigated his writings largely in the context of medieval Middle Eastern culture, Sufi tradition, and a philological framework, and oftentimes in a comparative context with European literature and theory as well. The studies I am referring to include Hellmut Ritter's classical work *The Ocean of The Soul*, Lewisohn's study of ʿAṭṭār's esoteric poetics in "Sufi Symbolism in the Persian Hermeneutic Tradition: Reconstructing the Pagoda of ʿAṭṭār's Esoteric Poetics," Franklin Lewis's analysis of the politics of conversion and Christian love in "Sexual Occidentation: The Politics of Conversion, Christian-Love and Boy-Love in ʿAṭṭār," and Fatemeh Keshavarz's discussion of the nature of poetic logic in ʿAṭṭār's *Manṭiq al-ṭayr* (*Conference of the Birds*) in "Flight of the Birds: The Poetic Animating the Spiritual in ʿAṭṭtār's *Manṭiq al-ṭayr*," to name but a few. Of course, there have also been a few works on Sufism engaging with modern theoretical perspectives—to which I owe my approach—such as Michael Sells and James Webb's discussion of the affinities between the Lacanian "real" and mystical language in "Lacan and Bion," Ian Almond's comparative study of Derrida and Ibn ʿArabī in *Sufism and Deconstruction*, and Mahdi Touraj's analysis of Rūmī's bawdy tales using Lacanian psychoanalysis in *Rūmī and the Hermeneutics of Eroticism*. However, research that reads ʿAṭṭār's works contrapuntally with medieval European literature and modern theory in regard to the notions of transgression and the law, human diversity, inclusiveness, and the construction of subjectivity has been limited.

Given that these concepts are in the spotlight today, it is essential for scholars of medieval studies to investigate whether modern insights and theoretical notions can help us better understand medieval works such as ʿAṭṭār's, or whether their application should be limited to the scholarship concerned with contemporary issues. It is also equally important to explore the possibility of medieval works such as ʿAṭṭār's shedding light on our understanding of these modern concepts, which have occupied the minds of modern theorists for so long. Without such an analysis we will be left with an inadequate understanding of both medieval and modern cultures and literatures. This book endeavors to remedy this gap in the literary criticism on ʿAṭṭār's works by examining the ways in which modern theoretical notions interact with ʿAṭṭār's writings and medieval European writings, and vice versa. In pursuing this argument, I will draw on cross-cultural and cross-historical interactions between ʿAṭṭār's ideology, European literature, and modern theory such as Foucault's in regard to their understanding of these concepts. Although I will trace the roots of the concept of transgression back to the works of Sade, Nietzsche, and Bataille, on whose works Foucault built his, I will also briefly refer to other modern thinkers such as Emmanuel Lévinas, Jacques Lacan, Julia Kristeva, and Judith Butler in regard to their suggestions about the self and the other, and the construction of subjectivity, in various chapters. I choose to focus mainly on Foucault's notion of transgression and summon him into conversation with ʿAṭṭār because Foucauldian notions of the self and the other, boundary crossing, and the spiral movement between the proper and the improper have produced much of our contemporary cultural theory that is preoccupied with the concept of "difference" in regard to class, gender, race, ethnicity, and sexuality. Foucault's notion of transgression, which introduces the relationship between the individual and social subject, has become important to all areas of cultural theory, including anthropology, history, sociology, philosophy, and literature. His understanding of transgression has become an important concept for interpreting how liminal or minority experiences help to form larger social and cultural boundaries. Insofar as this book is concerned with the liminal experiences of sexual, social, cultural, and religious transgressors and their shaping of subjectivity in medieval European and Persian literatures, particularly in ʿAṭṭār's poetry, and because Foucault's understanding of violation of the law sums up the modern theoretical perspectives on these notions, it would be appropriate to invite Foucault and ʿAṭṭār to have a conversation with each other, and read their works alongside European literature for this study.

However, since works on transgression occupy the landscape of premodern Persian poetry, and ʿAṭṭār's poetry is no exception, it is equally important to ask: Why ʿAṭṭār, and what can we learn from ʿAṭṭār's particular kind of transgression? I suggest that the writings of ʿAṭṭār stand out due to his unique understanding of love in Sufism, and the way Sufis illuminate the path of love through the art of storytelling. Furthermore, due to this love, those who violate the law in order to shape their subjectivity and emerge as new individuals are fully accepted in his poetry. None of ʿAṭṭār's predecessors came near his straightforward and lucid storytelling technique. Although his narratives are mostly symbolic and allegorical, they can be easily understood even by a layperson because of the familiar subjects and characters he tends to employ. Those acquainted with Sufi principles can learn the lessons of morality and humanity that ʿAṭṭār strives to convey in his stories. Those not familiar with Sufi thought may simply enjoy the plain subjects and commonplace characters of these stories (see Bayat and Jamnia 49). Although ʿAṭṭār's characters, such as Maḥmūd, Ayāz, Majnūn, and Lailā, are types that can be found in earlier classical Arabic and Persian literature, ʿAṭṭār's achievements lie in his adding fine nuances which introduce infringing yet acceptable approaches to the dominant tradition. My reading of ʿAṭṭār's works suggests that his poetry is an attempt to remove the barriers that denote exclusion. In his poetry, ʿAṭṭār recognizes people's equality and interdependence in the face of their differences. Hence, ʿAṭṭār portrays his true surrender and submission to the divine as a Sufi by accepting and embracing human diversity. Accepting and recognizing the diversity of God's creations rather than shoring up sociocultural boundaries characterize ʿAṭṭār's way of loving divinity. ʿAṭṭār's love of the divinity and humanity allows him to create empowered characters who are able to cross social, moral, ethical, class, gender, and sexual boundaries, to de- and reconstruct their identities through the annihilation of the self and union with the societal other and the divine other. ʿAṭṭār's outcasts and peripheral characters are worth studying because they are complex and interesting, and this comes out in the subtle choice of words and actions that ʿAṭṭār ascribes to these characters.

My fascination with integrating medieval and modern concepts is not unique. Foucault has already done so, as can be maintained by the following remark where he speaks about the blending of the past and the present in his method of analysis: "I set out from a problem expressed in current terms today, and I try to work out its genealogy. Genealogy means that I begin my analysis from a question posed in the present" ("The Concern for Truth" 262). Similarly, this method is apparent in *Discipline and Punish*, where Foucault contemplates his reason for being interested in obsolete systems and periods: "[Is it] [s]imply because I am interested in the past? No, if one means by that writing a history of the past in terms of the present. Yes, if one means writing a history of the present" (31). What Foucault has done is exactly what I set out to do in this book. My interest in the past lies in the fact that medieval works such as ʿAṭṭār's are not mere historical texts, but living texts that can reveal as much about our present selves as they do about the past. Hence, I begin with the concept of transgression and the limit that occupies the minds of many modern scholars, and trace its genealogy back to the past via literature.

Regarding this intertwinement of the past and the present, Aranye Fradenburg argues likewise in *Sacrifice Your Love*: "We are creatures not only of our time, but also of our highly particular histories—our families, their families, the other families they know, and our phantasmic transformations of them into memories, ideals, expectations, disappointments, responsibilities, and utopian desires" (48). It is true that this challenges the established and definitive view of temporality, where all events occur in their proper time order. However, as Fradenburg argues,

> "Becoming medieval" does not require complete identification with the past; for one thing, that is impossible, and for another thing, even if we could do it, we would not be "becoming." Sometimes we should approach medieval texts with critical languages that differ from those their authors, even their audiences, might have approved. We cannot confine the work of knowing the Middle Ages to replicating, however hopelessly and/or heroically, medieval cultures' self-understanding. We also should explore how medieval cultures, like all others, may have misunderstood themselves. (77–78)

Therefore, the medieval period cannot be limited to the past, for it plays a major role in shaping our present world and us as scholars of medieval studies. Congruently, our present, along with its modern perceptions, is equally significant for perceiving the medieval period as it was and as it could have been. This interplay between stories of different periods has the potential to embody the relation between history, theory, and literature.

By pursuing the genealogy of these concepts I hope to illustrate that explorations of medieval subjectivity can contribute to understanding subjectivity in our modern world and vice versa. My purpose is not to construct a new truth, but rather to dismantle the narratives, concepts, ideas, and truths that constitute our present experience and (mis)perceptions regarding the study of medieval texts and our understanding of modern concepts. I do so through an examination of literature because literature (and generally art), be it medieval or modern, reflects an image of the real. As Plato formulated it, art mirrors our own world and makes it seem familiar yet foreign. It produces a copy of what already exists in the real world even though that copy might be imaginary. However, it produces an image of the real that competes with the idea of the real, for, as Lacan puts it, "The picture does not compete with appearance; it competes with what Plato designates for us beyond appearance as being the Idea" (*Four Fundamental Concepts* 112). It is at this moment that the distinction between the symbolic and imaginary aspects of literature comes into play and encourages us to question what is beyond the sociocultural imaginary, the truth. As Lacan would argue, it allows us to look behind the veil.

Hence, in reading ʿAṭṭār's poetry alongside European literature and modern theory, I set out to trace the intersections of transgression, law, inclusion and exclusion, self and the other, and the construction of subjectivity in ʿAṭṭār's treatment of class, gender, sexuality, and religion. The aim in doing so is to reassesses the significance of the concept of transgression and the construction of subjectivity within select works of ʿAṭṭār. While other scholars have investigated ʿAṭṭār's poetry from within the confines of a critical analysis of the Sufi tradition, my research creates a bridge between medieval Sufi poetry, medieval European literature, and modern theory. Transgression is central to ʿAṭṭār's treatment of enlightenment with regard to class, gender, and sexuality. I contend that the way ʿAṭṭār frames the concepts of transgression, construction of subjectivity, and inclusiveness in his poetry can be brought into conversation with medieval European literature and modern theory. In my study, the relation between transgression and the law is not one of liberation from oppressive restrictions, but of undoing the structures that produce constraining binaries. In this book, the law is not viewed as a limiting force, but one that allows alternatives. In my analysis, transgression, as a force, undermines the law, violating what is normative, necessitating acceptance, encouraging openness, and producing possibilities for the construction of a variety of subjectivities. My comparative inquiries into ʿAṭṭār's poetry and modern theory can help intensify our understanding of the notions of transgression and construction of subjectivity advanced in both the medieval and the modern world. This comparative analysis is of course only possible through the study of these cultures, individually and interdependently, in the medieval and the modern period.

One of the most significant concepts discussed in this book is the transformative power of love, which has long been at the center of Islamic Sufism. ʿAṭṭār's use of the theme of transgressive love as he portrays society's marginalized pariahs, outcasts, and untouchables is particularly noteworthy because it shows how he frames the concepts of the construction of subjectivity and inclusiveness within the notion of human diversity. I examine four love stories that ʿAṭṭār used in his writings to comment on these concepts. I chose love stories because love is a key concept in ʿAṭṭār's spirituality, and it is through love that he invites his readers to transcendence. I look at the ways in which ʿAṭṭār engages with the underrepresented members of society and the social pariahs in his works through rewriting the established scripts, illustrating his love of both divinity and humanity. By placing modern theory and European literature alongside ʿAṭṭār's works, this book not only explores the reasons for ʿAṭṭār's inclusion of transgressors and peripheral characters in his works, but it also places the intertwined cross-cultural and cross-historical interactions of modern literary theory and medieval literary works into perspective for readers, questioning and challenging our understanding of subjectivity. After all, it is arguable that literature as an expression of human experience precedes theoretical articulations.

The European perspective adds further nuanced analysis to the book; however, I acknowledge that the works under comparative analysis in each chapter do not belong to the same traditions, genres, or even periods sometimes. I have tried to examine European works of mystical literature which correspond most closely with ʿAṭṭār's works regarding the concepts under analysis in this book. What I am interested in here is the similarity within the concepts of transgression of the law and inclusiveness in various cultures and regions of the world which help shape new subjectivities. In addition, since the concepts of gender, class, sexuality, religion, diversity, and inclusiveness cannot be used universally over time and place, I articulate my conceptualization of these terms in the context of the medieval Middle East and Europe separately in each chapter. Depending on the extent of information for each concept, this conceptualization is placed at times under a separate subheading, at other times, under one subheading.

In short, this book exemplifies the main tenets of comparative literature and cultural studies. While primarily focused on the study of Persian culture and literature, it also explores the relationship between literary knowledge production and Iranian history. It examines the works of the renowned medieval Persian poet ʿAṭṭār and addresses the significance of their production, distribution, reception, and dissemination. Adopting an empirical and systematic approach, this interdisciplinary study of ʿAṭṭār opens up a new space of comparison for reading and understanding medieval Persian and European literatures.

Traversing linguistic, national, and disciplinary boundaries, this book calls into question the presumed differences between medieval Islam and the West and makes possible a rich dialogue between civilizations that have historically been pitted against one another. I invite the readers on an intellectual journey that reveals exciting intersections that redefine the hierarchies and terms of comparison. In Steven Tötösy de Zepetnek's words, this book therefore works "against the stream by promoting comparative cultural studies as a global, inclusive, and multi-disciplinary framework in inter- and supra-national humanities" (3).

In chapter 1, "Sufism, ʿAṭṭār, and His Works," I trace the historical background of Islamic Sufism and its development back to the Quran, the Prophet Muḥammad's life and sayings, and to the sociopolitical conditions of the period. In many regions of the Near and Middle East, Islam grew within the predominantly Christian environment. The early Muslims had close social and intellectual contacts with their Christian neighbors and were directly influenced by the teachings of Christian mystics. Thus, I also discuss Christian mysticism, Christian saints, and their interaction with the Muslim societies that produced numerous literary, philosophical, and religious texts. Then, I briefly cover ʿAṭṭār's life, spirituality, and his works. I discuss the fact that ʿAṭṭār lived in Persia during the Seljuk Empire (1077–1307), a period of constant wars and battles, eroded ethical principles, social corruption, and economic crisis. This was a time when taverns spread across the region, and most of ʿAṭṭār's characters are drawn from people who frequented these taverns. I review Sufism and its emphasis on love, which is significant for understanding ʿAṭṭār's works. I particularly examine the correlation between earthly and heavenly love in Islamic Sufism: for Sufis, the love of every created object elevates the individual spiritually, bringing him or her closer to the love of God and beatific vision. Beginning with Plato's ideology, and its later emergence in the Muslim world, I explore the idea of the *ephebe* (the beautiful human being), which was used by Neoplatonists as well as by medieval Persian writers via the concept of *ʿishq* (profane love). *ʿIshq* and its derivatives were frequently used in classical Persian prose and poetry, and were how Sufis proceeded to contemplate divine beauty and love as manifested in human form and human (i.e., profane) love. This manifestation of love can be found in the writings of ʿAṭṭār and also in Aḥmad al-Ghazzālī (1061–1123), ʿAyn al-Quḍāt al-Hamadānī (967–1007), and Jalāl al-Dīn Rūmī (1207–1273), to name a few. In regard to ʿAṭṭār's specific interest in love mysticism, I refer to the influence of the Sufi Manṣūr al-Ḥallāj (858–922) on him, and the various anecdotes available about ʿAṭṭār's initiation into Sufism. The focus of the book is on ʿAṭṭār's three lyrical poems *Ilāhī-nāma* (*The Book of God*), *Muṣībat-nāma* (*The Book of Suffering*), and *Manṭiq al-ṭayr* (*Conference of the Birds*), along with his prose work *Tadhkirat al-awlīyā* (*Memoirs of the Saints*). In each one, I examine the ways ʿAṭṭār establishes correspondences between the divine and the human realm through his love narratives and analogies, incorporating unconventional lovers, transgressors, and marginalized members of the society as rightful lovers of the divine. I illustrate how transgressing the constructed barriers of one's mind and crossing conventional boundaries allow individuals to de- and reconstruct their identities, annihilate the ego, and (re)discover the divine through earthly love.

In chapter 2, "Modern Theory, Michel Foucault, and His Predecessors," I try to map out the genealogy of literary theory in regard to the concepts of transgression, the limit, and the construction of subjectivity. Although the overarching theory with which I am concerned in this book is Foucault's ideas of transgression of taboos and the consequent shaping of the self, since he was influenced by a number of other theorists before him, I delineate the development of these notions as well. I explore the theoretical discourses of Nietzsche, Sade, and Bataille, for whom the concepts of transgression and the limit have been central. I discuss how in their works, depicting a secular world, sexuality becomes the site of knowledge and power construction, and the traditional sacred-profane binary is replaced by transgression and the limit. Then, I invite modern literary theory into a conversation with ʿAṭṭār and explicate it in detail. Through reading ʿAṭṭār, medieval European literature, and modern theory, largely Foucault, I posit that through the breaking of taboos, the subjects under analysis in these literary works as well as the ones concerned in the theoretical texts transcend the barriers of their minds and emerge as new selves.

In chapter 3, "Rābiʿa al-ʿAdawiyya and Margery Kempe," focusing on ʿAṭṭār's *Tadhkirat al-awlīyā*, I discuss ʿAṭṭār's portrayal of an early female Sufi, Rābiʿa al-ʿAdawiyya (717–801), who transgressed gender boundaries. I show that contrary to the common view of Muslim women as subservient and passive, Rābiʿa is portrayed as challenging the established gender norms of her day in ʿAṭṭār's work. Rābiʿa's crossing of gender boundaries and her mysticism as portrayed in ʿAṭṭār's works can be seen both as defense mechanisms against her experiences of exploitation and as necessary steps to transcend the limits of her gender and feminine sexuality in order to reach the type of liberation that she so longed for. In order to elucidate issues of gender transgression, I draw parallels between her life and spirituality and the life and spirituality of her Christian counterpart, the English female mystic Margery Kempe (1373–1438). Margery is known for writing *The Book of Margery Kempe*, and her spiritual career begins after her traumatic experience of childbirth and her abject feelings about femininity and motherhood. Through her spirituality, Margery, like Rābiʿa, crosses the gender boundaries of her time and reshapes her identity to re-enter the world as a new self. Both Rābiʿa and Margery turn to divine love as a way to reconstruct their identities through the (re)discovery of and union with the divine. In addition to the analysis of Rābiʿa's and Margery's gender transgression, this chapter also argues that Rābiʿa and Margery owe their popularity to their male authors and scribes, respectively, who helped their texts travel through time and space. Indeed, despite their efforts, Rābiʿa and Margery both needed the acknowledgement of their contemporary male spirituals for the written transmission of their mystical experiences. In so doing, these male authors and scribes, including ʿAṭṭār, showed their acceptance of gender transgression and proved themselves as true mystics by embracing gender equality.

In chapter 4, "Maḥmūd and Ayāz, Sufi Homoeroticism, and European Same-Sex Relationships," I examine the poems that ʿAṭṭār wrote about the relationship between Sultan Maḥmūd of Ghazna (r. 998–1030) and his slave Malik Ayāz, which violated the sexual boundaries of the day. I examine their same-sex love narratives in reference to the philosophy of *shāhidbāzī* or *naẓarbāzī* (gazing at beardless adolescent boys) in Sufism, which conflated the contemplation of the beauty of adolescent boys with the contemplation of the beauty of the divine. Maḥmūd and Ayāz's relationship broke the rules and codes of the philosophy according to which such relationships were commonly practiced in confraternity communities, particularly in mystical initiations, and were expected to exist and be practiced merely for the love of God. In ʿAṭṭār's narratives, Sultan Maḥmūd's relationship with Ayāz's did not take place in a confraternity or in a mystical context, nor did it target God's love. In addition, the relationship is portrayed by ʿAṭṭār as sexually charged, reciprocated by the object of affection, indiscreet, and unusual in the sense that the beloved is an adult man rather than an adolescent boy. I argue that by not conforming to the standards of the philosophy, Maḥmūd and Ayāz violate the sexual and class boundaries of their day. By presenting their narrative, ʿAṭṭār challenges the contemporaneous gender and class hierarchies. In the meantime, I also initiate a conversation between modern theory and ʿAṭṭār's works regarding the acceptance of sexual transgressors, the violation of laws, and the construction of subjectivity. I closely read passages from Foucault alongside ʿAṭṭār's and create a dialogue between them to indicate that deviating from gender and sexual norms, forming subjectivity, and embracing the other are issues, which are still being discussed, in our modern times. I also believe that an exploration of ʿAṭṭār's acceptance of diverse human forms helps us to understand these critical concepts better. However, I acknowledge the differences between ʿAṭṭār's understanding of these concepts and Foucault's interpretation of them, which speaks about our understanding of modern subjectivity. To put this relationship into perspective, I also refer to a similar trend of same-sex desire in medieval Europe which was particularly common among high-ranking clerics and left a respectable body of literature dating from the eleventh and twelfth centuries; I discuss the possible Muslim-Christian interaction at that time with regard to this trend. My contrapuntal readings of ʿAṭṭār's works, European literature, and Foucault's ideas help us further understand medieval and modern subjectivities alongside each other, and illustrate that transgression of the laws that our minds have constructed can lead to transcendence of the worldly constructed paradigms and help us emerge as new subjects.

In chapter 5, "Majnūn and Lailā, and Lancelot and Guinevere," I examine the story of Majnūn's (known as "madman") excessive love for Lailā and his crossing of social boundaries. I first explore the background to the story and the multiple narrative lines which exist in Arabic and Persian literatures. I discuss several of the medieval Muslim writers' condemnation of love madness. Then, I look at ʿAṭṭār's poems and examine Majnūn's idealization of Lailā's beauty, his violation of social laws, and his consequent marginalization. I study the transformative power of love and how it leads the individual to union with both the earthly beloved and the heavenly Beloved. ʿAṭṭār's narratives of Majnūn and Lailā's love story illustrate that their love was adjudged to be forbidden not only because it was excessive and regarded as love madness, but also because it violated the traditional Islamic right of fathers or guardians to decide on the marriage of their children. Majnūn's obsessive behavior brought shame and dishonor to Lailā and her family. His constant visits to Lailā's home and his recital of love poems to her were the ways in which he publicly displayed his emotions for her. Such a public declaration of love went against the conventions of arranged marriages in the Islamic culture. Majnūn is portrayed as roaming the desert, living with animals, and being improperly clothed, all of which point to his rejection of familial and social ties. I argue that by including Majnūn's love story in his works, ʿAṭṭār shows his acceptance of this social pariah and undermines the established norms of his day in order to encourage openness to alternative ways of love. However, ʿAṭṭār regards Majnūn's love for Lailā as a threshold upon which divine love is found. Because Majnūn's love madness was comparable to the Sufis' moments of rapture, his story entered mystical works, including ʿAṭṭār's poetry. The demented lover, Majnūn, who contemplates Lailā constantly, becomes the model for transgressing the limits and transcending the earthly constructed paradigms of arranged marriages and expressions of love through Sufi love. Majnūn's subversive love of Lailā allows him to deconstruct and reconstruct his self and emerge as a new individual in full union with the divine. Again, in this chapter I engage modern theory and bring it into conversation with ʿAṭṭār to show that ʿAṭṭār's acceptance of social outcasts in the medieval period can help us to learn about modern subjectivity through reading literary texts as live entities rather than mere historical texts. In this chapter I also refer to the medieval European tale of courtly love *The Romance of Lancelot and Guinevere*. I discuss their adulterous relationship and consider the commonalities between this romance and that of Majnūn and Lailā with respect to subversive love, transgressing social barriers, and emerging as new subjects. Looking at ʿAṭṭār's invitation of his characters to transcend the constructed sociocultural barriers of their minds, I place him alongside modern theory and European literature, and view transgression of the limit as a means for the construction of subjectivity.

In chapter 6, "Shaykh Ṣanʿān and the Christian Girl, and Abelard and Heloise," I focus on the story of Shaykh Ṣanʿān, his love for a Christian girl, and his religious transgression. Shaykh Ṣanʿān is a prominent ascetic *pīr* (Sufi master) who falls in love with a Christian girl and subsequently breaks the laws of Islam—he burns the Quran, drinks wine, and converts to Christianity. I examine the shaykh's transformation from ascetic to mystic and his violation of the religious law through his subversive love for the Christian girl, which leads to construction of subjectivity for both of them. I also elaborate on the medieval religious paradigms, and discuss the trope of the Christian Child or the *Tarsā-bachcha.* The story of Shaykh Ṣanʿān's love and his religious transgressions speak to the understanding of religious laws in medieval societies and the power of love. Advancing a critical analysis of the story of Shaykh Ṣanʿān and the Christian girl, we can see that Shaykh Ṣanʿān's transgressions provide him with an opportunity to acquire an alternative spirituality and identity. The violation of the religious law and his transcendence of the constructed barriers of his mind allow him to accept her. Through this subversive love, the shaykh's being is made and unmade; his subjectivity is deconstructed and reshaped; and mutual transformation occurs. In this story, ʿAṭṭār illustrates the religious taboos which hinder individual and spiritual growth, and should be broken. By analyzing ʿAṭṭār's poetry and initiating a conversation between him and Foucault, I not only explore the rigid medieval policies resulting in theological and sexual repression in Middle Eastern societies, but also show the dominance of similar rigid religious policies today and their consequences regarding liminal experiences and subjectivity. In this chapter, I also refer to the story of the forbidden love of Abelard and Heloise and their religious nonconformities that led them to engage in premarital sexual intercourse. Here, again, I read ʿAṭṭār, Abelard and Heloise, and modern theory contrapuntally to illustrate that the transgression of the constructed barriers of our minds leads to the de- and reconstruction of subjectivities.

The concluding chapter, "Human Diversity and Inclusiveness," explores ʿAṭṭār's preference for marginalized members of society, such as women, homosexuals, religious and social transgressors, infidels, sinners, fools, and members of despised professions. Since the previous chapters explore love stories of transgressive couples, in this chapter, I look at individual characters, not couples. I assert that ʿAṭṭār integrates outcasts into society by including them in his works regardless of the dominant sociocultural discourses directed at regulating deviations. I argue that ʿAṭṭār himself becomes a transgressor through his performative acts of nonconformity, which results in the emergent world of numerous possibilities.

In brief, the purpose of this study is to show that whereas members of social, religious, cultural, and sexual minorities may not be fully integrated in modern Iran (and even in the West), inclusiveness was *thinkable* in the medieval period by such extraordinary Sufi writers as ʿAṭṭār. Through this contrapuntal reading of ʿAṭṭār's poetry and modern theory, we realize the interdependence of these periods, and through the exploration of them alongside one another, we learn as much about our present as we do about the past. All in all, my research redefines Sufi scholarship through engaging with modern theory, and reading medieval and modern, theory and literature alongside one another regarding transgression and the construction of subjectivity.

Chapter 1

Sufism, ʿAṭṭār, and His Works

Muslim-Christian Intellectual Encounters

The religious conscience of Muslim mystics centers upon the primordial covenant between God and future humanity referred to in the Quran, in Sūra 7:172, where God asks the question of Adam's offspring, "Am I not your Lord?" and they answer, "Of course. We testify." In the Quran, the spirit is identified by "three primordial moments: creation . . . ; prophecy . . . ; and the moment of truth or day of judgment in which the spirits return to the celestial analogue of the Kaʿba" (Sells, *Early Islamic Mysticism* 18). The first primordial moment is when Adam was created and God blew his soul into him. This is the day of *Alastu*—referred to in Sūra 7:172—returning to which is the goal of all Muslim mystics. This is the day "when only God existed, before He led future creatures out of the abyss of not-being and endowed them with life, love, and understanding so that they might face Him again at the end of time" (Schimmel, *Mystical Dimensions* 24). This moment when all dualities merge and unite with the divine is the only meaningful concept left. The self and the divine other, the created and the Creator, meet each other and become one. The eternal and the temporal lose their meaning. All boundaries between the physical and the spiritual are blurred. It is a transcendental moment.

The origins of Islamic Sufism should also be traced back to the Prophet Muḥammad's life and sayings, and to the sociopolitical conditions of the period in which he lived (570–632). Muḥammad's asceticism, piety, night vigils, and prayers were among the first models of conduct followed by the early Sufis, who focused on asceticism more than on anything else in their religious practices. It should also be noted that in many parts of the Near and Middle East, Islam grew mainly within a Christian environment. The Muslims of the period maintained close social and intellectual contacts with their Christian neighbors, were directly influenced by the teachings of Christian mystics, or had previously been Christians (Smith, *Studies in Early Mysticism* 244). This social and intellectual interaction deserves attention. During Muḥammad's lifetime, Christian-Muslim encounters were harmonious, though shortly after his death in 632, Muslims started displaying overt hostility towards Christians. Unlike the polytheists in Mecca and the Jews in Medina, the Christians that Muḥammad encountered were not a community but scattered sects, so the interaction between them and Muḥammad was relatively limited. Nonetheless, Muḥammad's religious movement was influenced by the ascetic lifestyle of Christianity, from which it developed the notion of "a creating, sustaining, and judging God" as well as many of its devotional practices (Waardenburg, *Muslims and Others* 98). During Muḥammad's conflict with the Jews in Medina in 627, he favored the Christians over the Jews because the Christians—who held varied political allegiances—were less of a threat in the political struggle between Medina and Mecca, and their pious lifestyle attracted Muḥammad. However, this amicable attitude changed in 630, by which time Muḥammad's religious movement endeavored to reform polytheism, Judaism, and Christianity, and refuted Christian doctrines about God's essence and his relationship with humankind. When Muḥammad encountered the Christian Arab tribes in the north in 630, he offered them a choice of either adopting Islam or pledging to pay him a monetary tribute to avoid war. The Christian Arab tribes resisted Muḥammad and his religious doctrines, and it is possible that this resistance precipitated Muḥammad's desire to more swiftly expand his ideology (Waardenburg, *Muslims and Others* 98). In order to implement his version of monotheism, Muḥammad had to reject all religions and beliefs that he deemed contrary to monotheism, and he consequently imposed Islam on both Christian and Jewish Arabs. In Jacques Waardenburg's words, the resistance of these communities paradoxically contributed to Islam's transition from a purificatory religious movement to a universal religion, called *dīn al-ḥaqq* (religion of Truth) by its followers (*Muslims and Others* 99).

Muḥammad's monotheistic message spread throughout the Arabian Peninsula and was accepted by many of its inhabitants by 632, that is, about the time of his death. However, after Muḥammad's death, several Arab tribes announced their rejection of Islam. They had accepted Muḥammad's leadership rather than his faith; therefore, they demanded to be independent after his death. Muḥammad's father-in-law, Abū Bakr (r. 632–634), was selected as the first of four "rightly guided" caliphs to lead the Muslim community. He was in charge of quelling those rebellions, but he lived for only two years after Muḥammad. His successor, ʿUmar ibn al-Khaṭṭāb (r. 634–644), the second caliph, had more of an impact. The Muslim community began to expand its influence during ʿUmar's time. The ancient tradition of launching raids into the surrounding rich territories of Syria and Iraq to the north still persisted in Arabia, and since Muslims had assembled a large army after the suppression of tribal rebellions under Abū Bakr, this tradition developed further under ʿUmar. At first, the main purpose of those ventures was enrichment; however, later, judging by the raids on the holy city of Jerusalem, it appeared that these were religiously motivated also. What distinguished those Islamic raids from the preceding ones was the collapse of the opposing armies of the Byzantine (330–1453) and Sassanian Empires

(224–651) at the battles of Yarmūk (636) and Qādisiyyah (637). Consequently, Palestine, Syria, Iraq, Egypt, and Persia fell to the Muslims (Goddard, *Christians and Muslims* 126–27).

By 732, the Muslim military forces had united and exerted their economic, political, social, and intellectual influence over a large territory outside Arabia. That territory became the core of the "Commonwealth of Islam." Since the region had expanded into the territories of the Roman and Persian Empires of Late Antiquity, it inevitably included areas that were predominantly populated by Christians. This group constituted the majority in the former Roman provinces within the limits of the Oriental Patriarchates of Alexandria, Antioch, and Jerusalem, as well as in North Africa and Spain. Numerically, Christians formed a considerable minority population in the Persian Empire (Griffith 11). Under Muslim rule, however, Christian populations gradually diminished in the commonwealth. Over the centuries, their numbers declined from a considerable majority before the Crusades (1096–1272) to a scattered minority by the beginning of Ottoman times (1299). It is hard to pinpoint all the reasons for this diminishment; however, one certain thing is that the new attractive religious allegiance could offer opportunities of upward mobility to individuals in the Christian communities. The social conditions for Christians under Muslim rule were another important factor in this decline. For instance, Arabic became the public and official medium of the society. In addition, during the formative period, the culture of Islam was displayed in public spaces and institutions (Griffith 14). In the time of the Umayyad caliph ʿAbd al-Malik (r. 685-705), Muslim authorities had begun to appropriate the conquered regions outside of Arabia for the Islamic Commonwealth. The display of Islam had two religiously significant purposes. One was to declare the Islamic *shahadah*, that is, the testimony of faith in one God and his prophet Muḥammad, everywhere. Another was to remove all Christian symbols from public spaces (Griffith 14). This antipathy to Christianity can be seen in the destruction of the cross, which was a spiritual, political, and ideological symbol of the Byzantine Empire (Goddard, *Muslim Perceptions* 30–31). The most dramatic campaign was the construction of ʿAbd al-Malik's monument in Jerusalem, "the Dome of the Rock," with its anti-Christian inscriptions. According to Sidney Griffith, an example of the most characteristic policy of those days was the effort by the caliph ʿUmar ibn ʿAbd al-ʿAzīz (r. 717-20) to advocate equality for all Muslims, regardless of whether they were Arab conquerors or new converts. These developments made Islam a more attractive option for the Christians interested in social growth and drew the authorities' attention to the development of policies which would regulate the social lives of non-Muslims (*dhimmī*) living within the Muslim polity (15). Gradually, the process of Islamization made life increasingly intolerable for those non-Muslims who refused to convert to Islam. For instance, they had to pay *al-jizyah* (the poll tax), which was imposed on the "People of the Book" living under Muslim rule. These non-Muslims were expected to be submissive and keep a low social profile. It was after the conquest and consolidation of Islamic rule that a legal instrument known as the Covenant of ʿUmar came into being; it mandated that Christians, Jews, and other non-Muslims pay the tax, and assigned them to lower social strata. Originally, this legal instrument evolved from the pact that Muslims concluded with the cities they conquered in the seventh century under the caliph ʿUmar ibn al-Khaṭṭāb. Over time, however, many stipulations changed, and by the mid-ninth century, several theoretical schemes for governing the non-Muslims had been elaborated, which included a series of stipulated civic and personal disabilities for the *dhimmī* populations (Griffith 15–16). *Al-jizyah* was believed to be the price that the "People of the Book" had to pay in return for receiving protection (*dhimmah*) from the Islamic government. Such protection was considered part of the government's responsibility to its non-Muslim dependent populations. The *dhimmīs* were governed by their own leaders who were responsible for tax payments on their behalf during the classical Islamic period. In Ottoman times, this arrangement was called the *millet* system. Griffith has termed the non-Muslim populations during these times as "second-class citizens," although he is uncertain about the use of the term "citizen" for a population that was merely tolerated within the body of Islamic politics. He exemplifies this by highlighting the legal conditions constraining those populations: they had to remain subservient, wear distinctive clothing, avoid public display of their religion, and refrain from proselytizing Muslims (Griffith 16). A case illustrating the consequences of the public display of non-Muslim religious allegiances is the incident that occurred under the Umayyad caliph al-Walīd ibn ʿAbd al-Malik (r. 705–715) when the chief of the Banū Taghlab was tortured and martyred for venerating the cross. However, the majority of Christians lived in peace, provided that they paid the monetary tribute, although the next caliph ʿUmar ibn ʿAbd al-ʿAzīz attempted to enforce a law under which no Christian could serve in the administration of the Islamic state (Goddard, *Muslim Perceptions* 31). These developments resulted in the gradual decline in the number of churches, monasteries, and Christian schools.

During the Umayyad dynasty (661–750), political power shifted from Medina to Damascus in Syria (Nashat and Tucker 45–55). This shift is considered one of the main reasons for the emergence of Sufism; however, we have little information about Sufism during the Umayyad dynasty (Awn, "The Ethical Concerns" 241). With the rise of the Umayyads and the constant expansion of the Islamic Empire, many pious Muslims became aware of the discrepancy between the quranic revelations about the end of the world and the Muslim conquest of the "lands of the infidels." The Umayyads were seen to be worldly and impious Muslims; therefore, the pious began resisting the government and did so increasingly as time progressed. There were many debates about the proper moral conduct of a Muslim ruler, and Sufi thought partially evolved out of these debates. The first Sufi ascetic who rose against the impious conduct of the government was al-Ḥasan al-Baṣrī (624–728). His teachings influenced many pious people in Iraq and elsewhere, and his fear of the Day of Judgment is reflected in his sayings. Al-Ḥasan al-Baṣrī's disciple, ʿAbd al-Wāḥid ibn Zayd (1311–1390), laid the foundations of the ascetic settlement in Ābādān, a city on the shores of the Persian Gulf (Schimmel, *Mystical Dimensions* 29–31). The works of these scholars contributed to the formation of the new Islamic religious discourse which was produced within the social context of the Muslim-Christian-Jewish encounter. In addition, the conditions in which the Christian *dhimmīs* lived caused them to become social minorities that were subject to discrimination and persecution. In response to these changes, Christians developed discourses of accommodation and resistance. For instance, they composed philosophical or religious discourses in Arabic as a clearer statement of their Christian faith. They also produced Christian-Arabic literature of resistance with more contentious intent (Griffith 17). These intellectual developments were instrumental in the emergence of Sufism in the following years. Under the caliph ʿAbd al-Malik and during the reigns of his sons and successors (707–750), Christian writers turned their attention from writing about their social invisibility and the new Arab faith to the theoretical and apologetic response to the Muslim challenge posed to the Christians in the conquered regions (Griffith 32). One of the earliest genres developed by the Christian writers was that of the apocalypse, which expressed Christian writers' reaction to Islam. Some authors wrote about natural disasters and plagues as tokens of the Arab affliction; others viewed them as omens of the end of the world. The most well-known work written in this genre is *The Apocalypse of Pseudo-Methodius* (Griffith 33). These developments provided the background for another variety of intellectual discourse in the writings of Christians under Islam. Two Christian scholars produced comprehensive summary compendia of Christian doctrine. St. John of Damascus (676–749/764) was the first in Christian intellectual history to write a *summa theologiae*. His work is called *Pege Gnoseos*, or *The Fount of Knowledge* (Griffith 40). Another scholar who lived in the region of Syria, Theodore bar Koni (fl. ca. 792), composed a summary of Christian teachings of the Church of the East. It contains a form of an extended commentary on the Bible, the Old and New Testament, and is called *Scholion* (Griffith 42–43).

By around 750, the boundaries of the Islamic Empire stabilized, expansion ceased, and consolidation accelerated. During this time, the Islamic religion developed its disciplines of theology, law, philosophy, and mysticism. This was the Abbasid period of Islamic civilization, which lasted from 750 until 1258 (Goddard, *Christians and Muslims* 127). The Abbasid Empire wanted to establish a truly Islamic state, different from that of the Umayyads. The Abbasids ruled society and state on the basis of the single official religion. This contributed to the connection between religion and political objectives; it also encouraged the development of *fiqh* (Islamic jurisprudence) and the use of *ʿilm al-ḥadīth* (the sayings of Muḥammad) in order to formulate the *sharīʾa* (Islamic law) for the Muslim community. At the same time, theologians began to elaborate the doctrinal system with which they identified Islam. Their *kalām* (theology) allowed space for a theological discussion between Muslims and non-Muslims as long as the basic tenets of Islam, such as the Quran and Muḥammad, were respected (Waardenburg, *Muslims and Others* 111). The most important cultural and intellectual exchanges that helped Islamic civilization to grow occurred during al-Mahdī's reign (r. 775–785). He was sympathetic toward non-Muslims and invited them to translate works written in Greek and Syriac into Arabic.

Translations that were undertaken during this period include al-Mahdī's astrologer Theophile b. Toma's translation of Homer and Aristotle from Greek into Syriac; Abū Nūh al-Anbarī's (fl. 775) translation of Homer and Aristotle from Syriac into Arabic; the Catholicos Timothy's (728–823) production of a series of books on various subjects, including history; and Isho Bokht's (730–780) translation of documents from Middle Persian sources into Syriac (Khanbaghi 48). Under the caliph Hārūn al-Rashīd (r. 786–809), Nestorians produced accomplished astronomers and mathematicians as well, such as Sahl ibn Rabn of Ṭabaristān (fl. 786), who translated Ptolemy's *Almagest* from Greek into Arabic (Khanbaghi 48). Also, during the reign of the caliph Abū Jaʿfar ʿAbdullāh al-Ma'mūn ibn Hārūn al-Rashīd (r. 813–833) there was a great deal of interaction between Muslims and Christians, when representatives of each faith were allowed to debate with each other at the court. Until the eleventh century, Christians helped translate Greek and Syriac scientific and cultural works into Arabic (Goddard, *Muslim Perceptions* 31). Ḥunayn ibn Isḥāq (809–873), a Nestorian Christian from Hira, is considered the greatest translator of that period. He translated around one hundred books from Greek and Syriac into Arabic (Khanbaghi 48). Some popular Nestorian philosophers of the tenth century include Israel of Kashgār (870–960), Yuḥannā ibn Ḥaylān (860–920) and Abū Yaḥyā of Merv (?–949). Though there was amicable collaboration between Muslim and Christian intellectuals in this period, it was a time of greater hardship for ordinary Christians in various regions of the Abbasid Empire. A characteristic example is seen in the revolt of the Coptic peasants in Lower Egypt in 832. The revolt was crushed savagely and marked the beginning of the large-scale conversion of Christians to Islam due to social and financial predicaments (Goddard, *Muslim Perceptions* 31).

Turning back to the development of Sufism, although Sufism emerged under the Umayyad dynasty, Islamic mysticism only began to flourish during the Abbasid Empire, when the capital was moved from Damascus to Baghdad and the majority of the non-Arabian population of the Middle East had converted to Islam (Nashat and Tucker 45–55). Over the centuries, one area in which there was always mutual interaction and influence between Christians and Muslims was mysticism. In the formative years of Islamic thought, early Sufis and Muslim mystics were influenced by the ideas and practices of Christian monks. Similar to Christian monastic life that emerged as a protest against the worldliness of the Roman Empire in the fourth century, Sufism also evolved as a protest against the worldliness of the officials and caliphs after the Muslim conquests. Of course, after having fully developed, Sufism influenced some of the Western Christian mystics as well, especially in Spain, from the twelfth to the fourteenth century. Ramon Llull (1232–1316) was one of the first Christian mystical writers to be influenced by Sufi ideas, and as a result of Llull's legacy, Sufi ideas became incorporated into the works of the Spanish Carmelite St. John of the Cross (1542–1591) as well. There are also parallels between the sayings of Muslim Sufis and Christian mystics. For instance, the statement uttered by the Sufi al-Ḥallāj, "I am the Truth," has a similar underlying meaning to the sayings by Christian mystics, such as those of Julian of Norwich (1342–1420), "And I sawe no dyfference between God and oure substance, / I saw no difference between God and our substance" (Norwich 84), and St. Catherine of Genoa (1447–1510), "My Me is God, nor do I recognize any other Me except my God Himself" (qtd. in Huxley 11). Therefore, in different periods of history we observe mutual interaction and influence between Christian and Muslim mystics, with ideas and practices passing both ways. Persia during the time of ʿAṭṭār was no exception to this.

ʿAṭṭār's Life, Spirituality, and Works

In *Tales of Love*, Kristeva writes: "Love is the time and space in which 'I' assumes the right to be extraordinary. Sovereign yet not individual. Divisible, lost, annihilated; but also, and through imaginary fusion with the loved one, equal to the infinite space of super-human psychism. Paranoid? I am, in love, at the zenith of subjectivity" (5). What Kristeva means here is that the power of love enables individuals to be extraordinary, to merge with the imaginary, and therefore to reach the zenith of subjectivity. Love empowers individuals to transgress social, moral, ethical, class, gender, and sexual boundaries, and to de- and reconstruct their identities through annihilation of the self.

The transformative power of love has long been at the center of Islamic Sufism. Love, in Sufism, leads to reconstruction of the self, initiating (re)discovery of, and union with, the divine beloved. Sufi writers spoke of two different kinds of love: that of God and that of the things that God loves. For Sufi thinkers, such as Aḥmad al-Ghazzālī, ʿAyn al-Quḍāt al-Hamadānī, Farīd al-Dīn ʿAṭṭār Nishāpūrī, and Jalāl al-Dīn Rūmī, profane love, perceived as love of the worldly beloved, was the first step on the path toward union with the divine. They believed that earthly love is the emanation of sacred love. In their eyes, the love of every created object elevates the individual spiritually so they move even nearer to the love of God and beatific vision. Nevertheless, the relationship between sacred and profane, earthly and heavenly love in Islamic discourse has long been a controversial one, often pitting orthodox religious theologians against liberal spiritual Sufis.

Plato was the first author to assert in *Phaedrus* that the experience of beholding a beautiful human being (*ephebe*) can instigate a vision of the absolute beauty of the divine; and, of course, Neoplatonists followed Plato in this thinking. The notion of God taking on a human appearance is also common in Christian teachings, as with the doctrine of the incarnation of Christ as the Logos. It originates from the Old Testament, where God creates humans after his own likeness. In Christianity, intimate contact with God is attained through Holy Communion. It is also attained by worshipping the images of Christ, the Virgin Mary, and the saints, and prostrating oneself before them, a common practice in the Christian tradition since the fifth century. Even concentrating on the suffering and asceticism of the crucified Jesus or the saints functions as an earthly medium employed by believers to experience the heavenly (Ritter 449). Through this amalgamation of the heavenly and the earthly, humans experience the sacred in the form of the profane. They are confronted by a mysterious act through which ordinary profane objects become sacred—that is to say, their nature changes—yet these objects continue to be what they are and keep their due place in the cosmic order. This is what occurs in the sacrament of Holy Communion where the host is an ordinary object—bread or wine—that becomes sacred, and the church is the sacred space that allows this to happen, shielding it from the profane world outside. Therefore, for religious and spiritual ends, the entire world of Nature has the ability to reveal itself as a "cosmic sacrality" (Eliade 11–12).

A discourse bearing similar features (i.e., focusing on earthly love as a doorway to spiritual love) evolved in Persian Sufi literature during the medieval period. The term *ʿishq* (profane love) and its derivatives were frequently used in classical Persian prose and poetry. Beginning in the middle of the eighth century and during the ninth century, some of the more determined Sufis used the term to express the relationship between the Creator and his creatures (Dehqani 117). However, before the tenth century, discussions of love and longing were mainly semantic in nature. The orthodox theologians had objected to the use of the word *maḥabba* (love), but when the word *ʿishq* was introduced to describe the relationship between the divine and his creations, even Sufis objected to its use since it referred to a passionate, overflowing kind of love and longing that they believed would not have been a quality of a self-sufficient divine being (Schimmel, *Mystical Dimensions* 137). Nonetheless, Sufis proceeded to contemplate divine beauty and love as manifested in human form. This human form was called *shāhid*, meaning an eyewitness or a testimony. The beauty of earthly human forms created by God was perceived as a testimony to the beauty and presence of the divine. Hence, the earthly was regarded as a key to the heavenly. ʿAṭṭār was one of the most significant authors to espouse and articulate the term *ʿishq* as a representation of both earthly and heavenly love. His poetic works, *Ilāhī-nāma*, *Muṣībat-nāma* and *Manṭiq al-ṭayr*, along with his prose work, *Tadhkirat al-awlīyā*, embody the crucial elements of Sufi discourse, and were widely read and imitated by later Sufis, such as Rūmī.

ʿAṭṭār lived in Persia during the Seljuk era, a time characterized by war, corruption, and financial crisis. The troubles of this period originated with the death of Malikshāh of Seljuk (r. 1073–1092) in 1092, when quarrels arose among his sons over the throne and the apportioning of the empire, which eventually caused the empire to be dissolved into smaller states. In 1118, Sultan Sanjar, who was initially the Sultan of Khurāsān, succeeded to the throne and became the leader of the great Seljuk Empire until 1153. Sanjar was constantly engaged in wars and battles during his reign, among them the battle against the Oghūz Turks, who captured him in 1153 and held him hostage until 1156, during which time the Oghūz Turks plundered Khurāsān and murdered innocent people (Maleki 7–8).

The constant wars and battles during Sanjar's reign eroded the ethical principles of the society and led to corruption. In addition, the economic crisis caused by the wars placed the poor under financial pressure, and governmental revenue decreased considerably. However, the taverns, which had spread throughout Persia in this period, and served as gathering places for gamblers, wine drinkers and libertines, became the main source of income for the government. The tavern goers, regardless of the differences between them, had one thing in common: they all openly lived a life of nonconformity. Thus, despite their transgressions, they could be said to be honest and authentic people. In the following chapters, we will see how in his works ʿAṭṭār praises such transgressors as symbols of honesty and freedom, and prefers them to Sufis (whom he characterizes as pretentious) and spiritual leaders (whom he characterizes as deceitful).

Unlike his contemporaries, ʿAṭṭār never dedicated his poetry to kings or to the rulers of the day (Zarrinkub, *Ṣidā-yi* 25). He did not merely avoid praising them but directly criticized their hypocrisy. Annemarie Schimmel writes that in ʿAṭṭār's works the old Sufi devices, such as poverty, are used to emphasize the richness of a true dervish's soul and his spirituality as opposed to a king's spiritual poverty. ʿAṭṭār portrays kings begging everyone for everything as opposed to dervishes who are spiritually rich (*Mystical Dimensions* 304). In his article "The Religious 'Mathnavīs' of Farīd al-Dīn ʿAṭṭār," John Andrew Boyle also argues that "towards the rulers of the world ʿAṭṭār, like most of the mystics, adopts a critical, not to say hostile attitude. He tells many tales of Sultan Maḥmūd, the conqueror of India, being admonished or rebuked by humble folk whom he encounters while hunting or campaigning" (12). ʿAṭṭār's critical view of the rulers who were his contemporaries prevented him from joining the court but allowed him to indulge in his personal experiences among the common public (Zarrinkub, *Ṣidā-yi* 34). While he admonished wealthy kings and rich rulers for their spiritual poverty, he embraced and admired peripheral individuals and societal outcasts in his works.

ʿAṭṭār wrote several books of poetry which together contain 45,000 verses. His books include: *Ilāhī-nāma*, *Pand-nāma* (*The Book of Counsel*), *Dīwān* (*Collection of Poetry*), *Mukhtār-nāma* (*The Book of the Empowered*), *Muṣībat-nāma*, and *Manṭiq al-ṭayr*, along with his prose work, *Tadhkirat al-awlīyā*. Since the focus of this book is on *Ilāhī-nāma*, *Muṣībat-nāma*, *Manṭiq al-ṭayr*, and *Tadhkirat al-awlīyā*, these works will be briefly reviewed here, respectively.

Tadhkirat al-awlīyā, which consists of seventy-two chapters on the life and spirituality of the famous Sufis, is ʿAṭṭār's only surviving prose work. It begins with the biography of the sixth Imam of Shi'ism, Imam Jafar Sādiq, and ends with al-Ḥallāj's biography. It also includes stories about the life and spirituality of the first female Sufi, Rābiʿa al-ʿAdawiyya. According to Reynold A. Nicholson, "it is the oldest work of the kind in Persian and . . . although deficient in dates and biographical details of any sort, it contains a large amount of material which is not to be found in the later Biographies" (*Tadhkirat al-awlīyā* 5). Despite the fact that it is not a well-documented record of the Sufis' lives, its literary value lies in its being an early example of Persian prose.

ʿAṭṭār's *Ilāhī-nāma* is a poetic work which consists of 6,511 verses. It begins with the praise of God, the Prophet Muḥammad, and his companions. The main story line revolves around the conversation between a king and his six sons, each of whom demands materialistic and worldly things from their father. The king tries to expose the transient and temporal nature of his sons' demands through a number of spiritual stories. The demands of the sons encompass many of the common matters and popular urges of the day, such as the desire to marry a beautiful girl or to possess magical powers. *Ilāhī-nāma* provides the readers with responses to questions about worldly matters and human desires. It also addresses the way human beings must choose if they are to liberate themselves from these worldly desires in a transient life that ultimately ends in death. The book explains that seeking the Truth and walking on the divine path involves renunciation of all worldly desires and attachments. Mojdeh Bayat and Mohammad Ali Jamnia posit that in *Ilāhī-nāma*, ʿAṭṭār "likens human beings with faculties of ego, imagination, intellect, thirst for knowledge, thirst for detachment, and thirst for unity to a king with six sons. The lesson he teaches the sons is to pursue the Eternal Presence of God as the highest goal" (51). Therefore, *Ilāhī-nāma* has been considered as an allegorical work which focuses on the exploration of the renunciation of worldly desires in favor of the more exalted heavenly longing. In *Ilāhī-nāma*, ʿAṭṭār criticizes superstitions and beliefs of perfunctory common people and the elite of his time alike, using the demands of the king's sons as a point of reference. ʿAṭṭār not only offers moral and social advice but also admonishes the spreading of false beliefs by some of the hypocritical spiritual leaders of his time. The book contains more spiritual stories than any of ʿAṭṭār's other works; in it, he dedicates a considerable number of stories to the renunciation of worldly matters, the fear of death and the future, and the merits of piety. *Ilāhī-nāma* also contains stories about popular Persian national figures, such as Sultan Maḥmūd of Ghazna (r. 998–1030) (Furūzānfar, *Sharḥ-i Aḥvāl* 95–99).

Muṣībat-nāma is a collection of 7,000 verses. It is a masterpiece in which ʿAṭṭār depicts the endless pain and suffering of the wayfarer who seeks the Truth. The wayfarer grieves all along his way and finally reaches nothing but bewilderment (Zarrinkub, *Ṣidā-yi* 86). In this work, ʿAṭṭār uses poetry as a way of praising God. He draws a link between *shiʿr* (poetry), *sharʿ* (divine law), and *ʿarsh* (the divine throne), based on a pun in the Persian language (Zarrinkub, *Ṣidā-yi* 112). *Muṣībat-nāma* describes the quest of a Sufi for the divine during the forty days of his seclusion. The Sufi travels throughout the world of creatures, from the noblest to the lowliest of them. He listens to the *lisān ul-ḥāl*, the "tongue of the state," "of wind and earth, of fire and sea, and hears the endless yearning of all creatures for their original home" (Schimmel, *Mystical Dimensions* 306). The seeker relays his experience of encounters with forty creatures to the *pīr* hoping to receive explanation. However, it is only through the intercession of the Prophet Muḥammad, the foremost mystical master, that the seeker finds the way into his soul "where all longing ends" (306). Nevertheless, the journey toward God is not the end of the way, but only the beginning of the journey into *baqā* (survival).

Like *Muṣībat-nāma*, *Manṭiq al-ṭayr* is also a story of Truth-seeking. In *Manṭiq al-ṭayr*, a gathering of different kinds of birds seeks to elect a *pīr* to lead them through the challenges of life. Each one of the birds comes up with an excuse to not set out on the difficult path in search of the *sīmurgh* (their ultimate goal). However, the hoopoe (a species of bird) persuades them to begin the journey, and is chosen as their *pīr*. The hoopoe leads them through the seven valleys of *Ṭalab* (Quest), *ʿIshq* (Love), *Maʿrifat* (Understanding), *Istighnā* (Detachment), *Tawḥīd* (Unity), *Ḥiyrat* (Bewilderment), and *Faqr* (Poverty). Having overcome hardships and trials along the way, only thirty birds reach the destination, but the *sīmurgh* is not there. They wait fruitlessly for the *sīmurgh* for so long that they finally realize that they, the thirty birds (in Persian, *sī murgh*), are the *sīmurgh* and that the Truth resides in each of them. ʿAṭṭār illustrates, here, how the seeker searching for the Truth can reach the highest degree of purity along the way, and, moreover, that the Truth resides inside the seeker. Schimmel considers *Manṭiq al-ṭayr* a "standard work of Sufi literature," and one which inspired mystics and poets for many generations (*Mystical Dimensions* 305). She writes, *sīmurgh* "is the most ingenious pun in Persian literature, expressing so marvelously the experience of the identity of the soul with the divine essence" (307). In comparison with two of ʿAṭṭār's earlier works, *Ilāhī-nāma* and *Muṣībat-nāma*, *Manṭiq al-ṭayr* is a more developed mystical work. Its spiritual allegories and narratives are more profound. Even ʿAṭṭār's use of literary figures of speech, such as the pun on the word *sīmurgh*, is more professional. *Sīmurgh* epitomizes the mystical notion of the annihilation of the self, losing oneself in the divine, and the union of the lover and the ultimate beloved. In *Manṭiq al-ṭayr*, the birds succeed in seeing their true selves through a mirror, represented by the *sīmurgh*, but their true selves are also their beloved, and the fervent mystical love they experience is the love of the divine. The observer and the observed are one, and the seeker and the sought are the same. Therefore, *sīmurgh* represents the amalgamation of the earthly and heavenly beloved in its heavenly form (Purnamdarian 103–12).

In each one of these works, ʿAṭṭār establishes correspondences between the divine and the human realm through his love narratives and analogies, foregrounding unconventional lovers, transgressors, and marginalized members of society as the true lovers of the divine. ʿAṭṭār demonstrates in his works how deviating from the moral codes and crossing conventional boundaries allows the violators to annihilate the ego, de- and reconstruct their identities, and (re)discover the divine through earthly love. But, how did this thread of spirituality come to run through ʿAṭṭār's writing? There are several accounts of how ʿAṭṭār became attracted to Sufism. One of them is found in *Nafaḥāt al-uns* (*Breaths of Intimacy*), where Maulānā ʿAbd al-Raḥmān Jāmī (1414–1492) relates that one day ʿAṭṭār was busy in his shop when a dervish entered, begging ʿAṭṭār to give him something in the name of God. ʿAṭṭār ignored his request, and the dervish asked ʿAṭṭār, "Sir, how will you pass away?" ʿAṭṭār replied, "Just as you will." The dervish put his wooden bowl under his head, lay down, invoked God, and passed away. ʿAṭṭār, baffled by this incident, left his profession to become a devotee of Sufism (24). Daulatshāh Samarqandī (1439–1495) also relates that ʿAṭṭār turned to Sufism after his encounter with a dervish who admonished ʿAṭṭār for his infatuation with worldly matters and riches (141). However, Badiʿ al-Zamān Furūzānfar argues that ʿAṭṭār was attracted to

Sufism since his childhood (*Sharḥ-i Aḥvāl* 17). It is also believed that ʿAṭṭār joined a Sufi settlement under the guidance of Rukn al-Dīn (1261–1336), a shaykh of the Kubrawīyya order, after which he travelled to Mecca on pilgrimage. It can be assumed that he went to Mecca upon completing a certain phase of his spiritual development. After the pilgrimage, he began writing (Bayat and Jamnia 50). Many individuals have been mentioned as ʿAṭṭār's masters, but considering the time in which he lived, only Najm al-Dīn Kubrā (1145–1221) could have possibly been one (Reinert 20–25). ʿAbd al-Husayn Zarrinkub writes that although there was great respect between the two and Najm al-Dīn's master, Majd al-Dīn of Baghdad (d. ca. 1209–1216), ʿAṭṭār himself was considered a complete and perfect shaykh who did not need a master (*Ṣidā-yi* 36). On the other hand, Jāmī considers ʿAṭṭār to be an Uwaysī Sufi, after Uways al-Qaranī (1197–1259), having al-Ḥallāj in mind, since it was believed that in Uwaysī school of Sufism spiritual knowledge could have been transmitted between two individuals without their physically having met or interacted. However, Hermann Landolt in "ʿAṭṭār, Sufism and Ismailism" concludes that "it is not even certain whether ʿAṭṭār belonged to a particular Sufi group, let alone a Sufi order (*silsila*), for he himself never identifies anyone by name as his Sufi master, nor does he ever adduce any *silsila* to show his credentials as a Sufi" (3–4). There is much uncertainty about ʿAṭṭār's participation in Sufi orders and settlements, but though he might not have had a master, there is no doubt that he was inspired by al-Ḥallāj's love mysticism.

ʿAṭṭār derived his philosophy, spirituality, and interest in love mysticism from several centuries of earlier Sufi writings on love. In the initial years of Islam, Sufism mainly focused on asceticism; however, in the eighth century it evolved from its original ascetic form into a doctrine of selfless love for the divine. In such a state of selflessness, Margaret Smith writes, the Sufi "cease[s] to exist and pass[es] out of self. [S/he is] one with Him and altogether His" (*Rābiʿa the Mystic* 110). Sufis also based their understanding of love on the quranic verse that referred to the precedence of man's love for God above anything else (Sūra 5:59). Generations of Sufis gave love and intuitive knowledge of the divine preeminence over discursive learning and knowledge of the divine. Sufis strove to return to the origin from which everything proceeded. They wanted to reach the state in which they were before they existed, that is, the state of the primordial covenant when the divine was alone and nothing yet existed. In that moment, God breathed into man and created Adam in his own image so that man became the perfect image of the divine, like a mirror reflecting his qualities. It is only through the return to the perfect image of the divine that Sufis believe they can reach union with the divine. They believe that God created man as his highest manifestation because he wanted to be known: "I was a hidden treasure, and I wanted to be known, so I created the world." Sufis believed that the divine is "closer than the jugular vein" (Sūra 50:16), so they needed to look into their own hearts to find the divine (Schimmel, *Mystical Dimensions* 189). This concept can be found in ʿAṭṭār's *Muṣībat-nāma*, where the wayfarer finds peace and love in the divine.

Regarding the significance of love in Sufism, Schimmel writes:

> Mysticism can be defined as love of the Absolute—for the power that separates true mysticism from asceticism is love. Divine love makes the seeker capable of bearing, even of enjoying, all the pains and afflictions that God showers upon him in order to test him and to purify his soul. This love can carry the mystic's heart to the Divine Presence "like the falcon which carries away the prey," separating him, thus, from all that is created in time. (*Mystical Dimensions* 4)

In their writings, many Sufis distinguish between asceticism and mysticism. For instance, Jāmī explains the difference between austere asceticism and true Sufism as follows: "The ascetics regard the Beauty of the Otherworld with the light of faith and certitude and despite the world, but are still veiled by a sensual pleasure, namely the thought of Paradise, whereas the true Sufi is veiled from both worlds by the vision of the Primordial Beauty and Essential Love" (*Nafaḥāt* 10).

At the beginning of the Abbasid period, Sufis and ascetics who admonished the rulers for their wrongdoings and criticized them boldly were tolerated. However, gradually, the rulers began to treat them with less forbearance. One such example was the execution of al-Ḥallāj. He had recklessly expressed the sentiment "I am the Truth" (*ana'l-ḥaqq*) on his way to the execution. When asked what made him so excited in the face of approaching death, he replied that death was his way to heaven and to the union with the absolute (Zarrinkub, *Arzish-i* 64). Al-Ḥallāj's belief was that the relationship between the Creator and his creations was reciprocal, and that God had created man in his own image. He held that God had shaped man like a mirror so that he would be able to see his love in him, and that this love was the secret of creation. Al-Ḥallāj's love mysticism was thus an amalgamation of earthly and heavenly love (Dehqani 116–19). Many later Sufis were inspired by al-Ḥallāj's spirituality and referenced him in their works. One such reference is found in *Tadhkirat al-awlīyā*, where ʿAṭṭār relates that while al-Ḥallāj was waiting in prison to be executed, a dervish asked him, "What is love?" He replied, "You will see it today and tomorrow and the day after." Al-Ḥallāj was then executed on the same day, burnt on the next day, and had his ashes given to the wind on the third. ʿAṭṭār writes, "This is love" (*Tadhkirat al-awlīyā,* trans. Losensky 403). This peculiar type of al-Ḥallājian love mysticism was subsequently embodied in ʿAṭṭār's writings. Through this story, ʿAṭṭār tells about the life and spirituality of a Sufi who became "a symbol for both suffering love and unitive experience, but also for a lover's greatest sin: to divulge the secret of his love" (Schimmel, *Mystical Dimensions* 64).

Al-Ḥallāj's execution, in Majid Fakhry's words, was "a stark reminder of the dangers inherent in the doctrine of the 'essence of union,' which al-Ḥallāj interpreted as simply the manner in which the mystic becomes an instrument of God, speaking and writing on His behalf" (*A Short Introduction* 77). Al-Ḥallāj was executed for the boldness of his mystical interpretation, which was deemed to be blasphemous self-deification. Through this boldness, he had transformed Sufism and brought it out of the *khāniqāh* (convents) into the public to be disseminated among the lay people. This transmission of Sufism into the public, which was in fact a form of social protest, obviously threatened the rulers. Unlike al-Ḥallāj, many ascetics and Sufis of the time chose to ignore the wrongdoings of the rulers and resorted to seclusion in convents (Maleki 214). Gradually, social criticism gave way to a form of seclusion and asceticism whose goal was not mastery over one's soul but over other beings. The outcome was the emergence of different groups of Sufis who departed considerably from the earlier principles of Sufism. In such conditions, the true Sufis who stayed faithful to those principles were stranded between two different groups: the earthly rulers on one side, and their followers, the pretentious Sufis and ascetics, on the other. The true Sufis had no other choice but to either stay silent and ignore the corruption of society or be loyal to their principles and accept death as a result (215). Al-Ḥallāj chose loyalty and death; therefore, he became the epitome of suffering on the path to divine love and submission to the unity of the divine beloved. He believed that the essence of God and the creation was love, and that *ʿishq* (profane love) was the doorway to divine love. Many Sufis, such as Aḥmad al-Ghazzālī, ʿAyn al-Quḍāt al-Hamadānī, and Ibn al-ʿArabī (1165–1240) followed al-Ḥallāj. However, in Iran, ʿAṭṭār—and later Rūmī—are considered to be part of the al-Ḥallājian mystical tradition.

Regarding love in Sufism, ʿAṭṭār believed that love was not limited to humans. He saw love in all creatures as emanations of divine love. He loved the entire world and all creatures in it. For him, God's motivation for creating the world and the people in it was love. For ʿAṭṭār, all the elements of the universe, from the lowliest to the noblest, were in constant motion towards one destination—God; and the reason for this attraction is nothing but love. The entire universe is in love with God and seeks its origin in him (Maleki 263–64). ʿAṭṭār's works portray the constant seeking and progression of the seeker's soul towards its goal and origin. ʿAṭṭār exposes the endless longing of the human soul to go through the different stages of development and annihilation of *nafs* (the lower self) before becoming perfect.

However, as it was with al-Ḥallāj and his mysticism, walking on the path towards the divine is fraught with pain and suffering. For ʿAṭṭār, Sufism begins with pain and reaches perfection through pain (Zarrinkub, *Ṣidā-yi* 157–58). Regarding the theme of pain and suffering in ʿAṭṭār's spirituality, Schimmel associates ʿAṭṭār with al-Ḥallāj's mysticism as well. She views al-Ḥallāj's spirituality as inspiration for ʿAṭṭār's initiation on the divine path. She writes that ʿAṭṭār's biography of al-Ḥallāj in his *Tadhkirat al-awlīyā* is very touching and "has shaped the image of al-Ḥallāj for all subsequent generations" (*Mystical Dimensions* 305). It is from al-Ḥallāj that ʿAṭṭār learned to endure suffering and pain on the path of divine love. Schimmel characterizes ʿAṭṭār as "the voice of pain, the voice of longing and of searching" in the Persian mystical tradition (305).

The al-Ḥallājian mystical tradition and the selfless love it pursued are reflected in many of the later Sufi works and literature. From the twelfth century onwards, Persian literature had been subject to several developments. One such development was the emergence of the ghazal and lyrical poetry as a medium for expressing sacred as well as profane love, that is, the kind of love between the Creator and the created about which al-Ḥallāj preached. Poets began to employ erotic language in their works to describe unearthly love (Seyed-Gohrab 72–73). The increasing use of poetry by Sufis further influenced the fusion of the erotic and the mystical and promoted the use of erotic vocabulary in mystical writings. Sufis had quite an extended erotic vocabulary which they employed in their writings to express their fervent love for the incorporeal beloved (13). However, in order to avoid criticism, Sufis used erotic language metaphorically, for which reason mystical poetry is somewhat obscure. It leaves readers to draw their own conclusions about the eroticism and esotericism of mystical poems. This type of mystical love, fused with erotic language and incorporating liminal characters, is what we frequently encounter in the works of ʿAṭṭār.

Using an ambiguous language, ʿAṭṭār believed that even in the physical world, love is the main element on the path leading to union with the divine. According to ʿAṭṭār, a true *sālik* (wayfarer) should seek (earthly) love on the divine path and relinquish the ego through love in order to find God and reach divine union. Oftentimes, a Sufi's profane love, representing the heavenly, guides him or her to transgress earthly boundaries and reject the status quo. This is the moment when a Sufi faces the Kristevan zenith of subjectivity, that is, the point when a Sufi wayfarer de- and reconstructs herself or himself and emerges as a new subject who is able to cross earthly boundaries with the means of divine love. However, despite her or his transgression of these boundaries, this new subject is an individual totally submitting to the will of God. This is how the zenith of subjectivity is reached in a Sufi way.

At the zenith of subjectivity, ʿAṭṭār's spirituality and his love of divinity allowed him to love all creations of the divine, including the transgressors, although the concepts of transgression, the law, and inclusiveness were different in the medieval Middle East than they are today. In the medieval Middle East, "justice" was administered by a ruler appointed by divine blessing and providence to protect the state from internal and external enemies. This required a strong military force and wealth. At the top of the society, a king secured justice for his subjects. In return, he relied on those in the lower social ranks, such as peasants, to provide the revenue. Therefore, in the context of the medieval Middle East, justice as a concept signified more than the equality of society's members under the law. It presumed the provision of "peace, protection, good organization, and a functional infrastructure" (Darling, "Medieval Egyptian" 1; see also Darling, "Do Justice;" "Circle of Justice"). This ideology has been called the "Circle of Justice" and it engendered a special literary genre which advised kings and other royal members of the values that were of merit both in kings and in the general population in the Islamic world. This genre is also called "Mirror for Princes," and one of its remarkable examples is Kai Kā'ūs Iskandar's *Qabūs-nāma*, in which he advises his son on matters of kingly etiquette and values. Since divine blessing in the medieval Islamic society was of paramount significance, and the notion of justice referred to the relationship between individual citizens, the divine, and the ruler, ʿAṭṭār's tendency to be socioculturally inclusive can be considered the result of his affiliation with Sufism and his devotion to the divinity.

ʿAṭṭār's opposition to the mainstream social ethics of his day, however, becomes apparent in his rejection and criticism of the rulers of the time and his total submission solely to the divine. In this way, ʿAṭṭār's spirituality allowed him to exercise a great degree of openness and acceptance of outcasts, marginal figures, and the societal other in general. This particular vision of ʿAṭṭār becomes explicit in his works due to their language and content, which are inclusive and conscious of issues related to gender, sexual, religious, and sociocultural diversity. After ʿAṭṭār, Sufi poetry reached its peak with Rūmī. According to Jāmī and later Daulatshāh, Rūmī met ʿAṭṭār in Nishāpūr on his way from Balkh to central Iran with his father. During this visit, ʿAṭṭār gave his book *Asrār-nāma* (*The Book of Secrets*) to Rūmī. Although this story has not been recounted in any of Rūmī's own biographies, it may be believed to be accurate since ʿAṭṭār was still alive when Bahā al-Dīn Walad (1152–1231), Rūmī's father, passed through Khurāsān. At the time, it was customary for the Sufis to visit their fellows wherever they traveled. Therefore, it is possible that Bahā al-Dīn Walad and his son Rūmī visited ʿAṭṭār on their way (Daulatshāh 193). Furūzānfar also indicates that since the spiritual connection between ʿAṭṭār and Rūmī is evident in Rūmī's *Masnavī* (an extensive Sufi poem in six books), and many stories from ʿAṭṭār's works can be found in Rūmī's as well, it is possible that Rūmī had read all of ʿAṭṭār's works and was inspired by him (*Sharḥ-i Aḥvāl* 70). His famous verse praising Sanāʾī Ghaznavī (1080–1141) and ʿAṭṭār is memorable: "Sanāʾī was the spirit, and ʿAṭṭār his two eyes / we have come after Sanāʾī and ʿAṭṭār." This line cannot be found in Rūmī's own works, however. It is believed that it was coined by his son Sultan Walad (1226–1312) and repeated in several of his ghazals. Nonetheless, the fact that more than thirty-five of Rūmī's stories in the *Masnavīs* are derived from or inspired by ʿAṭṭār's works attest to ʿAṭṭār's great influence on Rūmī and on the Persian Sufi tradition and literature of the following generations.

Chapter 2

Modern Theory, Michel Foucault, and His Predecessors

ʿAṭṭār's love mysticism allowed him to be socioculturally, religiously, and sexually inclusive. His works are a testimony to his openness and acceptance of transgressors, outcasts, peripherals, and the societal other. In his works, ʿAṭṭār advocates pushing the limits, which leads to the construction of new subjectivities. We can find a similar encouragement to violate the law and shape subjectivity in modern theory. Although I will mainly initiate a dialogue between Foucault and ʿAṭṭār regarding these concepts, it is essential to look at the development of these concepts in the works of post-Enlightenment intellectuals such as Friedrich Nietzsche, the Marquis de Sade, and Georges Bataille.

The Marquis de Sade's (1740–1814) philosophy was at the forefront of the emerging post-Enlightenment movement that sought to break the moral, social, and legal boundaries which defined the civil state after the French Revolution (1787–1799). Sade's *Philosophy in the Bedroom*—advocating erotic fantasies with an emphasis on violence and brutality against the Catholic Church—and his advancement of extreme freedom were picked up as a philosophy of transgression with sexuality at its center in the nineteenth and twentieth centuries. In *Philosophy in the Bedroom*, Sade uses the exchanges between the inexperienced character, Eugénie, and the worldlier characters, Dolmancé, Madame de Saint-Ange, and Le Chevalier de Mirval, in order to expose the libertine way of life. A large part of this exchange deals with explicit sexual material, but the characters also discuss religion, politics, crime, and nature. Sade begins with an introduction which prepares readers for what they are about to read. He urges readers to give in to their desires, regardless of how unconventional they may be, as human desires are a part of nature, and acting against them in any way is acting against nature. From the beginning, Sade alerts readers to the fact that the characters are meant to serve as models of specific types of people, and that the play will serve all those along the spectrum of transgression, from "lewd women" to "young maidens" to "amiable debauchees" (185). All of these characters work together to show the reader how transgression is one of the only ways that human beings can derive pleasure from this potentially miserable existence. As Sade says, these acts are the only chance that man has "to sow a smattering of roses atop the thorny path of life" (185). He addresses the fact that many people are reluctant to give themselves fully to their desires, as many of their wishes would go against the laws put in place by moralists who wish to strip people of the pleasures they could be experiencing.

In "Dialogue the First," Sade introduces all the libertine characters and addresses their various transgressive acts. Bisexuality, sodomy, and incest are all referenced within the first two pages of the play. Sade does this in an attempt to shock the reader from the start, so as to normalize the language surrounding the activities in which the libertines partake. It is important to note that these characters are not acting transgressively simply for the sake of going against what society has deemed appropriate, but because they feel that ignoring their desires would be a crime against nature. The reader is also introduced to the ways that the characters speak to and about one another, which can be jarring at times. Le Chevalier, in speaking to his sister, Madame de Saint-Ange, refers to Dolmancé as "the most evil individual, the greatest scoundrel in the world" and "the most profound seducer, the most corrupt, the most dangerous man" (188, 190). Despite these seemingly deterring descriptions, Le Chevalier reveals that he has had sexual experiences with Dolmancé in the past, and he continues to have them throughout *Philosophy in the Bedroom.* In this chapter, the primary plot of the play is also introduced when Madame de Saint-Ange tells Le Chevalier that she is bringing a young woman to their estate in order to educate her in the ways of libertinage. In "Dialogue the Second," the shortest in the entire play, Eugénie arrives and is welcomed by Madame de Saint-Ange. This section also reveals the conflict between Eugénie and her mother, Madame de Mistival, who is deeply religious and conservative, and thus does not approve of the education that her daughter is about to receive. Eugénie also tells Madame de Saint-Ange that she will only be in her care for two days. "Dialogue the Third" does the most in the way of Eugénie's development into a libertine. At the beginning of the section, when faced with any display of sexuality, she is awkward and uncomfortable. Madame de Saint-Ange and Eugénie enter the bedroom and are surprised to find Dolmancé waiting for them, and Eugénie blushes at his very presence. He tells her that "modesty is an antiquated virtue" and that decency is "A Gothicism not very much defended these days" that is "hostile to nature" when she resists his advances (197). However, by the end of the page, Eugénie willingly throws herself into his arms and kisses him passionately. After examining her physique, Madame de Saint-Ange and Dolmancé begin to instruct Eugénie in the lifestyle of the libertine, which makes up the majority of the section. The basis of the lectures given by Madame de Saint-Ange and Dolmancé is nature, which they claim is more important than the laws laid out by the moralists in charge of society. First, they instruct her on the particulars of human anatomy and sexuality, primarily by demonstrating on each other. Once Eugénie begins to question them on the morality of these acts, the conversation turns to virtue and religion. Eugénie is shocked to learn that her mentors believe God to be an illusion, but Dolmancé provides a lengthy explanation as to why he does not believe in God. The central element of his diatribe against religion, like the rest of the discussion, is focused on nature (210). Both mentors agree that Eugénie must abandon her attachments to religion in order to fully give in to libertinage. "Dialogue the Fourth" is mainly concerned with Eugénie's sexual experiences, and she is introduced to Le Chevalier, who takes her virginity. Together with Madame de Saint-Ange and Dolmancé, the four perform an orgy in order to aid in Eugénie's sexual education. This leads to the introduction of Augustin, the gardener, in "Dialogue the Fifth." This section of the play begins with more sexual exploits, this time incorporating Augustin as well as the original four characters. Eugénie questions the libertine view of sodomy, and Dolmancé explains in a long lecture why it should be an accepted sexual act. Essentially, he claims that the moralist notion of "sex only for procreation," which assumes that nature would not allow human beings to feel sexual attraction or arousal unless they were able to create human life at that very moment, is misinformed. Throughout the work, through each character, Sade repeatedly emphasizes the link between nature and following one's desires. He makes it clear that there is no such thing as good or evil when one is giving in to desire and that even committing murder would not be going too far. This idea comes to fruition in the final act of the play, when Eugénie's mother comes to claim her but many different characters brutalize her. She is whipped, beaten, and raped, but those involved—particularly Dolmancé, Madame de Saint-Ange, and Eugénie—are not disturbed by their actions. The play ends before the reader is able to see whether or not they reflect upon their treatment of Madame de Mistival, but it can be assumed that they do not regret what they have done, as it was all done for the sake of the pursuit of pleasure. Because of these violent acts, "Dialogue the Seventh and Last" is perhaps the most transgressive of the entire play, as it shows what happens when the libertine will truly stop at nothing, even ruthlessly violating her own mother in Eugénie's case, to get what she desires. Throughout the entire work, Sade illustrates how sexuality for pleasure's sake is essential. This is how the notion of subversive sexuality became central to discussions of transgression against institutional religion and morality in later philosophical works such as Bataille's.

Bataille (1897–1962) adopted Sade's ideas of sexuality in theorizing his own understanding of transgression and the limit. Bataille's work is concerned with the relationship between the sacred and the profane, and how the sacred creates human society. At the core of his philosophy on economic and social relationships are the concepts of surplus, excess, and waste. Bataille considers excess as whatever challenges an economy of production and consumption, and focuses on waste products of the body, society, and thought, which include madness, poetry, excrement, sexuality, and obscenity.

Bataille published his first novel *L'Histoire de l'oeil* in 1928 (*The Story of the Eye*). In this novel influenced by Sade, he explores erotic fantasy. The novel outlines the ways through which a literary text can explore the boundaries of the modern subject. For Bataille, the divisions between economic, moral, and ethical boundaries constitute the individual subject. When the subject crosses these boundaries, she or he becomes aware of the imposition of the limits on herself or himself. This experience of boundary crossing is accompanied by the pleasure and joy of moving from an ordered realm to a chaotic one.

The Story of the Eye is a short tale of a young boy who discovers his sexuality with the help of a young woman named Simone. The unnamed narrator begins the book by saying, "I grew up very much alone, and as far back as I recall I was frightened of anything sexual" (Bataille 9). This is an interesting way to start, as the next seventy pages are spent primarily with the narrator detailing his sexual adventures with Simone, and he immediately jumps into describing their first sexual encounter. At first, it appears that Simone is the more transgressive of the two, as he says that "on a sensual level, she so bluntly craved any upheaval that the faintest call from the sense gave her a look directly suggestive of all things linked to deep sexuality, such as blood, suffocation, sudden terror, crime; things indefinitely destroying human bliss and honesty" (11). The actual timeline of the story is unclear, so the narrator's transition from a shy, terrified boy to a sexually deviant one could either have been quite sudden or have taken place over a great amount of time. Regardless of the time it takes for the narrator to change, it is clear that this alteration does take place. This becomes apparent from as early as the book's first chapter, when he and Simone take advantage of Marcelle, a young girl who lives nearby. While he describes it primarily as a threesome, it seems to be more like rape. Marcelle happens upon the narrator and Simone in a field, and when she realizes the sexual nature of their positions, the narrator says she "suddenly collapsed and huddled in the grass amidst sobs," after which the two lovers "hurl [themselves] upon a self-abandoned body" (12). Even after this sexual assault, Marcelle chooses to spend time with Simone and the narrator, but it becomes clear that she suffers from emotional trauma and is thus placed in a sanatorium. During their separation from Marcelle, Simone and the narrator obsess over her and are unable to endure any sexual activities without imagining her "piercing cries" (21). Eventually, Simone and the narrator break her out of the asylum, but it is clear that Marcelle is too traumatized to cope with the real world and she kills herself. Her death is the most easily discernable climax of the story, and it causes the narrator's transition to be fully realized. Just after releasing Marcelle from the sanatorium, the narrator has an epiphany regarding his sexual tastes. He tells the reader, "I did not care for what is known as 'pleasures of the flesh' because they really are insipid; I cared only for what is classified as 'dirty' . . . My kind of debauchery soils not only my body and my thoughts, but also anything I may conceive in its course, that is to say, the vast starry universe, which merely serves as a backdrop" (42). He is only satisfied, then, when his transgression occurs on a level much higher than himself. Like the libertines in *Philosophy in the Bedroom*, the narrator does not desire to take part in debauchery simply for debauchery's sake. He does, however, take pleasure in the corruption of purity as a coincidence or side effect of his satisfaction. While Marcelle's death seems to make the narrator more confident in claiming his desires and putting them into words, it has a different effect on Simone. After they discover

Marcelle's body, the narrator describes their relationship as "very remote from anything we touched, in a world where gestures have no carrying power, like voices in a space that is absolutely soundless" (Bataille, *The Story of the Eye* 44). Because of this eerie distance, Simone begins to retreat into herself, and the narrator feels as if he must make more of an effort to understand her. Like most other things in the story, the narrator explains this search for Simone in a sexual way, comparing her orgasms with the laughs of "savage Africans" (46). He aligns her with these mysterious people by saying that when laughing, they "have long-lasting spasms, with all parts of the body in violent release, and they go whirling willy-nilly, flailing their arms about wildly, shaking their bellies, necks, and chests, and chortling and gulping horribly" (46). By comparing Simone to a race that was largely misunderstood during the time in which the story takes place, the narrator emphasizes how distanced he feels from his lover. Once the narrator establishes the shift in their relationship, the two flee the country to Madrid to avoid any legal repercussions from Marcelle's death. A major part of their stay in Madrid is concerned with bullfights, which they connect deeply with sexuality. The narrator claims that "any spectator has that feeling of total and repeated longing typical of the game of coitus" and that "the utter nearness of death is also felt in the same way" (47). The narrator's description of bullfights follows a sexual pattern, in that it builds up to a climax and ends abruptly.

The climax comes in the tenth section, titled "Granero's Eye," in which the narrator, Simone, and Sir Edmund (who helps them flee to Madrid) attend a bullfight together. It is mentioned earlier that the testicles of the first bull killed are typically cooked and served to one of the bullfighters seated in the front row of the arena, but Simone begs Sir Edmund to obtain them for her raw. She receives them and immediately tells Sir Edmund and the narrator that she wants to insert one into her vagina, but the men attempt to convince her otherwise. Eventually, Simone's desire becomes too intense and she succumbs to it, which coincides with Granero, the young bullfighter, being gored by a bull. Bataille describes these two events in the following way: "A shriek of unmeasured horror coincided with a brief orgasm for Simone, who was lifted up from the stone seat only to be flung back with a bleeding nose, under a blinding sun; men instantly rushed over to haul away Granero's body, the right eye dangling from the head" (*The Story of the Eye* 53). This ends the chapter, and at the beginning of the next one, the reader is told that "everything was promptly back to normal" (54).

The rest of the book plays out in Madrid and is primarily concerned with the three protagonists interactions with a young priest named Don Aminado. These final three chapters signal the first major discussions of religion, and what triggers this discussion is their arrival at the church of Don Juan; Don Juan being one of the most canonical literary libertines. This tale presumes not only that Don Juan was a real man, but also that he repented from his life of libertinage to found a church. Don Aminado is the resident priest of this church, another irony that is not to be ignored, as he engages in sexual activities with Simone during her confession. Just as Don Juan had to deal with his own transgressions, Don Aminado eventually faces torture at the hands of Sir Edmund, Simone, and the narrator, and is eventually murdered by them. While in Don Aminado's chambers, Sir Edmund comes upon the wafers and chalice used for communion, which he uses as an opportunity to express his opinions about the true meaning of communion. When Simone states that the wafers smell like sperm, Sir Edmund says,

> Precisely, . . . the hosts, as you see, are nothing other than Christ's sperm in the form of small white biscuits. And as for the wine they put in the chalice, the ecclesiastics say it is the *blood* of Christ, but they were obviously mistaken. . . . since they employ only *white* wine, they are showing that at the bottom of their hearts they are quite aware that this is urine. (Bataille, *The Story of the Eye* 61)

This is perhaps the most transgressive passage of the entire book, but it expresses a different type of transgression than the rest of the story. After explaining his logic behind this belief, Sir Edmund joins Simone and the narrator in attacking the young priest, ultimately killing him by choking him while he has an orgasm. All of this happens abruptly in the last few pages of the book. Once the priest is dead, the three protagonists leave Madrid in disguise and continue to flee from any legal consequences of their actions. As we observe, the narrator, Simone, and Sir Edmund take pleasure in boundary crossing and entering a chaotic realm; however, they also become conscious of the imposition of the law and are constantly on the run. Bataille's later works, such as *Inner Experience*, explore these dualities and paradoxes, and the existence of infinite definitions in the law in a world without God as well.

In *Erotism: Death and Sensuality* (1986), Bataille situates eroticism and death at the core of the human experience. Examining these two concepts defined as taboo, Bataille delves into themes which relate to transgression. Contrary to scientific approaches, he explores how these aspects of being human relate to each other rather than looking at them separately. The book is divided into two parts. The first part, "Taboos and Transgressions," explores the nature, purpose, and development of taboos. In this section, he draws on prehistoric experiences and discusses how taboos emerged in those times. He suggests that along with taboos, the idea of breaking those taboos also emerged as an integral part of the human experience. Bataille defines transgression as an urge to transcend the limit while simultaneously trying to maintain it. For Bataille, transgression is always associated with an imposed, existing limit. He believes that transgression prevails along with our understanding of the taboo and our ability to reconcile respect for the law with violation of the law; eventually, these violations result in an individual's awareness of law. Bataille writes, "The inner experience of eroticism demands from the subject a sensitiveness to the anguish at the heart of the taboo no less great than the desire which leads him to infringe it. This is religious sensibility, and it always links desire closely with terror, intense pleasure and anguish" (38–39). Hence, Bataille claims that observing and submitting to the taboo is an unconscious process. However, violation of the taboo is accompanied by an internalized, individual mental anguish, thus maintaining the taboo's existence. This internal process situated within a social setting leads to both transgressing and maintaining prohibition. Within this system, transgression can never amount to abolition of the law, specifically because it does not liberate an individual from all of its socially and historically constructed limits. An important touchstone of this section is the issues that Bataille explores in regard to Christianity and how it has played a defining role in the evolution of the taboos. In the Christian world, the taboo was absolute. As he explains, "Transgression would have made clear what Christianity concealed, that the sacred and the forbidden are one, that the sacred can be reached through the violence of a broken taboo" (126). The second part of the book, "Some Aspects of Eroticism," takes a look at the Kinsey Reports, which offered the first comprehensive scientifically based research into human sexuality in the 1950s. Bataille uses the report to support his own argument in recognizing sexuality, but he also comments that the reports are flawed and limited. In this part, Bataille takes under consideration Sade's works and discussions on suffering and sexuality which led to the coining of the term "sadism" to describe the gratification and pleasure some people receive from pain. Then, he moves to Claude Lévi-Strauss, who is known for his explorations of the relationship between eroticism and incest. Lastly, Bataille probes the link between sexuality and spirituality, and draws parallels between those who live intensely spiritual lives and have emotionally and physically ecstatic experiences, such as mystics, and those who have an intense experience from sexual pleasure. He writes:

> The trances, the states of rapture and the theopathic states prolifically described by mystics of every religious discipline—Hindu, Buddhist, Moslem or Christian, not to mention the rarer ones who have no religion—all have the same significance: non-attachment to ordinary life, indifference to its needs, anguish felt in the midst of this until the being reels, and the way left open to a spontaneous surge of life that is usually kept under control but which bursts forth in freedom and infinite bliss. The difference between this experience and that of sensuality is only a matter of confining these impulses to the domain of inner awareness, without the intervention of real and intentional physical activity (or if the body does come into play it is in a minimal fashion, even in the breathing exercises that Hindus deliberately practise for certain effects). (*Erotism* 246–47)

Bataille's philosophy of transgression—which, for him, is an act that disintegrates the traditional philosophical distinction between subject and object and between the self and the other—and the constant breaking of the limit have had a great impact on Western philosophy. For example, Foucault takes up Bataille's insights about the significance of the irrational in human actions and social relationships. Foucault, also like Bataille, sees sexual transgression as key. However, Nietzsche's works and his idea that God is dead also impacted Foucault in his belief of "will to power."

Friedrich Nietzsche's (1844–1900) philosophy is significant in this discussion insofar as it directly impacted Foucault's understanding of the notions of transgression and the limit. With Nietzsche's idea of the "death of God," the main hermeneutic object which can provide us with a definite definition is lost, which means that there can be infinite ways of understanding and interpreting a concept. We can find this possibility of infinite number of definitions in the law in Bataille's works as well. Nietzsche's reworking of human existence in regard to the Greek gods Apollo and Dionysus have been influential in the formation of the definition of transgression as we know it today. Nietzsche uses these concepts in *The Birth of Tragedy*. He begins the book by explaining the central duality of art as the opposition between Apollonian and Dionysian characteristics. He believes that the introduction of Dionysus represents the birth of Greek tragedy. This is because Dionysus symbolizes wilderness and madness, and thus directly opposes the Apollonian perspective of comfort and boundaries. Nietzsche illustrates duality by showing how dreams and drunkenness are opposing states. Nietzsche says of dreams, "We take pleasure in the immediate apprehension of form, all shapes speak to us, and nothing is indifferent or unnecessary. But even when this dream reality is presented to us with the greatest intensity, we still have a glimmering awareness that it is an illusion" (15). We can thus take comfort in dreams, even the unpleasant ones, as we can dismiss them upon waking. Nietzsche associates this notion with Schopenhauer's concept of *principum individuationis*, or principle of individuation. This means that under the influence of Apollo, man is able to distinguish between appearances and reality as well as between himself and his fellow man. These distinctions, while at times necessary, are not conducive to artistic processes or interpersonal relationships. Drawing on the idea of turning Beethoven's "Hymn of Joy" to a painting with no restraint, Nietzsche illustrates the harmonic power of the Dionysian world by describing it in the following way: "Now the slave is a free man, now all the rigid and hostile boundaries that distress, despotism or 'impudent fashion' have erected between man and man break down. Now, . . . each man feels himself not only united, reconciled, and at one with his neighbor, but one with him, as if the veil of Maya had been rent and now hung in rags before the mysterious primal Oneness" (17). This certainly seems to be the artist's dream, living in harmony with his fellow men, no boundaries separating people or art forms. Nietzsche suggests that in order to create art, the artist must succumb to Dionysian madness, which signifies the artist's call to transgress. By associating Dionysus with drunkenness, a less socially accepted state than Apollo's association with sleeping, he immediately signifies to the reader that Dionysian artists are on the fringes of society. It is possible to be an artist without transgressing, but Nietzsche calls these artists naive and believes that they are focused only on aesthetics, with no attention paid to things lying just beneath the surface. At first, it appears as if Nietzsche is saying that the Apollonian impulse should be entirely ignored in favor of the Dionysian, but he then explains the importance of Apollo in transforming Dionysus from a force of destruction to one of redemption and harmony. Once Apollo confronts Dionysus, his power is utterly transformed. It can be gathered, then, that Apollo's influence on Dionysus transformed him from a destructive presence in society to a productive one. It is important that Nietzsche says that "the chasm has not been bridged," as this would imply that one of the two forces no longer exists (20). Both forces are essential to society and to art, for the artist must maintain his transgressive position, which would be impossible without the Apollonian force. Dionysus remains an agent of chaos, but the type of chaos that is sustainable. Hence, Nietzsche considers the Apollonian as the realm of individual and cultural limit while the Dionysian realm represents chaos and motion, which the Apollonian tries to control and confine. The Apollonian is all about form, structure, and rational thought. The Dionysian, on the other hand, is all that breaks away from structure, such as madness, ecstasy, and drunkenness. According to Nietzsche, it is in a state of ecstasy and madness that individuals give up their self to submerge with a greater whole. This dichotomy and the responses to it extend to the West and Western culture and art, and represent the opposition between nature and culture as well.

For Michel Foucault (1926–1984), the relationship between the forces of Apollo and Dionysus, chaos and order, and instinct and reason unfolds in a spiral manner. In his essay "Preface to Transgression," the Apollonian proposed by Nietzsche becomes the limit and the Dionysian translates into transgression. The Apollonian limit represents post-Enlightenment reason, which controls and limits Dionysian chaos, both on an individual and cultural level. In this post-Enlightenment era, where reason has replaced the sacred, Foucault, like Bataille, centralizes sexuality as the borderline between the Apollonian and the Dionysian. In this way, Foucault examines the underlying assumptions of Western culture beyond a simple dichotomy. He sheds light on the importance of understanding these concepts in a spiral manner rather than as a dichotomous entity as Nietzsche did. Nietzsche's work influenced Foucault in his re-theorizing of the concepts of power and desire, which constitute human subjects. Hence, Foucault conceived new modes through which human subjects no longer needed power or control over the other. This was, of course, a new direction compared to former discourses about power, desire, and subjectivity.

Foucault also expanded on Bataille's narrower theory of transgression and developed his own, which engages literature and individual subjectivity—one of the main reasons why I engage with his theory in this book. Foucault begins "Preface to Transgression" by referring to Christian mysticism, then moves to the "Sade to Freud" period of modernism, and finally discusses his own notions of transgression and the limit in a postmodern era. He writes, "sexuality has regained, in contemporary experience, its full truth as a process of nature, a truth which has long been lingering in the shadows and hiding under various disguises—until now, that is, when our positive awareness allows us to decipher it so that it may at least emerge in the clear light of language" (29). Foucault uses the verb "regained" because he believes that sexuality was once at the heart of Christian mysticism but has been pushed into the margins. He hopes that it will come to light through his discussion of it. Foucault expounds that for a long time transgressive sexuality was integrated into a Christian hierarchy of experience and transcendence. Referring to Bataille's *Erotism*, Foucault presents us with a counterfactual belief, saying: "Yet never did sexuality enjoy a more immediately natural understanding and never did it know a greater 'felicity of expression' than in Christian world of fallen bodies and of sin" ("Preface" 29). Foucault notes how desire and the erotic lead to a center of "a divine love of which they were both the outpouring and the source returning upon itself" (29). Like Bataille, Foucault believes that the connection between the erotic and the divine can be captured in the mystics' raptures and ecstatic expressions. What is happening during these mystical raptures, in Foucault's terms, is that the transgressive nature of sexuality is being given a transcendental significance.

Foucault contrasts the accounts of sexuality in Christianity with the modern denaturing of sexuality from the "Sade to Freud" period, from which, in Foucault's words, sexuality needs to be liberated in the postmodern era. This "Sade to Freud" state of affairs is a discontinuous and denatured sexuality which constitutes the human—that is, logic and consciousness—as the limit. Foucault proposes that through being "denatured" and violated by logical human languages, sexuality has achieved its characterization. In this context, sexuality refers to nothing beyond itself. Thus, it is through its limits that sexuality is reestablished as modern and impossible to be further extended or translated. Foucault sees the contemporary consciousness of sexuality as an extension of sexuality to its limits rather than liberation. It is through this extension that the notion of infiniteness, and therefore God as the embodiment of infiniteness, is disrupted. According to Foucault, sexuality has been used to take us to the limit of our consciousness because it is the "sole substance of universal taboos" ("Preface" 30). Hence, he rejects the idea of absolute freedom: "no matter how terrifying a given system may be, there always remain the possibilities of resistance, disobedience, and oppositional groupings. On the other hand, I do not think that there is anything that is functionally—by its very nature—absolutely liberating" ("Space, Knowledge, Power" 354). The liberating engagement is transgressive eroticism, which is the means for transcending the human as the limit. Furthermore, it is aimed at the void where God once was. In this way, as the sexuality of Christian mystics was aimed at God's presence, the transgressive sexuality of postmodern humans is aimed at God's absence. Foucault believes that sexuality and its limit cannot liberate humans because God is dead.

It is because of this absence of God that Foucault invites his readers to equate the death of God and freedom from religion with the sexual liberation that language has experienced. For Foucault, any institutionalized knowledge, such as philosophy or religion, is an instrument of power which tries to gain control over the sexually deviant. Liberated from religious obligation, yet taken to its extreme, sexuality has managed to assist in bringing about the death of God. This is because God is the embodiment of the infinite, but with the presence of sexuality and its limit (as it becomes finite), God has lost meaning. Whereas Bataille postulates that we must not "spiritualise the domain of sexuality to exalt it to the level of ethereal experiences" (*Erotism* 245), Foucault suggests that "the language of sexuality had lifted us into the night where God is absent, and where all of our actions are addressed to this absence in profanation that at once identifies it, dissipates it, exhausts itself in it, and restores it to the empty purity of its transgression" ("Preface" 31). This is of course because sexuality has expressed its own finiteness and limit while destabilizing the influence of religion. Thus, even sexuality has its own limit, and cannot liberate individuals.

The death of God translates into an end to the Christian mystics' transcendental justifications for transgression. As Foucault puts it, "Profanation in a world which no longer recognizes any positive meaning in the sacred—is this not more or less what we may call transgression?" ("Preface" 30). In a world where the sacred has lost its meaning, human subjects (logic) become God, the limit. Now if there is no sacred reference and no transcendental justification, Foucault encourages us to question: what is the limit for transgression? Where does one draw the line? The death of God, as Foucault puts it, has denied us the "limit of the Limitless" and has produced for us "an experience in which nothing may again announce the exteriority of being" (32). Without God, there is nothing to refer our transgressions to, nothing to provide us with a rationale for exercising it, nothing to liberate us.

Although like Sade, Bataille, and Nietzsche, Foucault's work examines the central role of sexuality in a secular post-Enlightenment world, and replaces transgression and the limit with the sacred and the profane, what differentiates Foucault from his predecessors is his argument in "Preface to Transgression" which illustrates that transgression is an important concept for understanding the liminal experiences which shape social and cultural boundaries. Foucault explores the concept of transgression both individually and culturally in the context of social repression. For Foucault, the boundaries of the self and the other are illuminated through acts of transgression. Therefore, transgression is the continual crossing of boundaries through a process of construction and deconstruction of identities and through the separation of the self from the other. The other is frequently rejected and excluded at the social level. However, since the self and the other are interdependent, and since the other is both socially despised and desired, the self-other dyad is an integral part of the dominant culture's social imaginary. Thus, the other is simultaneously present on the periphery and in the center of society. Foucault argues that "the limit and transgression depend on each other for whatever density of being they possess: a limit could not exist if it were absolutely uncrossable and, reciprocally, transgression would be pointless if it merely crossed a limit composed of illusions and shadows" ("Preface" 34). For Foucault, "transgression is not related to the limit as black to white, the prohibited to the lawful, the outside to the inside" (35). It is not a sign of liberation; it is not associated with the ethics; "it must be liberated from the scandalous or subversive, that is, from anything aroused by negative associations" (35). Therefore, Foucault's ideas indicate that the relationship between transgression and the law is not an absolute one.

Insofar as sexual pleasure is concerned, we can track this obscurity in Jacques Lacan's (1901–1981) conceptualization of transgression, too, in its relation to law through exploring his idea of "jouissance." Lacan considers the Pleasure Principle as the means to limit jouissance. According to this definition, giving up jouissance becomes necessary for the attainment of subjectivity since jouissance is forbidden for the speaking subject, and the jouissance which has been sacrificed becomes the object which is desired but is unattainable. However, in this way, jouissance becomes pain because there is only a certain amount of pleasure that can be attained if the subject transgresses the prohibition. After that, there is only pain left and jouissance becomes the consequent suffering. Lacan argues that despite the dominance of law, we enjoy it; and we do so particularly because it prevails. This is how Lacan explains jouissance. For Lacan, jouissance is neither the instinctual urge for pleasure nor the fulfillment of such urges, both of which function in conflict with law. Jouissance is not organized through transgression of the law. On the contrary, it is organized in relation to the law. Lacan claims, "If there is no god . . . everything is forbidden" (qtd. in Žižek 9–10). Nonetheless, the absence of law prescribes universalization of prohibition because the enjoyment that we experience from transgression is in fact imposed. Our enjoyment always follows a certain law, the law of the superego.

In line with the arguments of all these thinkers, Foucault and ʿAṭṭār demonstrate that transgression measures up to the de- and reconstruction of subjectivity through the crossing and recrossing of boundaries, and they both agree that transgression is important for our understanding of liminal experiences. ʿAṭṭār's works examine the sociocultural, religious, and sexual taboos and the violation of these taboos. ʿAṭṭār shows that the violation of the law does not fully liberate individuals from the historically constructed limits; however, he suggests that this violation can offer ways for rewriting the structured and established narratives. Like Foucault, ʿAṭṭār views the boundaries between the individual and the cultural as emerging through transgression. Foucault defines individual and collective subjectivity by means of the demarcation between appropriate and inappropriate values to the other, such as normative heterosexuality versus deviant homosexuality. This is how Foucault introduces the notion of the "destabilized subject" as one who is not rational. Foucault posits that in a secular world without the sacred, transgression is the site for profanation, and sexuality is the only source of differentiation in a world where there is no space, object, or human to be violated; hence the reason for sexuality being the central limit. For ʿAṭṭār, however, love takes center stage, and although it does not amount to full liberation from all historically constructed barriers, it offers myriad ways for living and loving. Foucault's notions of boundary crossing, transgression, and acceptance of the other shapes much of the cultural productions of contemporary cultural theory, which is preoccupied with acceptance of sexual, cultural, social, and religious diversity. It is part of his larger antihumanist argument which illustrates that human reason has further enslaved humans rather than liberated them. Through his theory of transgression, he questions the underlying ideas of the humanism and Enlightenment tradition which argue that humans are stable and unified subjects. Transgression, therefore, is an important concept for understanding the liminal experiences discussed in modern cultural theory.

The remainder of this book will focus on the ways that Foucault and ʿAṭṭār can be brought into a dialogue regarding transgression, the limit, and the construction of subjectivity. It is within the contradictory space of the medieval and the modern, theory and literature, and Western and Middle Eastern that I would like to initiate this discussion. Through analyzing ʿAṭṭār's works in the coming chapters, we will see that ʿAṭṭār is accepting of transgressors and liminal individuals through love and spirituality. He encourages violation of the limits (social, cultural, sexual, and religious taboos) as a means of opening infinite ways of living and of loving, and of human forms. Although such violation of the law does not fully liberate individuals from all historically constructed limits, he introduces ways for disrupting the established narratives. In his spiritual world, with God as the embodiment of infiniteness, spirituality aids the self to be open to infinite others, merge with them, and emerge as a new subject.

This contradictory fusion is what helps the self to reconstruct its subjectivity in relation to the other. The construction of subjectivity through the fusion of the self and the other via violating the constructed barriers in our minds is where Foucault and ʿAṭṭār agree; hence, both believe in the significance of liminal experiences and transgression for the shaping of cultural and social boundaries. While ʿAṭṭār emphasizes the presence of the divine, Foucault reiterates the absence of God. However, if we translate Foucault's God to human logic and consciousness, then both ʿAṭṭār and Foucault seem to advocate liberation from that logic through the crossing of the barriers that human consciousness and reason has constructed, and while for Foucault sexuality is central, for ʿAṭṭār spirituality takes the spotlight. The analysis of ʿAṭṭār's works alongside medieval European literature and modern theory, particularly Foucault's, will in turn demonstrate that medieval works such as ʿAṭṭār's are not mere historical entities but texts that can reveal as much about medieval subjectivity as they do about our modern understanding of subjectivity. In the following chapters, I will mainly focus on ʿAṭṭār but will also read medieval European literature, and closely read theoretical passages from Foucault, and sometimes from other thinkers as well, such as Julia Kristeva, Emmanuel Lévinas, Jacques Lacan, and Judith Butler, contrapuntally.

Chapter 3

Rābiʿa al-ʿAdawiyya and Margery Kempe

Background Information

In his *Tadhkirat al-awlīyā*, ʿAṭṭār devotes an entry to Rābiʿa al-ʿAdawiyya. She gained considerable recognition throughout the Muslim world as the first female Sufi, and for her introduction of the theme of love into the Islamic mystical tradition. Narratives and legends about her life indicate that she was born between 714 and 717/18 and died in 801 in Basra, that is, modern day Iraq. Medieval sources locate Rābiʿa's tomb on the outskirts of Basra, not in Jerusalem or Egypt as some other sources have claimed. ʿAṭṭār and other scholars have suggested that Rābiʿa was an orphan and a non-Muslim slave who converted to Islam. It is also related that Rābiʿa was a client of the clan of al-ʿAṭīk, which was a subclan of ʿAdī ibn Qays, which was, in turn, a clan of the Quraysh tribe of Mecca, the tribe of the Prophet Muḥammad. After the conquests of Islam until the end of the Umayyad caliphate (634–750), non-Muslims could convert to Islam under the sponsorship of an Arab patron, who either adopted the convert into his or her clan or maintained the convert in a state of clientship, which was often formalized by a contract of mutual assistance. Rābiʿa, who was one of these clients, seems to have been both non-Arab and non-Muslim, and the al-ʿAṭīk clan had sponsored her conversion into Islam (al-Sulamī 74). Various legends affirm that after being freed, Rābiʿa lived the celibate life of an ascetic in a desert cell her entire life. She is known for her spirituality, asceticism, and selfless love of God, for her wit and wisdom, her strong and public criticism of men, and her constant refusal to marry.

This chapter proposes that contrary to the common view of Muslim women as subservient and passive, Rābiʿa is portrayed as challenging the established gender norms of her day in ʿAṭṭār's *Tadhkirat al-awlīyā*. Rābiʿa is illustrated in ʿAṭṭār's works as a freedwoman who refuses all worldly pleasures such as marriage and is a harsh admonisher of her fellow male Sufis and her male disciples. Rābiʿa has oftentimes been characterized by her male counterparts as desexualized. Having abandoned the typical feminine emotions and sensitivities ascribed to the women of the period, probably because of the physical, emotional, and sexual exploitation she may have suffered as a slave, she is shown as taking refuge in God and Sufism. Rābiʿa's crossing of gender boundaries and her mysticism as portrayed in ʿAṭṭār's works can therefore be seen both as defense mechanisms against her experiences of exploitation and as necessary steps to transcend the limits of her gender and feminine sexuality in order to reach the type of liberation that she so longed for.

In order to have a more nuanced view of medieval female mystics' gender transgression, in this chapter I will also look at a similar gender transgression in Rābiʿa's Christian counterpart, the Englishwoman Margery Kempe (1373–1438). Although Rābiʿa and Margery lived centuries apart, and although they belonged to two different spiritual and religious traditions, much of what ʿAṭṭār writes about Rābiʿa's gender transgression and its relation to her emotional, psychological, and spiritual experiences can be found in the accounts of Margery's spiritual path in *The Book of Margery Kempe* (*The Book* hereafter), which she wrote with the help of her scribes. In this book, she chronicles her numerous pilgrimages to holy sites, as well as her mystical conversations with Jesus Christ, the Virgin Mary, and St. Anne, and the tension in late medieval England between institutional orthodoxy and public modes of religious expressions such as Lollardy. Margery was born Margery Brunham in King's Lynn, Norfolk, and married a Norwich man named John Kempe with whom she had fourteen children. Margery's public expression of spirituality as a laywoman was unusual among the more traditional holy exemplars of her time, such as Julian of Norwich, who was a cloistered anchoress. Throughout her spiritual career portrayed in the book, Margery is challenged by both the church and the civil authorities on her adherence to the teachings of the institutional church; however, she proves her orthodoxy in each case. In her book, Margery's spiritual career begins after her traumatic experience in childbirth and subsequent abject feelings about femininity and motherhood. Through her spirituality, Margery, like Rābiʿa, is shown as crossing the gender boundaries of her time and reshaping her identity to reenter the world as a new subject. Both Rābiʿa and Margery turn to divine love as a way to heal their earthly wounds. I argue that the power of divine love and the encounter with the divine other allow these two women to transgress gender boundaries, to de- and reconstruct their identities through annihilation of their selves, to rediscover the ultimate reality, and to unite with the divine.

In this chapter, I draw on the parallels between these two women's experiences and place them in conversation with modern theoretical works such as Lacan's and Foucault's. Reading passages contrapuntally from each text, I illustrate how both medieval and modern texts emphasize the importance of breaking away from social restrictions in order to forge one's identity. By crossing the sociocultural boundaries and barriers constructed by their own minds, these women not only show their independence, but also reconstruct their subjectivity and emerge as new subjects able to survive without male intervention, except for the transmission of their writings. This chapter also examines the role of Rābiʿa's and Margery's male counterparts in the shaping of their spirituality and subjectivity. Although Margery's book is the best source available for a middle-class woman's experience in the Middle Ages, like Rābiʿa, Margery owes her popularity to her male scribes and confessors who helped her text travel through time and space. Indeed, despite their efforts, Rābiʿa and Margery both needed the acknowledgement of their contemporary male spirituals for the written transmission of their mystical experiences, which is further proof of their day's male dominance and testimony to their own boundary crossing. Margery's scribes, by writing her experiences, and ʿAṭṭār, by including Rābiʿa in his *Tadhkirat al-awlīyā*, not only revere these women's spirituality, but also illustrate their own tendency towards pushing the social, cultural, and gender boundaries of the day, which used to exclude the female voice from the public, official space. I argue that these male authors, too, embrace gender diversity, which is a crucial step in proving their own mysticism and submission to the divine.

Gender Demarcations in the Medieval Muslim World

The dominant religion of the Mediterranean Middle East before Islam was Christianity, although Jews and Zoroastrians dwelled in the region too. The emphasis on transcending the body and the value that the church put on women's virginity and sexual purity in accordance with the view of women as essentially biological beings was dominant in most of the cultures of this region. Although female celibacy was valued, the independence it gave to women to act on their own was a challenge to male authority and to socioreligious notions about women (see Ahmed, *Women and Gender* 24; Keddie, *Women in the Middle East*; Najmabadi, *Women with Mustaches*). The idea that sex was only acceptable for procreation, but sinful otherwise, mostly focused on women's sexuality and bodies; the female body was considered shameful. These notions mandated men to avoid contact with women; therefore, even the sight of a woman was threatening to men. Consequently, the female body was to be covered and veiled, and strict segregation of the sexes was emphasized (Ahmed, *Women and Gender* 35).

When Islam emerged in the seventh century, it identified with the Judeo-Christian monotheism of the region. At the time of the Muslim conquests, the region was mainly under the influence of the Christian church, which had already legitimized misogyny by referring to biblical stories. As the new religion of the region, Islam incorporated this scriptural misogyny into its socioreligious world (Ahmed, *Women and Gender* 36). Within a decade of Muḥammad's death (632), the Arab conquests had transferred Islam to lands different from Arabia. These societies were urban and had already developed legal, religious, and social mores and traditions. They were also restrictive toward women and even more misogynistic (67).

After the conquests, wealth and slaves flooded into the Muslim communities of Arabia. At this time, Muslim elites owned thousands of slaves; even ordinary soldiers had a few to serve them. Because of the slave market, women were treated as commodities and had little power over their sexual, psychological, and emotional lives. Male masters owned, rented, or sold them (Ahmed, *Women and Gender* 80). During the transitional period of the Muslim community from its first decades to the Abbasid era, attitudes toward women and marriage changed even more. Marrying non-virgins became shameful. Women's participation in society and in religious matters was further restricted. The trend was towards women's absolute closure and diminution (67). In this period, the words "woman" and "slave" became synonymous with objects for sexual use. This trend was prevalent in Iraq, too, Rābiʿa's home country, where the Sassanian Empire was located (80).

The Arab conquests aimed at Islamization and Arabization, but at the same time integrated Judeo-Christian customs and traditions. The misogynist attitudes licensing polygamy, concubinage, and easy divorce for men were allowed in the urban Middle East before Islam; however, Islam further endorsed and gave religious sanction to negative conceptions of women. Consequently, the abuse of women became legally and religiously sanctioned practices in the Muslim world. Abbasid society gave extreme importance to androcentric teachings in Islam in matters of relations between men and women (Ahmed, *Women and Gender* 80). Rābiʿa, being a female Sufi, lived most of her life under such conditions.

However, matters were slightly different in Sufi circles. Sufi movements, which challenged the norms of the day, including gender norms, emerged during the Abbasid era. By simply allowing women to practice religion and to maintain control over their sexuality, the Sufis affirmed the importance of the spiritual over the biological. Sufi ideas challenged the way Islam conceptualized gender (Ahmed, *Women and Gender* 66). Piety, asceticism, the renunciation of materialism, the emphasis on celibacy, and the rejection of unbridled male sexuality all had political dimensions as well. Through their nonconformity to the mainstream, Sufis wanted to show their opposition to the government and established religion (95–96). The Sufi ethos countered that of the dominant society. Sufis demonstrated that gender arrangements are social decisions. Rejecting the gender arrangements of society, Sufis honored the contribution of female spiritual leaders such as Rābiʿa. However, this is not to say that all male Sufis embraced female spirituality equally.

Medieval Male Sufis' View of Rābiʿa's Spirituality

Although some male Sufis were accepting of female spirituality, the ideal of medieval Sufism was male, and the stance that male Sufis adopted toward women in the medieval period was unclear. For instance, male Sufis such as Sanāʾī (1080–1131), who were not favorable toward women, at times claimed that "A pious woman is better than a thousand bad men" and at other times, such as in the *banat an-naʿ sh* (daughters of the bier), implied that "daughters are better on the bier than alive" (qtd. in Schimmel, *Mystical Dimensions* 426). Rābiʿa's faithfulness to God granted her significant status in male Sufi circles, although she was not the only female spiritual in the eighth century. Nonetheless, she was the only female Sufi who was to a certain degree accepted by male Sufis and in male Sufi circles, even by those who largely disfavored women. A statement indicating the acceptance of female spirituality in the medieval period appears in ʿAṭṭār's famous line in *Tadhkirat al-awlīyā*, where he states that in the realm of the divine union, gender differences lose their earthly significance (Losensky, 97; Nicholson, *Tadhkirat* 59):

> In unity, how can the existence of "me" and "you" remain, much less "man" and "woman"?
>
> در توحید وجود من و تو کی ماند تا بمرد و زن.

Rābiʿa's spirituality granted her an entry or a reference in most of her contemporary or later biographers' or authors' books. The first author who referred to Rābiʿa is al-Jāhiz of Basra (776–869) in his books the *Kitāb al-Ḥayawān* (*Book of Animals*) and the *Kitāb al-Bayān wa al-tabyīn* (*Book of Clarity and Clarification*). He was a literary man and a prolific prose writer who wrote essays under the influence of Greek logic. He portrays Rābiʿa as a self-denying ascetic, who renounces all worldly things and, contrary to the typical "weak" woman of her time, has strong self-control. Several references to Rābiʿa appear in Abū Ṭālib Muḥammad ibn ʿAlī Makkī's (?–996) *Qūt al-qulūb* (*The Nourishment of Hearts*). Another Sufi author who wrote about Rābiʿa briefly in his *Kitāb al-Taʿarruf li-madhhab ahl al-Taṣawwuf* (*The Doctrine of the Sufis*) is Abū Bakr al-Kalābādhī (fl. late tenth century). A writer who makes frequent references to Rābiʿa in his *al-Risāla al-qushayrīyya* is Abū al-Qāsim al-Qushayrī (986–1072) from Nishāpūr, Khurāsān. Al-Qushayrī's treatise includes material on Sufism, its philosophy, its terminology, and the biographies of exemplary Sufis. His portrayal of Rābiʿa is that of a female spiritual teacher and guide to men, something that was not common at the time. Rābiʿa is depicted in al-Qushayrī's work as a wise mystic who instructs others, has no weaknesses, and lacks worldly desires. Among Persian Sufi writers who mention Rābiʿa are Shams al-Dīn Aḥmad Aflakī (?–1360) in *Manāqib al-ʿārifīn* (*Feats of the Knowers of God*), and Jāmī in his *Nafaḥāt al-uns* (*Breaths of Intimacy*). Jāmī was not particularly favorable toward women, yet he wrote the following lines about Rābiʿa:

> If all women were like the one [Rābiʿa] we have mentioned,
> then women would be preferred to men,
> For the feminine gender is no shame for the sun,
> nor is the masculine gender an honor for the crescent moon.
> (*Nafaḥāt al-uns* 615)

Despite Jāmī's attempt to maintain gender equality, by writing that neither being a woman is shameful nor being a man is honorable, he still conforms to a gender binary and makes the reader wonder why there has to be a preference of one over the other, and why the woman has to be placed in a category of "shameful" while the man is placed under "honorable." In addition, reference to the feminine gender as shameful reminds the reader of the cultural and religious beliefs of the time, which held that the female body and sexuality are shameful and should be veiled. Jāmī's privileging of one gender over the other appears in the line that if all women were like Rābiʿa, "then women would be preferred to men." Here, Jāmī seems to be giving Rābiʿa's spirituality some credit; however, his comparing men and women, hierarchizing one over the other, as if they are mutually exclusive, is proof of the persistence of the dichotomy and the stance that Jāmī, and possibly other male Sufis, too, took with regard to women. Furthermore, he conforms to the gender binary in yet another metaphorical use, that of the sun and crescent moon imagery, as linguistically in Arabic the sun is feminine and the crescent moon is masculine.

Like Jāmī, al-Jāhiz and al-Qushayrī highlight Rābiʿa's gender by portraying her differently from a typical woman of her time, providing evidence that in medieval society gender hierarchies were of paramount significance. Among other early writers on Sufism who referred to Rābiʿa in their books are Abū Naṣr al-Sarrāj (?–988), who was born in Ṭūs (an ancient city in Khurāsān) and mentioned Rābiʿa in his treatise on Sufism, *Kitāb al-Lumaʿ fil Taṣawwuf* (*Book of Flashes*); al-Hamadānī (1098–1131) in *Shakwā al-gharīb min al-awtān* (*Complaint of a Stranger Exiled from Home*); Abū Nuʿaym al-Iṣfahānī (947–1038) in *Ḥilyah al-auliyā wa ṭabaqāt al-aṣfīya* (*The Adornment of the Saints and the Ranks of the Spiritual Elite)*, also known as *Ḥilyah al-abrār*; Sarrāj al-Qārī (ca. 1026–1106) in *Maṣāriʿ al-ʿushshāq* (*Gates of the Lovers*); Muḥammad al-Ghazzālī (1058–1111), who referred to Rābiʿa's love of the divine and celibacy in *Iḥyāʾ ʿUlūm al-Dīn* (*The Revival of the Religious Sciences*); and Ghānim al-Maqdisī (?–1279) in *Kashf al-asrār wa manāqib al-abrār* (*The Unveiling of the Mysteries and Merits of the Just*).

While all these entries and references are significant, Rābiʿa's most complete biography was written by ʿAṭṭār in *Tadhkirat al-awlīyā*. It is noteworthy that out of seventy-two biographical entries, ʿAṭṭār has devoted only one entry to a female Sufi while the rest are devoted to men. ʿAṭṭār portrays Rābiʿa as a strong, wise woman who is equal, and oftentimes superior, to men in spiritual matters, and who freely criticizes male Sufis for their shortcomings in spirituality. In *Tadhkirat al-awlīyā,* ʿAṭṭār defines Rābiʿa's rank in Islamic Sufism as (Losensky 97; Nicholson, *Tadhkirat* 59):

> Veiled with a special veil, hidden by the curtain of sincerity, burned up in love and longing, enamored of proximity and immolation, deputy of the virgin Mary, accepted among men, [Rābiʿa al-ʿAdawiyya]—God most high have mercy upon her. If anyone asks why we placed her memorial among the ranks of men, we reply that the Master of the Prophets (peace and blessing be upon him) declares: God does not regard your forms. It is not a matter of form but of right intention. If it is right to derive two-thirds of religion from [ʿAʿisha]-ye Sadeqa (God be pleased with her), then it is also right to derive benefit from one of his maid servants. When a woman is a man on the path of the Lord most high, she cannot be called woman.

آن مخدره خدر خاص ، آن مستوره اخلاص ، آن سوخته عشق و اشتیاق ،
آن شیفته قرب و احتراق ، آن گمشده وصال ، آن مقبول الرجال ثانیه مریم
صفیه ، رابعه العدویه رحمةالله علیهما. اگر کسی گوید ذکراو در صف

رجال چرا کرده ای گویم که خواجه انبیا علیهم السلام می فرماید :ان الله لاینظر الی صورکم الحدیث . کار به صورت نیست به نیت است . کما قال علیه السلام یحشر الناس علی نیاتهم . اگر رواست دو ثلث دین از عایشه صدیقی رضی الله عنها فراگرفتن هم روا بود از کنیزکی از کنیزکان او فایده دنیی گرفتن . چون زن در راه خدای مرد بود او را زن نتوان گفت . چنانکه عباسه طوسی گفت :چون فردا در عرصات قیامت آواز دهند که یا رجال ! نخست کسی که پای در صف رجال نهد ، مریم بود علیها السلام .

The fact that ʿAṭṭār needs to justify his reason for placing Rābiʿa in the rank of men by citing the Prophet and later comparing her to the Prophet's wife, ʿAʿisha, only further highlights the presence of the dominant gender binary. It also sheds light on ʿAṭṭār's own consciousness of the conventional and cultural gender demarcations of his day. Sells observes that this introduction is "an immediate and dramatic highlighting of the gender issue" (*Early Islamic Mysticism* 152). What is even more worth noting here is that whereas ʿAṭṭār mentions the Prophet's reference to the triviality of the outward forms, he himself attributes an alternative outward form to Rābiʿa by symbolically transforming her from female to male. Sells argues that "ʿAṭṭār appeals to historical precedent: the formative role of ʿAʿisha" and "to the tradition according to which Maryam, the mother of 'Isa (Jesus), will be the first among the 'ranks of men' at the final resurrection." Then, with a more abstract appeal to the importance of the person's inner intention, not the outward form, he finally "ends with a justification based on a mystical notion of unity" (152). This mystical notion of unity between all genders in matters of spirituality is what ʿAṭṭār wrote about in the line mentioned previously. ʿAṭṭār's vocabulary is also important in this passage as he uses the Persian terms *rijāl* and *mard* to refer to Rābiʿa, which, according to Dihkhudā's *Lughat-nāma* (Dihkhudā's dictionary), refer to either male sex and masculinity or well-known and famous men, though he could have instead used the more general terms *insān* and *bashar*, meaning a person or the entire humankind, equally encompassing all genders.

In another anecdote highlighting gender boundaries, in *Tadhkirat al-awlīyā*, ʿAṭṭār relates that al-Ḥasan al-Baṣrī once commented that he had spent an entire night with Rābiʿa without feeling that she was a woman (Losensky 104; Nicholson, *Tadhkirat* 65):

> I was with Rābiʿa for one full day and night. I was talking about the path and the truth in such a way that the thought "I am a man" never crossed my mind, nor did "I am a woman" ever cross hers. In the end when I got up, I considered myself a pauper and her a devotee.

یک شبانه روز در بر رابعه بودم و سخن طریقت و حقیقت گفتم که نه در خاطر من بر گذشت که مردی ام و نه بر خاطر او بگذشت که زنی ام آخر الامر چون بر خاستم نگاه خویشتن را مفلسی دیدم و رابعه را مخلصی.

In yet another narrative, which I will discuss shortly, ʿAṭṭār writes that al-Ḥasan was one of Rābiʿa's suitors who desired to be united with her in matrimony. Placing these two narratives side by side and examining them, it seems contradictory that al-Ḥasan could have spent an entire night and day with the woman that he wanted to marry and be oblivious to her femininity. As Leila Ahmed notes, this narrative repudiates the underlying "notion of sexuality as governing male-female interactions" (*Women and Gender* 96). In addition, whereas al-Ḥasan claims not to have been aware of her sexuality while in her presence, in another passage, he advises others to stay away from virgins like her because of the temptations that their proximity could generate. According to Margaret Smith, al-Ḥasan gave the following three pieces of advice to his fellow ascetics: "Set not your feet upon the carpet of kings (i.e., have no dealings with them); sit not alone with any virgin, even though it were Rābiʿa; and lend not your ear to others" (*The Way* 176). It is therefore paradoxical that al-Ḥasan, who had once asked for Rābiʿa's hand, appeared to be oblivious to her femininity, but simultaneously included her as a source of temptation and threat to male purity. Narratives like this complicate the gender-related issues of the time. On another note, ʿAṭṭār's reference to al-Ḥasan's comment that, to him, Rābiʿa seemed like a devotee in whose presence he felt like a pauper, "reverses the dominant society's valuation of male over female by representing not merely any man but one of the more revered male Sufi leaders describing himself as [a pauper] compared with a woman of truly superior merits" (Ahmed, *Women and Gender* 96). This is one of the moments when ʿAṭṭār himself seems to be trying to rewrite the dominant scripts pertinent to gender hierarchy in Sufism too.

These references illustrate that although some male authors referred to or devoted an entry to Rābiʿa in their works, they represented her in a way that served the sociocultural needs of the patriarchal society of the time. Pushing Rābiʿa's femininity into obscurity, they produced an image of Rābiʿa which was comprehensible only in the light of her male counterparts. Reading the comments and descriptions of Rābiʿa's contemporary male Sufis, her biographers, and other male scholars of the medieval Muslim world, one thing that strikes the reader is the attempts they made to undermine Rābiʿa's femininity. One may assume that this was done to justify the elevated status of this woman in the male-dominated realm of Sufism, where the ideal was male. In *Teachings of Sufism*, Carl W. Ernst astutely questions this type of writing: "How many times has it been said of an impressive woman, that she was, as it were, a man in the form of a woman? This sort of negative compliment seems to be the last resort of the male hagiographer who is perplexed and bewildered (and struck with admiration) by the spiritual power of a woman" (181–82). To Rābiʿa's contemporary, and later, male Sufis, she embodied the masculine traits that the medieval Sufi world revered. To maintain that long-enduring ideal of the male-dominated realm, however, these Sufis could do nothing but repudiate her femininity. Thus, even though Rābiʿa was spiritually endowed and revered, she was seen and defined in the light of contemporary men. After all, to maintain gender divisions, Rābiʿa, who was blurring the borders, would have to be controlled.

Gender Paradigms in Medieval British Society

Medieval British society was also no exception in terms of its restriction of the female voice. On the one hand, women were classified based on their marital status and their relation to men as maidens, wives, or widows, and on the other hand based on the binary of the sacred Virgin Mary versus the tainted Eve. Maidenhood, wifehood, and widowhood largely took on meaning according to women's subordination to masculine authority. This subordination was of course impacted by the church, which both limited "women's authority as wives and [expanded] it as virgins and visionaries" (Williams 2).

Regarding this duality, several significant historical and social events, such as the development of affective piety and increasing lay control over marriage, played important roles in late medieval British history. These changes opened up new female roles and new ways of thinking about and describing femininity. With the growth of affective piety and the emphasis on personal communication with the divine, both married and single women gained more authority. Women no longer had to be nuns or anchoresses to be considered spirituals. They could integrate their spiritual devotions into their secular, everyday lives (Williams 5).

However, fourteenth-century Britain was not yet completely familiar with the cults of female ecstatic piety and the public expressions of spirituality that were considerably popular in Europe at the time. Lollardy was also at its height. Lollards were the followers of John Wycliffe who advocated lay preaching and believed that everyone could interpret the scriptures if it was translated into the vernacular. Regardless of the substantial number of nuns and anchoresses, laywomen like Margery—who chose a singular vocation of charity, pilgrimage, fasting, penance, chaste living, preaching, and teaching and were popular for their public trances, visions, and ecstasy—were viewed as eccentric transgressors. Margery's knowledge of the scriptures as a laywoman and her preaching aroused feelings of antagonism and provoked the possibility of her being labeled a heretic.

Late medieval spirituality was impacted by the increase in the transformation of women's roles, which had been fundamentally limited to the private domain of domesticity. A great number of laywomen were attracted to spirituality, as it could assist them to move out of the private domain of the household and into the public sphere of religiosity. The era was highly influenced by the rise of heretical challenges to the church's authority and the great number of pilgrimages taken by pious women (Bynum, *Holy Feast* 16–20). These historical and social developments raised questions about the existing meanings and models of womanhood in late medieval Britain, and Margery Kemp was a target.

Medieval Clerics' Acceptance of Margery Kempe

Margery's father, John Brunham, was the popular five-time mayor of King's Lynn and one of two parliamentary members from the city. Her husband, John Kempe, though less notable than her father, was a burgess of King's Lynn. However, Margery, a woman in the household of the mayor, was left illiterate, although literacy had a different significance in medieval Europe than in the modern world. According to Michael T. Clanchy, in the medieval period after 1300, literacy was described as the ability to read Latin, but not necessarily to write it, while before 1300, literacy signified the ability to read, write, compose, understand, and express feelings in Latin (181–87). Margery's education was limited to the sermons that she had heard in the church, and the biblical parables and the saints' stories which were read to her. She would later also have heard itinerant and traveling preachers while on her extensive pilgrimages. It is clear that a common medieval Christian laywoman, even though a mayor's daughter, was not supposed to be well educated; rather, she was expected to listen to public sermons silently and remain intellectually confined. Thus, Margery, who showed great knowledge of the Bible and communicated with the divine directly, although not formally educated, seems to have crossed the gender boundaries of her day and appears as a transgressor. Margery was also well informed about continental women's cults, as she refers to Mary of Oignies and Bridget of Sweden in her book; this awareness, too, was a challenge to the authority of the church.

Due to the socioreligious conditions in England and the cultural notions of women as merely domestic wives and mothers, doing business and defending their estates only in the absence of their husbands, the incompatibility of Margery's spiritual vocation and pilgrimages with her expected maternal role seems to have been another threat to the dominant masculine authority, and oftentimes attracted enmity. In the Middle Ages, British mothers were expected to be loving and nurturing figures who provided early religious and moral instruction for their children within their homes. Margery reshaped this concept of motherhood by drawing on a wide variety of maternal experiences and images while exploiting the relationship between physical and spiritual motherhood (Williams 130–31). Margery's strong presence outside the domestic sphere was therefore viewed as subversive.

In *The Book*, Margery consciously manipulates even gendered vocabulary in dictating her experiences to her scribes in order to address the gaps inherent in existing ways of defining women. She explores questions about female power and authority. Rather than using the word "womanhood," Margery refashions motherhood. Since motherhood derives from both secular and spiritual sources, it offers a greater degree of access to power. Through motherhood, Margery reforms the traditional stereotypes and creates new possibilities for imagining femininity in the vernacular. By increasing the value of motherhood, Margery revalues womanhood. By becoming an author (dictating to her scribes) and a spiritual figure, Margery expands potential female roles (Williams 114–16). As Tara Williams argues, "Margery explicitly exploits her physical motherhood to gain the authority of spiritual motherhood and combines maternal with sexual imagery to express her extreme intimacy with Christ" (128). Margery links the sexual, maternal, and devotional to create authority for herself and her text (130). She gives value to physicality and to fleshly aspects of femininity, emphasizing that womanhood is not limited to concepts such as virtuosity, chastity, and virginity (146–47). It is because of her peculiar expression of femininity and motherhood, which she infuses with her spirituality, that Margery encounters numerous trials on her path. Of course, it should not be forgotten that despite many trials and inquisitions, she never views her singular vocation in opposition to the church and the clergy. The respect that Richard Caister, the vicar of St. Stephen's Church in Norwich, showed to her; the way Thomas Arundel dealt with the convictions brought to him by the clerics; and the reverence of the scribes, who ultimately helped her to write her book, indicate that the antagonism between the clergy and the pious laywomen in Britain should not be overgeneralized. Both Rābiʿa as a freedwoman and Margery as a mother-wife were expected to remain within the private confines of medieval domesticity. They were both impacted by the patriarchal worlds in which they lived; crossing the lines of demarcation would displace the authorities. Medieval societies (Muslim and Christian) desired to inscribe upon women their notions of what it meant to be a woman. Gender was restrictive of possibilities and alternatives, and these two women felt compelled to challenge the inequality and injustices that arose from it. This nonconformity was seen as a major deviation from the mainstream.

Sexuality and Trauma

Rābiʿa's sexuality and the suffering she endured are tightly intertwined in ʿAṭṭār's *Tadhkirat al-awlīyā*. There are several passages, such as the one mentioned previously about al-Ḥasan's description of Rābiʿa's femininity, where she is portrayed as a desexualized woman. ʿAṭṭār also highlights her suffering by telling us that she is an orphaned child, and that after a famine she is separated from her sisters and falls into the hands of an evil man (Losensky 98–99; Nicholson, *Tadhkirat* 60):

> a great famine occurred in Basra. The sisters were separated, and [Rābiʿa] fell into the hands of a wicked man who sold her for a few dirhams.
>
> در بصره قحطی افتاد و خواهران متفرق شدند رابعه بیرون
> رفت ظالمی او را بدید و بگرفت بس بشش درم بفروخت.

The emphasis on the wickedness of the man in Persian is shown by the use of the term *ẓālim* to describe him in the narrative. Dihkhudā's *Lughat-nāma* defines *ẓālim* as "oppressor" or "tyrant." Reading this narrative, the first questions that come to the reader's mind are: Who is this wicked man and how does Rābiʿa fall into his hands? And how does the wicked man treat Rābiʿa before he sells her as a slave? The commodification of slaves, male or female, was of course not unprecedented in medieval Muslim societies. As Janet Afary writes, "A male slave (*gholam*) and a female slave (*kaniz*) could be sold, exchanged, rented, inherited, or owned by several masters" (55). As mentioned earlier, following the Islamic conquests of the Middle East and the economic growth during the Abbasid period, free women's confinement and seclusion was further intensified. This economic expansion allowed the presence of domestic female slaves in Islamic society and sanctioned sexual relations between female slaves and their masters (Nashat and Tucker 52–54). On female slavery, Nikki Keddie also writes, "Slaves were often sexually subject to their masters. Although slavery was less onerous than, say, in the New World, it still entailed a lack of freedom and a sexual subjugation that were more severe than those experienced by free women" ("Introduction" 11). Keddie's comment highlights the fact that the concept of sexual abuse as we know it today might not have existed in the medieval period, and that the performance of sexual acts might have been taken to be part of the female slave's duty to her owner. Nevertheless, as Keddie adds, because female slaves lacked freedom and privacy, generally, and over their bodies, specifically, the oppressiveness of their conditions were intensified. On Rābiʿa's slavery, ʿAṭṭār briefly comments that her master put her to long and hard work. While ʿAṭṭār does not provide us with detailed information on Rābiʿa's life as a slave, Jennifer Heath furnishes interesting details. She writes that at the time of the sale exchange, Rābiʿa is eleven years old and very pretty. She notes that her master teaches her to sing, to play the oud and the flute, and to perform at parties and weddings. According to Heath, the demand for Rābiʿa is high because there is "something in her songs that lifts hearts. She is singing to her Beloved" (Heath 171). After a while, Rābiʿa's own heart is awakened and she begins praying and fasting, and refuses to perform in public, for which her master beats her severely. Then one night the master wakes up while Rābiʿa is praying and sees a light over her head, which has illuminated the entire house. He gets scared and frees her the next day (172). This narrative shows that in addition to being commodified in the sale exchange, Rābiʿa was physically and emotionally exploited during her enslavement—as can be seen in the long hours of strenuous physical labor and the nonconsensual singing and dancing in public—which is of course not surprising. Even though there is no solid information on her being sexually exploited as well, considering that "slave owners also had easy sexual access to their *kanizes* or *gholams*," sexual exploitation was a likelihood (Afary 55).

Rābiʿa's emotional insecurity is emphasized in the narrative right after the slavery transaction. In *Tadhkirat al-awlīyā*, ʿAṭṭār portrays Rābiʿa as a helpless child at the mercy of a *nā-maḥram* (a male stranger). She runs away, falls down, and breaks her hand; and this is the moment when she is illustrated as communicating with God, asking for his help (Losensky 99; Nicholson, *Tadhkirat* 60):

> One day on the street, she fled from a stranger. She fell and broke her hand. She put her face on the ground and said, "My God, I am homeless without mother and father. I am a captive, and my hand is broken. None of this saddens me. All I need is for you to be pleased with me, to know whether you are pleased with me or not."
>
> یک روز می گذشت نامحرمی در پیش آمد رابعه بگریخت و در راه بیفتاد و دستش از جای بشد روی بر خاک نهاد و گفت بار خدایا غریبم و بی مادر و پدر یتیم و اسیر مانده و ببندگی افتاده و دست

گسسته و مرا ازین غمی نیست الا رضاء تو می بایدم که دانم که تو راضی هستی یا نه.

What makes Rābiʿa so frightened of this stranger? Does Rābiʿa observe, experience, or undergo something so repulsive from this stranger that it makes her flee? If we consider the meaning that Dihkhudā's dictionary provides for the word *nā-maḥram*, which can roughly be translated as impudence or shamelessness—used frequently in sexual contexts—we might interpret this passage to mean that Rābiʿa was frightened of being sexually assaulted.

Some of Rābiʿa's actions might be comprehensible in this context. Victims of physical and sexual assault usually experience a long-lasting impact on their lives. They undergo phases of identity confusion, loss of trust, feelings of guilt, loss of self-esteem, and have difficulty forming intimate relationships. Susan Brison, a victim of sexual assault herself, writes about sexual violence, its aftermath, the skepticism victims face, and the disintegration of the self that the victims may experience ("Surviving" 13). After her freedom, Rābiʿa begins singing and dancing again for a while (Losensky 99). Can we propose that this is a phase of identity loss and confusion for her (or the only way she can earn a living)? Later, she feels guilty for performing and repents. After repentance, Rābiʿa is pictured as a devout worshipper of God. Her strict and disciplined mysticism and her lack of interest in marriage can be related to her debilitating experiences as a female slave, too.

A parallel to Rābiʿa's possible traumatic experience with sexuality as a slave and her consequent walk on the path of spirituality can be seen in her English counterpart's experiences, although in a different context. *The Book* recounts that Margery's spiritual vocation begins after her laborious experience of childbirth and her abject feelings about her femininity and motherhood. Reading Margery's book, the first thing that strikes the reader is that while the book is full of references to her father and her husband, there is no mention of her mother; and there is little information about her children, except when she speaks of the birth of her first child in book 1 and her prodigal son in book 2. Margery never talks about her maternal emotions or duties and *The Book* presents her first childbirth as a crucial moment of crisis in her life. Why does Margery, either consciously or unconsciously, avoid any reference to the female figures in her life? Why does she not allude to any of her children, and her own maternal bond with them? After all, what is so strange about femininity that Margery endeavors both to embrace it—by relating her own experience of childbirth and reliving those of the Virgin's and St. Anne's later in her visions—and to shun it by avoiding any reference to the female figures in her life?

Reflecting on Margery's feelings about femininity during and after childbirth, one thing is definite: the traditional Christian notions about the female body had a great impact on Margery. These traditions identified women with the flesh or the body, thus implying they were inferior, and men with the soul or the intellect, implying they were superior. The idea of the inferiority of the female body, its permeability and unreliability, was mainly derived from the Apostle Paul, St. Augustine,

Bernard of Clairvaux, and Aristotle. Some of the most widespread notions about the inferiority of the feminine body revolved around the concept of Eve's temptation and fall and women's sexual physiology. Medieval women were considered corporeal and sensual; they bore "the taint of Eve" (see Lochrie 19–27; Bynum, *Holy Feast* 15–16, 261–62; Voaden 7–40).

Margery's experience of femininity and motherhood begins with her pregnancy and childbearing, and, as shown in *The Book*, it is an onerous one. She is "labored with great attacks of illness" (Staley 6) ("labowrd wyth grett accessys"; Meech and Allen 6) until the child is born. Her choice of the term "labowrd," signifying the lengthy labor, and the word "grett," defined as "distressing or grievous" in the *Medieval English Dictionary* (*MED*), emphasize the traumatic impact of childbirth on her. In Jennifer Hellwarth's words, this distressing impact of childbirth "was common among women of medieval and early modern Europe and was grounded in infant and maternal mortality rates" (46).

However, a more religious interpretation can be suggested, because immediately after her laborious childbirth, Margery "sent for her ghostly father" (Staley 6) ("sent for hyr gostly fadyr"; Meech and Allen 6), so that she could confess of a "thyng"—a vice or a sin—tormenting her, but her confessor silenced her before she could confess. In the theological context of the medieval period, the tormenting sin that Margery refers to, but never talks about explicitly, refers to Margery's internalization of the medieval notions of femininity, female reproduction, and female carnality; Eve's fall from Grace (Genesis 3:16); and St. Augustine's suggestion in *City of God* that sex for mere pleasure and excitement causes the mind to be oblivious to God and, therefore, a sin (577). She feels this sense of sinfulness and the need for confession only after her marriage, sexual experience, and childbearing: "She had a thing in conscience which she had never shown before that time in all her life" (Staley 6–7) ("Sche had a thyng in conscyens whech sche had nevyr schewyd beforn that tyme in alle hyr lyfe"; Meech and Allen 6–7). *The Book* illustrates how due to her sexual pleasure, Margery, possibly associating herself with Eve, temptation, and the fall, feels a strong awareness of the deep chasm produced by that "thyng" between her and the divine. Hellwarth suggests that this "thyng" tormenting Margery could be the result of the fear of death after childbirth because of the high mortality rates of the time; but it can also be suggested that Margery felt an urge to repent her supposed sin before dying. Whatever the reason, the opening birth scene "illustrates well the emotional and spiritual travails that come with pregnancy and childbirth" (Hellwarth 46–47).

The fact that Margery cannot name this "thyng" also suggests that it is beyond language. Perhaps the confessor fears the "thyng" and wants it to be kept out of language. In fact, Margery intends to voice a "thyng" which has possibly not been articulated publicly before and has no place in the public accepted language and law, as Lacan would put it. And, insofar as it is never spoken in the text, it is beyond language for us, too.

This "thyng" is of course the word used by Lacan in his consideration of the "real" in *The Ethics of Psychoanalysis*. In examining the psychoanalytical aspects of the "thing," reference to Lacan's essay "Das Ding," in which he elaborates on the concept of the "thing" in psychoanalytical terms, based on the Freudian pleasure and reality principles would not be out of place here. Freud's pleasure principle, which dominates the id, states that we are ruled by the desire for pleasure, the urge to satisfy our physical and psychological needs, and to avoid pain. Lacan maintains that when "the signifying structure interposes itself between perception and consciousness . . . the unconscious intervenes . . . the pleasure principle intervenes" (*The Seminar VII,* 51). However, the pleasure principle can only dominate strongly early in life; when the subject becomes mature, the reality principle, because of the "exigencies of life," redefines the gratification of the pleasure sought by the pleasure principle. This desire is, of course, balanced by the ego, "on that basis there enters into play what we will see function as the first apprehension of reality by the subject. And it is at this point that that reality intervenes, which has the most intimate relationship to the subject, the *Nebenmensch*. The formula is striking to the extent that it expresses powerfully the idea of beside yet alike, separation and identity" (51). *Nebenmensch*, a German term meaning "neighbor," introduced by Freud as the unconscious, is "separated into two parts, one of which affirms itself through an unchanging apparatus, which remains together as a thing, *als Ding*" (51). Therefore, through experiencing *Nebenmensch*, the subject is isolated from the *Ding* and seeks to find it again; however, "what is supposed to be found cannot be found again. It is in its nature that the object as such is lost. It will never be found again. This lost object is the *das Ding*, that is, it is "the absolute Other of the subject"' (52).

Therefore, considering the psychoanalytic definition of the "thing" or *das Ding*, which is only one of the many interpretations of the "thing," it can be inferred that Margery has experienced jouissance, desiring the absolute other—the mother or primary caregiver of the child—who is lost forever. Margery experiencing jouissance for her primary caregiver or for the absolute other first feels joy, then feels guilt, then suffers an unknown pain, and needs to repent. Whether in its psychological or theological terms, one thing is definite, and that is "the thing" is a reminiscence of what is felt to be lost and cannot be found again—be it the Lacanian absolute other, the biblical grace from which Eve fell, or any other lost thing.

Margery's first experience of intimate interaction with the divine begins after her "emotional and spiritual travails" of childbirth, her feelings of guilt, and the need for repentance, when she is in bed with her husband and she hears sweet heavenly songs for the first time and expresses regret for having committed sins (Meech and Allen 11). The stark contrast between the heavenly song that she hears and the supposed sins she has committed bespeaks the extent to which Margery has internalized the current beliefs about femininity, and represents her spiritual longings. Therefore, not surprisingly, after such a traumatic experience, Margery avoids details about femininity and the female figures in her life, even a midwife. Yet she utilizes her abject feminine body by "embrac[ing] [her] femaleness," (Bynum, *Holy Feast* 163) and "not by reversing what she is but by being more fully herself with Christ" (Bynum, *Fragmentation* 41) in order to redefine her femininity in a more subjective manner.

The traumatic experience that Margery goes through is immensely different from what Rābi'a endures, and even the traditions they belong to are very different from one another; however, the marks left from the experiences on each of these women lead them on a spiritual path where love of the divine other empowers them to cross the confining boundaries of their gender, overcome trauma, and emerge with a renewed subjectivity.

Rābi'a's Crossing of Gender Boundaries

Rābi'a's spiritual path is accompanied by her constant refusal of marriage proposals, and Margery's spiritual journey lies in the core of her desire to stay celibate inside her marriage. For both women, however, these decisions are accompanied by admonishments from men and criticisms from their contemporaries. 'Aṭṭār refers to several of Rābi'a's marriage proposals and her rejection of them in *Tadhkirat al-awlīyā*. Rābi'a's marriage proposals confirm the sociocultural expectations of her time: that a woman should not remain celibate because she is not capable of managing her life alone. It also emphasizes the fact that although celibacy was favored, the independence it granted women was seen as a threat to the dominant social system. In this regard, 'Aṭṭār writes that one of Rābi'a's suitors was her Sufi master, al-Ḥasan al-Baṣrī, previously mentioned, who once asked her (Losensky 104; Nicholson, *Tadhkirat* 60):

> "Do you long for a husband?"
>
> رغبت کنی تا نکاحی کنیم و عقد بندیم.

Al-Ḥasan al-Baṣrī's marriage proposal to Rābi'a seems very unlikely in real life since at the time of al-Ḥasan al-Baṣrī's death, Rābi'a was most likely a young girl. However, this might be a reference to a different al-Ḥasan that has been transcribed inaccurately as al-Ḥasan al-Baṣrī, or 'Aṭṭār merely used his name for characterization in his narratives. Nonetheless, note al-Ḥasan's use of the term *riqbat* (long) which is synonymous with *ṭama'* (desire) and signifies lack and wanting. Smith, quoting al-Ḥasan on the idea of self-discipline, writes that *wara'* (abstinence) is the root of religion and *ṭama'* (desire) corrupts abstinence (*The Way* 176). These two conflicting uses of the synonymous words *riqbat* and *ṭama'* by al-Ḥasan are noteworthy insofar as they contradict each other. In addition, although al-Ḥasan is asking for Rābi'a's hand in this narrative, he is not asking whether she longs for or desires marriage. He is rather emphasizing the notion of "desire" through his use of the word *riqbat*, which also signals his own desire. Al-Ḥasan, who condemned desire in another narrative, is now asking about desire, but what matters here is whose desire is being discussed. On the significant distinction between male and female sexual desire in Sufi discourse, Valerie Hoffman writes, "Despite the fact that a great deal of Islamic popular literature depicts women as lustful seductresses and the initiators of all illicit sexual liaisons, in stories about Sufi women it is men's sexual lust that is emphasized. It is also significant to note that the women who are mentioned in these dictionaries are mainly seen as teachers of men" (367). Rābiʿa's response to al-Ḥasan is exceptional as it clearly signifies her rejection of all worldly desires. Acting like a teacher, Rābiʿa says (Losensky 104; Nicholson, *Tadhkirat* 66),

> The marriage knot can only tie one who exists. Where is existence here? I am not my own—I am his and under the shadow of his command. You must ask permission from him.

> عقد نکاح بر وجودی فرو آید اینجا وجود بر خاسته است کی نیست
> خود گشته ام و هست شده بدو و همه از آن او ام درسایه حکم او ام
> خطبه ازو باید خواست نه از من.

Rābiʿa's love of the divine has resulted in the annihilation of her ego; she is no longer a separate being but one with the divine. This narrative illustrates how Rābiʿa surpasses her male colleagues in spiritual and intellectual forthrightness. Although al-Ḥasan is himself Rābiʿa's master in Sufism, it is very difficult for him to comprehend how Rābiʿa has attained this spiritual state. This highlights Rābiʿa's superiority over a man of her own rank and further nuances the gender hierarchy. By referring to spiritual marriage and union with the divine, Rābiʿa deconstructs the established narratives about heterosexual earthly marriages and suggests alternatives for unions. She also highlights gender equality in the spiritual realm.

Rābiʿa's other suitor was ʿAbd al-Wāḥid ibn Zayd (1311–1390), who was renowned for the asceticism and sanctity of his life, according to Abū Ṭālib Muḥammad ibn ʿAlī Makkī. Although ʿAbd al-Wāḥid was an ascetic and a pious man himself, Rābiʿa refuses his proposal by saying, "O sensual one, seek another sensual like thyself. Hast thou seen any sign of desire in me?" (al-Makkī, *Qūt al-qulūb* 57). It is noteworthy, however, that Rābiʿa does not renounce the concept of marriage itself all together although she rejects ʿAbd al-Wāḥid's proposal because of its worldly sensuality. In fact, she is condemning earthly "desire" as she did in response to al-Ḥasan's proposal. Even though ʿAbd al-Wāḥid is himself a man of God, Rābiʿa lacks the desire to divide her attention and love between the divine and another being. She openly condemns the sensuality of ʿAbd al-Wāḥid. Sensuality for Rābiʿa signifies fulfillment of one's own desires. It is attention given to one's ego, which has no place in the realm of the divine.

Smith relates several anecdotes about Rābiʿa's refusal to enter the bond of matrimony which are not mentioned by ʿAṭṭār. According to one of these stories, Muḥammad ibn al-Hāshimī (?–ca.776), the Abbasid amir of Basra, offers Rābiʿa one hundred thousand dinars and informs her that he has an income of ten thousand dinars monthly, all of which he will bestow upon her if she marries him. Rābiʿa replies, "It does not please me that you should be my slave and that all you possess should be mine, or that you should distract me from God for a single moment" (Smith, *Rābiʿa the Mystic* 10). The Abbasid amir blatantly offers Rābiʿa worldly wealth, commodifying her and devaluing the institution of marriage. Rābiʿa views his proposal as a distraction from the divine. Smith regards Rābiʿa's refusal to marry as a sign of her union with the divine and the spiritual marriage that she has contracted with the beloved. Comparing Rābiʿa's celibacy with her Christian counterparts, Smith comments, "like her Christian sisters in the life of sanctity, Rābiʿa espoused a heavenly Bridegroom and turned her back on earthly marriage even with one of her own inmates and companions on the Way" (*Rābiʿa the Mystic* 13). Smith parallels Rābiʿa's eschewing of marriage proposals with the admonition of the monk Aphraates to the Christian "Daughters of the Covenant." According to Smith, Aphraates advises them to say to those who seek them in marriage, "to a royal Husband am I betrothed, and to Him do I minister; and if I leave His ministry, my Betrothed will be wroth with me and will write me a letter of divorce and will dismiss me from His house" (*Studies* 186). Since the gratification of the desire of the beloved is the sole purpose of her life, Rābiʿa, like Christian celibate mystics, refrains from every corporeal matter.

Rābiʿa's rejection of all marriage proposals can also be perceived as the ramification of her extremely disheartened feelings about earthly love, possibly caused by the experiences during her childhood as a slave. ʿAṭṭār shows how not receiving sincere human love, Rābiʿa turns to God and puts all her trust in him. Rābiʿa circumvents the Sufi philosophy of contemplating divine beauty through earthly love and beauty here. She aims directly for the divine, bypassing the earthly. This is also an indication of a moment of Foucauldian transgression of the law, whereby the law is not a limiting force but one that offers alternatives when crossed. Reading Rābiʿa's mysticism alongside Foucault's description of mystics as "incapable of dividing the continuous forms of desire, of rapture, of penetration, of ecstasy, of that outpouring which leaves us spent" and his argument that "all of these experiences seemed to lead, without interruption or limit, right to the heart of a divine love of which they were both the outpouring and the source returning upon itself" ("Preface" 29), we can understand how through her mystical raptures and ecstasies, Rābiʿa overcomes her sexual and physical trauma, displaces desire, reorients her sexuality, crosses the limit, and aims for the heart of divine love, which is the origin and source of all humanity. As Amy Hollywood and Patricia Beckman put it, "Mystical sexuality is about the intense pleasure and pain that bodies inflict and receive and about ecstasy, standing outside oneself, the breathless arousal and rhythmic satisfactions that come from, and in, this experience" (*The Cambridge Companion* 331).

In line with Hollywood and Beckman's paralleling of sexuality and mysticism, Ahmed considers Rābiʿa's class background as a freedwoman important in understanding her refusal to marry; as a slave she would not have been in a position to renounce worldly attractions, but finds satisfaction in being able to do so as a free woman. Furthermore, Sufism also provided her with an opportunity to live an independent and autonomous life, which would have been otherwise impossible for a woman of low birth. The narratives chronicling her refusal of marriage proposals illuminate the degree of autonomy her spirituality afforded her to remain free from male authority and control (*Women and Gender* 98).

In addition to her refusal to marry, another reason for which Rābiʿa is seen as crossing gender boundaries is her public criticism of men and her witticisms. In an expressive narrative in *Tadhkirat al-awlīyā*, ʿAṭṭār writes about Rābiʿa's encounter with a man who has tied a bandage around his head due to headaches. Rābiʿa asks him how old he is, and he replies thirty. She asks if he has suffered from headaches all those thirty years, and the reply is "no." Rābiʿa retorts (Losensky 107; Nicholson, *Tadhkirat* 68):

> Have you ever, in these thirty years, tied on the bandage of gratitude? And now because you have a single headache, you tie on the bandage of complaint?
>
> سی سال تنت درست داشت هرگز عصابه شکر بر نبستی به یک
> شب که درد سرت داد عصابه شکایت در می بندی.

For Rābiʿa, suffering is a chance for purgation. Although this criticism could have been addressed to any human being, regardless of their gender, there is a reason why the narrative emphasizes the presence of a man. This narrative shows Rābiʿa's witty but harsh criticism of those who lack patience in spiritual suffering and have little sense of gratitude. In a way, by focusing on a male addressee, the narrative also implicates the gender-related hierarchies and Rābiʿa's transgression of those hierarchies as she appears totally dominant and not as a passive and subservient female, which would have been expected at the time. It also highlights Rābiʿa's spiritual superiority over men (and women), which is another transgression in the context of Sufism where the ideal is male.

Rābiʿa's wit is portrayed in yet another exceptional narrative in *Tadhkirat al-awlīyā*. ʿAṭṭār relates that a group of people attempted to challenge Rābiʿa's spirituality by arguing that men are superior to women in spiritual matters because all prophets have been men (Losensky 109; Nicholson, *Tadhkirat* 70);

> All the virtues have been dispersed among men. The crown of nobility has been placed upon the heads of men, and the belt of magnanimity has been tied around their waists. Prophecy has never descended upon any woman. What do you have to boast of?
>
> همه فضیلتها بر سر مردان نثار کرده اند و تاج نبوت بر سر
> مردان نهاده اند و کمرکرامت بر میان مردان بسته اند هرگز
> پیغمبری هیچ زن نیامده است.

Agreeing with them, Rābiʿa responds (Losensky 110; Nicholson, *Tadhkirat* 70):

> Everything you said is true. But egoism, egotism, self-worship, and *I am your highest Lord* have not welled up in any woman. And no woman has ever been a pederast.
>
> این همه هست ولکن منی و خودپرستی و انا ربکم الاعلی از گریبان
> هیچ زن بر نیامده است و هیچ زن هرگز مخنث نبوده است.

Rābiʿa proves her spiritual superiority by publicly criticizing men, and in so doing, she crosses the dominant gender boundaries by being insubordinate. She is also repulsed over abusive sexual matters such as pederasty, which were common at the time. The Persian word *mukhannas*, which has been translated as pederast in this passage, refers to a young boy or old man who is the passive object of a same-sex relationship. It can also be translated as "catamite." This refers to the fact that in same-sex relationships, the passive recipient is subject to social derision. This comment also makes one wonder whether this distinction between passive and active roles in sexual matters has anything to do with the dominant view and expectation of women to be passive and subordinate. The sharp reprimanding of men by medieval female Sufis has of course been observed as natural and indicative of women's spiritual superiority by other scholars as well. As Ruth Roded writes, "The women's retorts embody not only pride in their spiritual state but also an aggressiveness toward men they meet, which contrasts sharply with their self-abnegation and submission to God. They rebuke and even mock men they feel are lacking" (103). Perhaps Rābiʿa's aggressiveness toward men and her love of the divine are the ramifications of her own plight as a slave and her reactions to male sexual exploitation. Whatever the reason, Rābiʿa's criticism of men is an instance of transgression of gender boundaries, which allows her to de- and reconstruct her identity by becoming aware of the self and the divine other.

Margery's Violation of Gender Boundaries

Rābiʿa's spirituality is paralleled by Margery's, whose desire for spirituality is manifested, in this case, in her desire for celibacy within her marriage. Although marital intercourse was considered less sinful if it was performed for having a child, for paying the conjugal debt, or as a remedy to fornication, since the medieval Christian perceptions about female sexuality had an integral role in Margery's negative attitudes about herself and her body, she sought chastity within her marriage for years. However, celibacy in marriage in medieval Europe was a matter of much confusion. Sexual intercourse was one of the foremost practices through which husbands could assert their authority over their wives. Since transitioning "from a carnal to a spiritual marriage" would have been seen as undermining the husband's authority, and therefore threatened the masculine domain of both the canonists and the husband, Margery was for many years denied that freedom (Elliot, *Spiritual* 245). Much like Rābiʿa's refusal to marry, Margery's request was seen as an aberration of the codes of society. However, after fourteen children, Margery ultimately succeeded in achieving celibacy by going before the bishop with her husband and taking a vow of chastity (Meech and Allen 115). The condition was that Margery would pay her husband's debts in return for celibacy within their marriage. This sheds light on the late medieval European notions of the female body as a commodity to be traded. Thus, although not a slave, Margery went through a similar instance of commodification as Rābiʿa when she was sold as a slave. But whereas Margery could negotiate her freedom, Rābiʿa as a slave could not. It was only after divine intervention that Rābiʿa's master and Margery's husband agreed to grant them the freedom they longed for. Both Rābiʿa, by refusing marriage proposals, and Margery, by asking for a spiritual marriage, move out of the familiar space of marriage and marital intimacy into an unknown sphere; they seem to be reconstructing the concept of marriage and deconstructing the socially accepted meaning of "womanhood." They are undoing the structures that have produced the binaries of womanhood and manhood.

But this is not the only reason that they appear as deviators. Through their public presence and harsh criticism of men, they pose a threat to hegemonic male-dominated cultures. Like Rābiʿa, Margery publicly voices her opinion, as when she encounters clerical opposition. One of the significant instances of this is seen in *The Book,* where, in the city of Canterbury, she is attacked for Lollardy by religious clerics after attracting attention to herself by shedding copious tears. Although crying and weeping is one of the common tenets of Christian spirituality, which normally occurs during the *imitatio Christi*, what sparks antagonism toward Margery is mainly that she brings these excessive tears into the public domain, which women were not allowed to do in fourteenth-century England. In her defense at the inquisition, Margery calls upon a biblical story before the monks, but faces further opposition for this. The reason for the strong clerical reaction to Margery's responses was the archbishop of Canterbury Thomas Arundel's seventh constitution, which considered lay spirituality unorthodox and heretical. He had published his *Constitutions* in 1409 to establish the terms of religious orthodoxy and to combat the threat of heresy against the scriptures and the faith. The *Constitutions* retained its importance until and during the sixteenth century.

Another similar incident in Margery's spiritual career occurs at her trial when she is accused of preaching by the archbishop of York (Staley 192). At the time, the vernacular Bible was only accessible to the members of Lollard communities, and Margery, as an uneducated laywoman, could not have read the Bible in Latin. Yet, vernacular translation of biblical stories had been part of monastic literary production and evangelical preaching to the laity for centuries. The anti-Lollard point seems to be that only ordained priests could paraphrase the Bible, which meant that the problem did not lie in the translation itself, but in the individual who undertook the translation. This makes us ponder who really had access to power. Furthermore, the clergy's desire to limit Margery could have been easily anticipated because monasteries and anchorites were familiar and acceptable at the time in England, whereas Margery's mixed life of both conformity and singularity insinuated aberration. The threat of Lollardy, hypocrisy, and her own peculiar behavior undoubtedly worked hand in hand to further the formidability of Margery's vocation. However, each time, Margery proved her orthodoxy and faithfulness to the church by referring to the Bible.

Rābiʿa's and Margery's journeys of personal communication with God and their attaining of self-awareness as women remind us of Pierre Bourdieu's comment that "when the conditions of existence of which the members of a group and the product are very little differentiated, the dispositions which each of them exercises in his practice are confirmed and hence reinforced both by the practice of the other members of the group . . . and also by institutions which constitute collective thought as much as they express it" (167). Rābiʿa and Margery encounter numerous oppositions and are questioned constantly about their spirituality and life choices because they have chosen a vocation that is immensely different from the path followed by other women. Their uniqueness conveys messages of nonconformity and threat to the socioreligious authorities of the time. If what Bourdieu says is true, for Rābiʿa's and Margery's subjective experiences to be in harmony with social and collective institutions, the authority of those collective institutions should be imposed and adopted through submissiveness. This Bourdieu calls a "perfectly closed world, each aspect of which is, as it were, a reflection of all the others, a world which has no place for opinion as liberal ideology understands it" (167). This very much corresponds with Rābiʿa's and Margery's worlds, which have either limited or no place for "liberal ideology," particularly if that liberalism and desire for freedom and independence is heard from a female voice. In this world, then, the power struggle is between orthodoxy, "straight opinion," and heterodoxy or the "competing possibles"; that is, the existence of choices, which Bourdieu calls "heresy" (169). Rābiʿa's and Margery's understanding of the possibilities open to them is the main reason that they are criticized and seen as transgressors. The world they live in is one in which, as Bourdieu states, power struggles attempt to conceal its contribution to the "delimitation of the universe of the discourse, that is to say, the universe of the thinkable, and hence to the delimitation of the universe of the unthinkable" (170). The universe of this discourse is the universe in which the boundaries are between "what goes without saying" and "what cannot be said" because of power. To refer back to Bourdieu, the conventions, traditions, prescribed cultural perceptions, and established gender demarcations are what go without saying because the existing power makes questioning the established norms seem taboo. Rābiʿa's and Margery's questioning of the conventions is a threat to the dominant power; it has the potential to change the public discourse—the Lacanian symbolic order—and established narratives.

Rābiʿa's Union with the Divine

Regardless of the earthly oppositions that they face, Rābiʿa and Margery find themselves in full harmony with the divine. To highlight Rābiʿa's union with the divine, ʿAṭṭār portrays her as a steadfast believer, observing her prayers, fasting constantly, and refusing to waste a single moment contemplating earthly desires in *Tadhkirat al-awlīyā*. Her intention is to be in communication with the beloved and to satisfy him rather than please her own self (Losensky 99; Nicholson, *Tadhkirat* 61):

> She fasted continuously and prayed all night, remaining on her feet until daybreak.
>
> پیوسته بروز روزه می داشت و خدمت می کرد و در خدمت خدای
> تا روز بر پای ایستاده می بود.

Rābiʿa's direct and personal communication with the Creator is intensified by his response to her (Losensky 99; Nicholson, *Tadhkirat* 60–61):

> She heard a voice say. "Do not be sad. Tomorrow a grandeur will be yours such that the closest of the heavenly company will take pride in you."
>
> آوازی شنود که غم مخور که فردا جاهیت خواهد بود که مقربان آسمان به تو بنازند .

This mutual communication is illustrated in yet another anecdote in *Tadhkirat al-awlīyā*, where in a state of illumination, God orders Rābiʿa to renounce all worldly matters. ʿAṭṭār writes that a visitor brings Rābiʿa a bowl of food, and she accepts. She goes to fetch a lamp, but when she comes back, a cat has overturned the bowl. She goes to fetch a jug so that she can break her fast, but when she returns, the lamp has gone out. She tries to drink the water in the dark, but the jug slips from her hand and breaks. She inquires from God what is happening to her, and God replies that suffering and bliss cannot coexist. If she wants to walk on the divine path, she must suffer (Nicholson, *Tadhkirat* 69). When Rābiʿa hears this, she completely cuts off her heart from all worldly desires, and for the last thirty years of her life, she prays every time as if it may be her last prayer. The beloved asks her to renounce all her worldly desires and to aim at fulfilling his desire in order for them to be one and she complies. This compliance and union allows her to circumvent earthly demarcations and emerge as a new subject. This is a moment of ultimate fusion of the self with the divine other.

Margery's Union with Jesus Christ

For Margery this discovery and fusion occurs through interacting with Christ, the Virgin Mary, and St. Anne during her *imitatio Christi*. The dominant imagery in Margery's book is that of the motherhood of the Virgin Mary and St. Anne, who "symbolize for Margery the perfect spiritual maternal paradigm—immaculate conception, virginal and painless birth, and the promise of resurrection" (Bynum, *Holy Feast* 49). According to *The Book*, Margery's path begins with Christ encouraging her "to think on [his] mother, for she is the cause of all the grace that [Margery has]" (Staley 15) ("to thynke on [his] modyr, for sche is cause of alle the grace that [Margery has]"; Meech and Allen 18). Contemplating the Virgin Mary, Margery then sees "Saint Anne great with the child, and then she prayed to Saint Anne if she could be her maiden and her servant" (Staley 15) ("Seynt Anne gret wyth chylde, and than sche preyd Seynt Anne to be hir mayden and hir servawnt"; Meech and Allen 18). Margery not only thinks about the Virgin Mary as the mother of Christ, but she envisions St. Anne pregnant with the Virgin. The fact that she desires to be the "maiden" and the "servant" of St. Anne at the time of her pregnancy raises the irony of her being alone at her own childbirth. Moreover, the maternal bond, which is left ambivalent in Margery's book, is intensified by her longing to nurse the Virgin Mary's child: "she begged for our Lady fair white clothes and kerchiefs to swaddle her son when he was born, and when Jesus was born, she prepared bedding for our Lady to lie in with her blessed son" (Staley 15) ("Also sche beggyd owyr Lady fayr whyte clothys and kerchys for to swathyn in hir sone whan he wer born, and, whan Jhesu was born sche ordeyned beddyng for owyr Lady to lygh in wyth hir blyssed sone"; Meech and Allen 19). Margery's spiritual encounter with Christ, the Virgin Mary, and St. Anne opens up the possibility for her to reconcile with her own sexuality and motherhood.

Therefore, despite the fact that Margery avoids mentioning her own maternal bond with her children in *The Book*, she is drawn into the larger world of the maternal discourse with Jesus Christ and the symbolic mothers of all humankind, the Virgin Mary and St. Anne. It seems that Margery has crossed the border of private motherhood and entered the public realm to mother all humanity. Thus, Margery's moments of ecstasy in *The Book*, which are focused mostly on the Passion of the Christ, infused with images of motherhood, grant her "a new source of power and sanctity" through which she is enabled to cross gender lines, undergo a process of self-shaping, and emerge as a new subject (Lochrie 13).

Conclusion

ʿAṭṭār shows how Rābiʿa's enslavement and her social status influenced her spirituality and helped her in the reconstruction of her identity through her spiritual rediscovery of the divine. Similarly, in *The Book*, we see that Margery's social status, her upbringing, and her internalization of the notions of medieval Christian theology about the female body led her to redefine her subjectivity through spirituality. Revisiting the writings on Rābiʿa and Margery and their spirituality, we see how they are portrayed as moving out of the realm of preconstructed law and language where, for instance, marriage was expected from a Muslim woman such as Rābiʿa, and preaching was forbidden for a Christian laywoman such as Margery. Through this movement, they are represented as facing personal experiences that endow them with a new self and enable them to reenter the realm of law and language with a new perception and confidence, asserting themselves through their love of the divine. Their most significant accomplishment is to give voice to what was unthinkable before—female autonomy and independence. Their singular trajectory is also a representation of the temporality of all worldly constructed territories, all boundaries, and all limits.

Due to their frustration with men, Rābiʿa and Margery turn to God in order to be enabled to transcend the existing gender hierarchies. According to the texts, it seems that Rābiʿa's and Margery's gender identity and femininity are in direct correspondence with their desire to avoid lack and seek perfection in turning to the all-powerful. However, this desire turns out to be unattainable, and mysticism, as Simone de Beauvoir expresses it, is just another extension of the same limited sexuality and gender identity. This desire is closely associated with sexual difference and the unconscious, in Lacan's words. For Lacan, the kind of body (female or male) one has does not determine one's position in language; it is rather one's relationship to the phallus, "the transcendental signifier within male-dominant society through which meaning is fixed and grounded," that sets one's position (Hollywood, *Sensible* 154). Lacan closely associates women's mysticism and subjectivity with their lack—not having a phallus—and their desire to fill the lack, "for desire merely leads us to aim at the gap where it can be demonstrated that the One is based only on the essence of the signifier" (Lacan, *The Seminar, Book XX* 5). And since, according to Lacan, women more than men bear the burden of the lack of the signifier (i.e., the phallus) from a psychological point of view, they lack subjectivity as well, and become the object of "the other's" desire; therefore, they try to fill this lack by turning to mysticism where they attain subjectivity.

On the one hand, for Rābiʿa and Margery, the motivation behind their devotion to God might be the Lacanian psychological and emotional need for liberation (and lack thereof) from the trauma and the harm caused by the male figures in their lives. However, this lack provides them with possibilities. Luce Irigaray echoes this sentiment: "Mystical sexuality thereby configures bodily finitude not just in terms of lack but also in terms of possibility, of the possibility that the skin and bones and nerves and blood that separate us one from another might also draw us out of ourselves, join us to another, through the sensations evoked by a caress or embrace, by piercing or rubbing" (200). Mystical imaginings of sexuality therefore help these women dislocate their embodied selves and reimagine their selves in spaces and forms not regularly inhabited; hence, the reason they are considered to be violating normative standards.

On the other hand, both women owe their recognition as female saints to male Sufis and scribes and confessors who transmitted the information about them from one generation to the next. Even though women have also contributed to the oral transmission of stories, the textual proof of these two women's existence and the sincerity of their spirituality is only seen in the writings of men and their references. If medieval men had refused to recognize Rābiʿa and Margery as women of God and worthy of reverence, modern scholars would not have had access even to the very scanty and at times inaccurate information about them today. That is to say, despite medieval Muslim male authors' tendency to portray a highly spiritual woman like Rābiʿa as manly, their acknowledgement of her is in itself a major reason for modern scholars' ability to access information on a medieval female saint's spirituality. Although ʿAṭṭār, like other medieval men, conformed to the gender demarcations of his time by justifying his reason for including Rābiʿa in his work, the very fact that he granted her a full entry has helped her name and her unique spirituality travel through time and place. In Margery's case, although the official clerics opposed her spirituality in different ways, the reverence of some and the writings of her multiple male scribes allowed her spirituality to travel from the medieval world to the modern world.

Writing, or being written about, gave a new representation to these women, enabling them to signify. Through the written text, the public has come to know about their experiences. Although their voice might have been suppressed in their lifetime to some extent, the written text left after them grants them a subjectivity, which crosses all demarcations. However, since these written texts survive only because of their male peers' acknowledgements, one may submit to Hollywood's argument in *Sensible Ecstasy: Mysticism, Sexual Difference, and the Demands of History* that for true reciprocity, even in mysticism, women still need male recognition to gain autonomy and to be able to transcend their gender. To Hollywood, even in mysticism, female agency without male acknowledgement is an illusory concept. This is not to belittle women's spirituality, but to say that even in the realm of mysticism, women did not succeed in transcending the limitations of their feminine body and sexuality without masculine agency. However, this acknowledgement is simultaneously a great testimony to their impact on these male authors, scribes, or confessors, and to their significance in the social world of their time. Male acknowledgement did not come easy; these women had to pay a price to gain it: the price they paid was risking their lives through boundary crossings.

By writing about female mystics, these medieval men showed a willingness to push the boundaries of the established discourse by embracing female spirituality. In Rābiʿa's case, one may say that the transmission of the narratives of her life and spirituality illustrates ʿAṭṭār's pushing of the conventional gender boundaries and demarcations of his day. By including Rābiʿa, ʿAṭṭār makes his point about Sufi love, which is aimed at a more transcendental goal than worldly matters such as gender distinctions. ʿAṭṭār portrays his true surrender and submission to the divine by accepting and embracing gender equality through his inclusive spirituality, which might characterize him as a transgressor of the conventions and ideologies of his day. The same argument can be made about Margery's scribes. Whereas many clerics showed strong opposition to Margery's spirituality, others such as her scribes embraced her peculiar devotion, and this might attest to their position as true servants of God.

This male dominance also speaks to the fact that desire has always been masculine while women's desires have always been suppressed or misplaced. At the core of the mystical experience, however, there is the desire for a union with the divine. Hence, Rābiʿa's and Margery's desire for union with the divine echoes their desire for freedom from all confinement and all limits—a desire for subjectivity through the divine. As Susannah Chewning writes: "The nature of mysticism—a loss of identity and selfhood through immersion in the power of the Divine—requires that which, it might be argued, is culturally denied to women: subjectivity" (127). Through our reading ʿAṭṭār's representation of Rābiʿa, Margery's descriptions of her own life in *The Book*, Foucault's notions of breaking the taboos, and, partly, Lacan's ideas, in this chapter, we can conclude that Rābiʿa and Margery attain the subjectivity denied to them through an immersion in the divine.

Chapter 4

Maḥmūd and Ayāz, Sufi Homoeroticism, and European Same-Sex Relationships

Redefinition of Desire

We encounter a set of love narratives in ʿAṭṭār's works that connects the love and contemplation of the beauty of adolescent boys with the contemplation of divine beauty and love. This kind of love frequently occurs between a roaming dervish and an adolescent boy—a common practice and acknowledged part of Sufi philosophy in ʿAṭṭār's day. Oftentimes we find in ʿAṭṭār's poetry descriptions of the beauty of a prince or a vizier's son whose lover is a wandering dervish. Such narratives conform to the standards of the Sufi philosophy known as "gazing at male beauty" or "the love of beautiful youth" (*shāhidbāzī* or *naẓarbāzī*) and are therefore not necessarily transgressive.

However, ʿAṭṭār also writes narratives about love between men outside of these motifs. A considerable number of his homoerotic narratives are dedicated to the love affair between Sultan Maḥmūd of Ghazna (r. 997–1030) and his slave Malik Ayāz. Sultan Maḥmūd was the most important ruler of the Ghaznavid Empire (975–1186), who turned the small city of Ghazna, which is in today's Afghanistan, into the wealthy capital of his empire, which extended from present-day Afghanistan to Iran, Pakistan, and the northwest of India. Ayāz was a Turkic servant who became an officer and then a general in the army of Sultan Maḥmūd and later rose to the rank of king of Lahore in 1021 in reward for his devotion to Maḥmūd. Although there are both positive and negative aspects to the Ghaznavid Empire, Sultan Maḥmūd is generally remembered as a great fighter for the faith and a despotic ruler of the magnificent empire (Bosworth, "Maḥmūd of Ghazna" 85). Examples of narratives about Sultan Maḥmūd as a ruler and fighter in ʿAṭṭār's works can be found in *Ilāhī-nāma* (discourse 15, part 1; discourse 5, part 7) and in *Muṣībat-nāma* (discourse 13, part 2; discourse 30, part 11). ʿAṭṭār also provides us with a representation of the sultan as both a despotic and a benevolent ruler. He praises Maḥmūd for some of his deeds but admonishes him strongly for others. These narratives, of course, conform to the standards of the genre of "mirror for princes," where kings and royalty receive advice on the treatment of their subjects. Through these stories, ʿAṭṭār not only supplies advice for the later rulers but also shows his disapproval of the sultan's preferential treatment of his subjects.

Leaving aside Sultan Maḥmūd's portrayal as a despotic ruler, we now turn to the focus of the current chapter: ʿAṭṭār's depiction of the sultan's homoerotic relationship with Ayāz. This is most noteworthy because it is one of the occasions on which ʿAṭṭār breaks away from the rules and codes of the philosophy of *shāhidbāzī*. Reading the narratives of Maḥmūd and Ayāz's relationship, it is difficult to assume that their love was of the kind practiced by Sufis in their brotherhood and confraternity circles—the mystical love of God and contemplation of the divine through the beauty of adolescent boys. In the medieval period, *shāhidbāzī* was commonly practiced in confraternity communities, particularly during mystical initiations, and was expected to exist and be practiced merely for the love of God. However, ʿAṭṭār's narratives show that Sultan Maḥmūd's relationship with Ayāz did not take place in a confraternity or in a mystical context, nor was it pursued for the sake of the love of God. Homoerotic affairs between masters and slaves were common in medieval Iran; however, their purpose was to experience sexual pleasure rather than the love of God (El-Rouayheb 118). In addition, we can infer from these narratives that Ayāz is not an adolescent boy but an adult man. Therefore, it seems obvious that Maḥmūd and Ayāz's relationship deviated from the standards of the philosophy of *shāhidbāzī*.

While this homoerotic love affair does not conform to the ideals of Sufi philosophy, ʿAṭṭār portrays it as a relationship that is simultaneously spiritual and earthly. In this chapter, I focus on ʿAṭṭār's decision to write about a homoerotic relationship that did not fit with the ideals of the philosophy of *shāhidbāzī* and was therefore condemned even by some Sufis. The remainder of this chapter examines ʿAṭṭār's treatment of this homoerotic love relationship and concludes that by including deviators, ʿAṭṭār shows his own nonconformity to the philosophical standards and sociocultural paradigms of the day, as he essentially embraces sexual diversity. In doing so, he proves to be a true Sufi and lover of all creations of the divine.

In this chapter, I also initiate a conversation between Foucault and ʿAṭṭār regarding the violation of laws and taboos, transcending the limiting standards of the day, and the construction of subjectivity. ʿAṭṭār's poetry illustrates transgression of the law as a way to transcend the worldly constructed paradigms, enabling the acceptance of those who are different from us. To create a more nuanced perspective of *shāhidbāzī* and ʿAṭṭār's treatment of those who deviated from it, I will also examine a similar trend in medieval European literature.

Shāhidbāzī or The Philosophy of Gazing at Male Beauty

Shāhidbāzī or *naẓarbāzī* originated in ancient Greece and penetrated the Muslim world as early as the middle of the ninth century. The followers of this philosophy in the Muslim world based their understanding of it on the popular *Ḥadīth al-ru'yā*, according to which the Prophet saw God in his dream, or during the ascension, in the form of a beardless youth (Ritter 459). In the Muslim tradition, references to God having human form can be found in the teachings of Hishām ibn Sālim al-Jawālīqī (?–799), who notes that although God has human form, He does not have flesh and blood and is like a radiant light; and those of Abū Isā al-Warrāq (?–861) who refers to God's black hair (461). Some Sufis, such as Tirmidhī (824–892) and Rūzbihān Baqlī (1128–1209) even claimed to have seen God themselves. Of course, it should be noted that these teachings were subject to orthodox criticism. For instance, Muḥammad al-Ghazzālī tries to refute the anthropomorphic interpretation of these dreams, saying that "what the one asleep sees in a dream is not the form of God—God is exalted above image and form—but only a symbol, a likeness. Radiant light and beautiful forms are but likenesses of real, non-physical beauty which has no form" (*al-Risāla* 29–32). Another group of Sufis called *Ḥulūlīs* went even further, teaching that God resides in people or animals. The practice of gazing at the beauty of youths and contemplating divine beauty is believed to have emerged out of the *Ḥulūlīs'* ideas and was likewise condemned by orthodox theologians and strict Sufis. The practice, however, was maintained in Sufi circles, with reference being made not to *ḥulūl* (incarnation) but rather to *shāhid*. Dihkhudā's *Lughat-nāma* defines *shāhid* as witnessing divine beauty perceived through the beauty of a male, and *shāhidbāzī* as the act of falling in love with a beautiful male, which is also synonymous with *liwāṭ* (sodomy).

Some Sufis, such as Muḥammad ibn al-Ḥusain al-Sulamī (937–1021) and Majd al-Dīn al-Fīrūzābādī (1329–1415) who spoke of *shāhid*, based their teachings on the sayings of the Prophet, who recommended contemplating beautiful objects. Others, such as Muḥammad ibn Ibrāhīm Abū Ḥamza (?–883) and Abū al-Qāsim al-Junayd (830–910) are believed to have tried to combat sensuality during their practice of contemplation, but it proved to be very difficult. The practice of contemplating beautiful objects appears in the Iranian philosophical works of Abū Naṣr Muḥammad al-Fārābī (872–950) and Ibn (Abū Alī) Sīnā or Avicenna (980–1037) in the ninth century. In his *Risāla fi'l 'ishq* (*Treatise on Love*) discussing this philosophy, Ibn Sīnā condemns gazing at youths and loving them if there is physical attraction and sexual desire involved. However, he approves if it is done for the sake of the union with the ultimate beloved (115–17). Among Sufis who condemned gazing at the beauty of youths were Muḥammad al-Ghazzālī, Abū al-Qāsim al-Qushayrī, 'Alī ibn 'Uthmān al-Jullābī al-Hujwīrī (ca. 990–1072), Shahāb al-Dīn Suhrawardī (1155–1195), Bahā Walad, and the Hanbalite Abū al-Faraj ibn al-Jawzī (1116–1201). In *al-Risāla fī 'ilm al-Taṣawwuf* (*Epistle on Sufism*), al-Qushayrī warns against the practice of *shāhid* and rejects the idea that it does no harm to the soul (184). Hujwīrī also rejects the practice altogether, announcing that "looking at youths and associating them are forbidden practices, and anyone who declares this to be allowable is an unbeliever" (416). Likewise, Ibn al-Jawzī, warning dervishes against loving the sons of kings, writes in his *Talbīs Iblīs* (*The Devil's Delusion*), "Don't fill your eyes with the sons of Kings, for they represent a temptation which is worse than the temptation of maidens!" (293; see also 235–40, 352–64, 447–58). The fact that all these theologians and Sufis felt the need to warn society against contemplating the beauty of youths makes us question whether the practice was exclusively intended for divine contemplation or it did in fact cross the spiritual boundaries and enter the realm of sensuality.

Ideally, the practice was expected to be confined to spirituality, without any accompanying feelings of physical attraction or sexual encounters. It was also supposed to be discreet and unexposed to the public eye, and not reciprocated easily and publicly by the beloved. There were many warnings against the dangers of gazing at the beauty of adolescent boys because it was regarded as a potential prelude to a sexual encounter, one of the major sins in Islam, *liwāṭ*, considered a transgression against *ḥaqq Allah* (a right of God) (El-Rouayheb 118). Another reason for these warnings was the potential for *shāhidbāzī* to disrupt traditional gender roles. Like many other cultures, Islamic culture had developed gender roles, where women were expected to be timid and passive while men were expected to be aggressive and active. These features demarcated boundaries between the male and the female spheres, the crossing of which would be a transgression. Since gazing at the beauty of adolescent boys could have led to sexual consummation, one partner would have to be active and the other passive. The passive partner would have therefore crossed gender boundaries by allowing himself to be emasculated and feminized (25). Hence, the reasons for warnings and condemnations against this philosophy largely derived from the discrepancy between its ideals and certain attempts to practice it.

In addition to medieval scholars, several modern scholars have discussed this ancient Greek and Arabo-Muslim cultural philosophy, which appears very different from our modern understanding of same-sex relationships. Michel Foucault, Dror Ze'evi, Khaled El-Rouayheb, Afsaneh Najmabadi, and Janet Afary are only a few who have examined this philosophy and asserted that "homosexuality" is too inadequate a term to define the experience of a male taking pleasure in relationships with adolescent boys. Further examination of the philosophy and its codes and laws offered by these scholars would not be out of place here.

Beginning from where it originated, in *The History of Sexuality*, Foucault notes that for the ancient Greeks, "love for one's own sex" and love for the opposite sex were not mutually exclusive emotions. The boundaries were not drawn based on the sex of the beloved or the lover but on their ethical viewpoints (187). According to ancient Greek thought, being inclined toward men or women represented "the appetite that nature had implanted in man's heart for 'beautiful' human beings," whatever their sex (188). The notion of two different desires assigned to different individuals did not exist in ancient Greek society. Both desires could coexist within the same person without being at odds with each other. It was considered merely a different way of taking pleasure and "more suited to certain individuals or certain periods of existence" (190). Thus, enjoying both adolescent boys and women was not inherently contradictory. A man who preferred adolescent boys to females was not considered naturally or socially different from those who were inclined to women. In that sense, in that culture, there was no socially imposed distinction between these two types of love. The preference for adolescent boys seemed more a matter of taste than an inherent persuasion. In the same context, Afary also writes that premodern Iranian men were not necessarily identified by their sexual desires but rather by their positionality in sexual relationships, being either active or passive. Same-sex relationship between an adult man and an adolescent boy, as long as it was implicit and "discreet," was a tolerated cultural practice in Mediterranean Muslim societies (*Sexual Politics* 107).

Regardless of the fact that this type of love was widely practiced and tolerated, it was subject to numerous condemnations and complications. Therefore, the practice was inhibited by rules and disciplines that had to be followed and decoded. For instance, the first thing to be taken into consideration was the difference in age and status between the lover and the beloved. A relationship between two men of the same status and age would result in the assumption of passivity in one partner. Since adult male passivity was abhorred, the adult who submitted passively would become a subject of derision (Foucault, *History* 193–94; Afary, *Sexual Politics* 107). Despite the rules about age and status difference, it would be wrong to assume that all same-sex sexual relationships were limited to adult men and adolescent boys. The same kind of relationship could be found between two men of the same age and status or two young boys. One other rule imposed in ancient Greece was the ritual of courtship. To make a relationship "a culturally and morally overloaded domain," there was a complete set of appropriate behaviors to be followed. The purpose was to endow the relationship with a beautiful form which would make it "aesthetically" acceptable as well. The roles of partners in the process of courtship were of utmost significance, too. The lover had certain "rights and obligations." In return, the beloved was expected not to submit too easily but show "gratitude." Although the relationship itself was expected to be kept discreet, the ritual of the adult male courting and pursuing an adolescent boy was practiced freely in public spaces such as gymnasiums (Foucault, *History* 196–97). It would continue up until a certain age, but upon the appearance of the signs of manhood, such as "the first beard," it was no longer appropriate for the adolescents to be the object of adult men's desire (199). It appears that love of adolescent boys was not initially forbidden, and nothing prohibited adult men from being in an open and free relationship with them. Adolescent youths were objects of adult men's desire and could be their "recognized sexual partners" (Foucault, *History* 217; see also Afary, *Sexual Politics* 79, 84–86).

Over time, however, the love for adolescent boys' beauty gradually transformed into a love "directed to the soul of boys rather than their bodies." This began with Plato, who established the inferiority of love of an adolescent boy's body as opposed to the love of his soul; and the soul that had not yielded was highly praised. The beauty of the soul was ultimately expected to make an individual gaze upon "the vast ocean of beauty" (Foucault, *History* 238–39). Hence, Plato structured the "love relation as a relation to truth; by . . . placing it in the one who is loved as well as in the one who is in love; and by reversing the role of the loved young man, making him a lover of the master of truth" (242). In this way, the Platonic erotics made the topic of Truth a pivotal element into this type of love relationship.

Consequently, men and women became beautiful objects of divine contemplation. However, since "the presence of women in a Sufi lodge would have caused more of an uproar in society, Sufis often chose pretty young male slaves or initiates, the ideal of beauty at the time, as their objects of loving contemplation" (Ze'evi 83). The Sufis were expected to admire the beauty of young boys which would lead them to Platonic Truth (83; see also El-Rouayheb, *Before Homosexuality* 12; and Bouhdiba, *Sexuality* 119–20). This was, however, the Sufi ideal; in practice, staying away from sexual activities proved to be difficult for the Sufis. Regarding this discrepancy between the ideal and the actual practice and its resultant sin, Afsaneh Najmabadi writes that the desire aroused by beauty "was not considered improper or sinful in itself. Sin belonged to the domain of deeds, for which reason there is plenty of literature warning against practices that might prompt a believer to engage in sinful acts" (*Women with Mustaches* 17–18). Therefore, it was the sinful acts and deeds following the gaze that were to be disciplined, which was the reason for so many advisories on how to control one's desire and gaze. It was the contradiction between the ideal and the practice which made this philosophy subject to condemnation. However, regardless of all warnings and denunciations, the philosophy and its practice survived and made their way into many literary works of the era.

The emergence of the philosophy in Iran resulted in two different kinds of same-sex relations. One appeared as a result of practicing the philosophy of "gazing at the beauty of adolescent boys"; the other emerged with the arrival of a large contingent of enslaved Turkish-speaking men and women who were to be used both in the army and for domestic purposes (Shamisa 15–16). Sirus Shamisa refers to *shāhidbāzī*, *naẓarbāzī*, *liwāṭ*, *bachchabāzī*, and so on as interchangeable terms used for the philosophy of gazing at the beauty of adolescent boys. The Ghaznavid Empire favored those Turkish slaves, and *liwāṭ* was a common practice in that period (39). Zarrinkub writes that one of the characteristic features of Iranian society from the Samanid era (819–999) to the Ghaznavid era was the presence of a great number of Turkish slaves in the Persian army who were bought either as prisoners of war or as presents for the rulers. They were promoted in the army quickly, often to the rank of commander, and considered close companions of the caliph. The youth and availability of those Turks made them highly demanded on the slave markets and a good topic for the poetry of the period. Hence, the term "Turk" became synonymous with "beloved" or *shāhid* in the Persian literature of the day (*Rūzigārān* 125). Shamisa also refers to the same points in *shāhidbāzī*. *Shāhid*, which also means witness to divine beauty, refers to a beautiful male in this context.

Classical Persian literature from the twelfth to the fifteenth century is imbued with themes of same-sex relations and homoerotic allusions and symbolism. Persian Sufi poetry overflows with rituals of courtship between people of "more or less equal status," such as the master-disciple relationship in Sufi orders within monasteries.

The poems disclose the sexual inclinations of the poet at times, and the poet's conformity to the general trend at other times (Afary 87–89). Hence, falling hopelessly in love with an adolescent boy became a familiar trope in Sufi literature, and this is no less so in ʿAṭṭār's works. One such narrative focusing on the love of a dervish or a Sufi for an adolescent boy is seen in the "Story of Fakhr al-Dīn Gurgānī and the Sultan's Slave" in ʿAṭṭār's *Ilāhī-nāma*. In this narrative, Fakhr al-Dīn Gurgānī falls in love with the sultan's slave at a feast. Although Fakhr al-Dīn keeps it secret, the sultan perceives his feelings and at the end of the feast presents the slave to him. Fakhr al-Dīn departs from the sultan's feast with the slave. However, on second thought, he decides not to take the slave with him because he is worried that the sultan, having presented the slave to him when he was drunk, might regret it the following day. Therefore, he leaves the slave in a vault of solid stone under the sultan's throne on a couch with two lit candles and sleeps before the door of that vault until daybreak. The next day, he meets the sobered king to make sure that the sultan is happy with his decision. When he goes back to the vault, he finds the slave burnt from head to toe by the fire of the candles which had fallen upon him. Out of sorrow for his beloved's death, Fakhr al-Dīn "rushe[s] into the desert and [makes] the story of 'Vīs and Rāmīn' his refrain" (*Ilāhī-nāma,* discourse 6, part 4). *Vīs and Rāmīn* is a popular Persian male-female love story composed by Fakhr al-Dīn Gurgānī. The plot line of the story is identical to *Lailā and Majnūn* or its Western counterpart *Tristan and Isolde*. This narrative illustrates the ways that Fakhr al-Dīn attempts to keep his love for the sultan's slave secret and discreet, which adheres to the standards of the philosophy of *shāhidbāzī*. To avoid temptation, he leaves the slave alone in the vault and sleeps at the door, outside the room—another moment of conformity to the codes of the philosophy that prescribes avoiding temptation. On the spiritual level, the story discloses the intense suffering of the seeker on the divine path, which can grow strong enough to drive him mad. Referring to the story, *Vīs and Rāmīn*, ʿAṭṭār makes use of the desert imagery as a symbol of hardships, trials, and pains of the Sufi. Through the earthly pain of losing his beloved, the Sufi will purify his soul along the divine path. Furthermore, both profane and sacred rhetoric are present in this story. The fire imagery is used not only as a metaphor for the fire of passion for the earthly beloved, but also as one of burning in the fire of desire for union with the heavenly beloved. Hence, the love of the earthly beloved becomes the threshold upon which Fakhr al-Dīn can perceive and reach divine love. Although in this narrative ʿAṭṭār conforms to the rules of the philosophy of *shāhidbāzī*, we will see later how he deviates from its laws in Sultan Maḥmūd's case.

ʿAṭṭār's works and medieval European literature have thematic affinities as regards the significance of love, its transformative power, and its prescription of subversion. A body of European literature depicting same-sex desire and love has survived from the High Middle Ages (c. 1001–1300), although, due to the religious prudery and obscurantism of subsequent generations, much of the information on this subject has been lost. What follows is an overview of the thinking on the matter among high-ranking clerics and the body of literature that has survived.

Same-Sex Desire in Medieval European Literature

In eleventh- and twelfth-century Europe, there emerged a trend of same-sex desire similar to the one that unfolded in the medieval Muslim world, particularly among clerics and high-ranking churchmen. As a result, a body of literature addressing same-sex desire has remained. There are striking similarities between the European literature of the time and the medieval Middle Eastern works considering the depiction of same-sex desire. For instance, at the center of the philosophy of *shāhidbāzī* lies the beautiful beardless adolescent boy that reminds us of portrayals of Christ in medieval paintings, which depict the ancient ideal of beauty. Another striking point is that in both Islamic and Christian literatures of the era, the subject of same-sex desire appeared in the writings of men of God and religious authorities, in the case of Islamic literature, in Sufi works.

Viewing the literature and art of the Middle Ages in Europe, therefore, we notice frequent references to same-sex desire between men and in men. For instance, in Marie de France's *Lais*, we read that in the twelfth century, if a man ignored a woman's sexual advances, he would be in danger of being called sodomite (65). Jacques de Vitry's description of Parisian pupils in the same era is another portrayal of that line of thinking; he writes that fornication was not considered a sin and "prostitutes dragged passing clerics to brothels almost [*sic*] by force, and openly through the streets; if the clerics refused to enter, the whores called them sodomites. . . . That abominable vice sodomy so filled the city that it was held a sign of honor if a man kept one or more concubines" (Rashdall 439). Late medieval Europe has frequently been considered intolerant of deviations and nonconformity, and the term "medieval" has been used to refer to oppression and intolerance. But it would be an overgeneralization to simply assume medieval society was characteristically intolerant of diversity.

Although Western European culture was strongly influenced by Germanic and Celtic traditions, its origins lay in Roman society. The Roman influence can be seen in every cultural and social aspect of the new societies. Notwithstanding the Roman inspiration, there is enormous difference between Romans and their heir societies regarding sexuality and tolerance. Almost none of the laws or taboos in the Roman Empire were used to regulate sexuality and love, particularly same-sex love. Roman society was tolerant of same-sex relations, and did not regard them as threatening, harmful, or immoral. Neither the law nor religion regarded same-sex relations as different from heterosexuality. As it was with Greek and Mediterranean societies, Roman society assumed that adult males could have sexual relations with both sexes. Thus, same-sex acts were not illegal. In Augustan Rome, the government taxed prostitutes who entered same-sex relations and granted legal holidays to boy prostitutes. Authors like Cornelius Nepos (c. 100–25 BC) who objected to same-sex relations regarded it as shameful or dishonorable but not illegal. Of course, this is not to say that there were no sexual taboos during this period, but that they were not directed at same-sex relations. In fact, as it was in other cultures as well, the passive partner in the relationship, if adult and a citizen, was subject to strong derision whereas noncitizens and young boys could be passive partners without loss of status if the relationship was voluntary. Similar to most cultures, gender-related concepts of behavior depended on cultural variables. Hence, it can be said that the culture of the early Roman Empire was the basis for social tolerance of same-sex relations in the West. However, writings on same-sex relations became rare after the third-century AD, beginning with the rise of legal actions against them (Boswell, *Christianity* 68–87).

With the decline of the Roman Empire and the rise of Christianity, social tolerance of same-sex desire declined as well. However, it is difficult to distinguish the extent to which Christianity affected this. The increasing ruralization of Roman civilization and the absolutism of Roman government are two aspects that might be considered influential in the decline of Roman tolerance of same-sex desire (Boswell, *Christianity* 119–21). The centuries during and after the fall of Roman urban culture witnessed the most hostile period of ecclesiastical thought on sexual matters and same-sex desire (206). After the breakup of the Roman Empire, the economy of Western Europe underwent enormous transformation between the tenth and fourteenth centuries. Domestic security had increased, there was economic stability, and many social and political institutions, technology, and agricultural techniques had advanced, and the population had grown. All these transformations were important for the growth of same-sex relations during the eleventh and twelfth centuries (207).

The literature surviving from the twelfth century depicts Christian writings celebrating personal affection, which transcends all moral, social, or familial obligations. This in itself is evidence of the dramatic social change of the time in European society. The literature is also full of references to mutual love, affection, and transformation. Love transformed the asceticism of the desert fathers to the passionate mysticism of St. Bernard (1090–1153). This sublimation of love was in fact accompanied by the development of urbanity and the veneration of humanism in social matters, and a respect for personal freedom, values, and feelings. These social shifts promoted public tolerance of all minorities that left long-lasting effects on cultural values and literature (Boswell, *Christianity* 241). The European literature of this period shares thematic affinities with the literature of the Muslim world regarding the significance of love and its transformative power.

Out of the High Middle Ages a body of literature depicting same-sex desire and love survived, although, due to ignorance, much of the information on the subject has been lost. For instance, the male statesman, orator, and general Alcibiades (c. 450–404 BC) appears as a female companion of Socrates (c. 470–399 BC) in many medieval literary works, and in Ovid's *Art of Love*, the phrase "A boy's love appealed to me less" was changed to "A boy's love appealed to me not at all" in order to show that Ovid was not a sodomite (Boswell, *Christianity* 18). Another body of same-sex literature has survived from the eleventh and twelfth centuries that deals mostly with religious themes of an orthodox nature regarding love. Many of the authors of these poems were prominent churchmen with significant ecclesiastical authority; however, none was accused of unorthodoxy (244). Twelfth-century

Europe saw a novelty in the overt expressions of the bishops and priests about same-sex desire and relationships. Earlier medieval poets such as Alcuin (740–804), Hrabanus Maurus (780–856), and Walafrid (808–849) had also referred to similar topics in their works, but theirs were less overt. The use of erotic language and themes referring to same-sex desire by high-ranking religious officials, who simultaneously wrote on conventional topics, was a new social development (250).

One of the most prominent topoi of the period was the emergence and adoration of the figure of Ganymede—the beautiful son of the king of Troy whom Jove had carried away to be his cupbearer in heaven. The term "Ganymede" became synonymous with "the beloved" in same-sex relationships in the High Middle Ages. Other terms that were frequently used to refer to youthfulness, same-sex desire, and intimacy were "boy," "game," and "hunting." Alcuin refers to a cleric he loved as a "beautiful boy"; Walafrid calls his fellow monk a "little boy"; St. Aelred of Rievaulx (1110–1166) refers to Simon, his lover, as a "boy"; and Marbod of Rennes (1035–1123) refers to himself as a "boy" in a love letter.

Marbod of Rennes' position as a master at a school in Chartres made his attitude toward same-sex desire influential throughout Europe, where copies of his manuscripts circulated widely. Using mostly religious themes, Marbod includes verses in his poem, "The Unyielding Boy," that satirize his subject. The reference to an unyielding boy is a reminder of the courtship rituals of the Sufi philosophy of *shāhidbāzī*, where the adolescent boy was expected to be coy and not to surrender easily. Marbod's language in his poem has both sexual and romantic overtones. For instance, the line "Who by the viciousness of his character denies the beauty of his body" has sexual undertones. Marbod asks the boy to surrender before he loses all his youthful beauty, which is transient. Marbod wrote a poem to a young boy whom he loved, but who was himself in love with a beautiful girl, who was, in turn, in love with Marbod. Marbod sends a command to his lover, who was away on business, to return if he wishes Marbod to remain faithful to him, because efforts were being made to woo him away. The unyielding, unattainable love object is a recurrent theme in his works.

The theme of an unyielding young boy can also be found in the works of a student of Peter Abelard (1079–1142), Hilary the Englishman (fl. 1125). Hilary complains about the arrogance of a young English boy in his poetry. Hilary's poetry is very personal in the way he expresses his anxiety over his feelings for a youth and his commitment to a woman at the same time. However, when Hilary's poems are addressed to women, they lack the emotional intensity of those addressed to a young male. Hilary makes use of the metaphor of "hunting" in his poetry and refers to himself as "the hunted," a reference to the helplessness of the lover in the face of an unyielding beloved. This metaphor is also found in ʿAṭṭār's works.

The appearance of the figure of Ganymede as a topos in medieval European literature is similar to the use of *shāhid* to refer to "the beloved" in Persian literature. The dominance of the imagery of hunting, the use of warlike language, and terms such as "game" can also be seen in the literatures of both cultures. Most significant is the presence of the young boy as a symbol for the beloved. Although these are very different concepts that appeared in different contexts, one cannot but notice the intellectual and cultural exchanges between Christian-Muslim and European-Middle Eastern societies in the medieval period in such matters.

After the twelfth century, because of this body of literature, the existence of men who had desire both for men and for women became common knowledge. As in Middle Eastern cultures, this desire was not considered a fixed sexual orientation in medieval Europe. Ruth Karras and David Boyd, in "Um cum muliere," explore sexuality in fourteenth-century England through examining the court documents and testimony of John Rykener, a cross-dressing prostitute who had sex with men, mainly clerics, in 1394. The authors discuss how Rykener's offense was not labeled prostitution, but a threat to public order. According to Karras and Boyd, Rykener's investigation raised questions about the role of sexuality in medieval culture because "the construction, or lack thereof, of specific sexualities; the deployment of the concept of sodomy to impugn the masculinity of celibate clergy; the relation between the grammatical subject/object relation and the social subject/object relation; and the medieval understanding of gender as performative and the issue of 'passing' were interlocked and conflated" (102–03). Since Rykener's sexuality is not defined clearly in the court documents, Karras and Boyd suggest two cultural categories in which Rykener could fit—prostitution and sodomy (103). Of course, it is striking that prostitution could be a sexual identity or orientation in the medieval period as it is, today, considered an act for soliciting money. It is also interesting that Rykener was not accused of prostitution. In regard to sodomy, although he never referred to himself as a sodomite, Karras and Boyd found the words "unmentionable," "unspeakable act," "abominable vice," and such terms—used to refer to sodomy in medieval Europe—in his confession in relation to his sexuality. Of course, Karras and Boyd believe that since a scribe wrote down his confessions, these terms were probably the scribe's (105). The authors note that sodomy in medieval Europe did not mean homosexuality as we know it today; legally, it was considered to be the act of anal intercourse and of course not all acts of anal intercourse were between two men (106). Thus, what was Rykener's offense? His offense was apparently the disruption of social norms—via gender and sexual transgression—which surfaces in legal and literary texts frequently in the medieval period. Regarding the construction of sexualities in the medieval period, Fradenburg and Carla Freccero write, throughout history, sexualities have been a "part of a history of 'discipline and punishment,' of 'social control,' of the ways communities construct people's bodies and touch them in rage or in welcome" (*Premodern Sexualities* viii). In the following section, I examine the ways that ʿAṭṭār constructs Sultan Maḥmūd's and Ayāz's sexuality.

ʿAṭṭār's Portrayal of Maḥmūd and Ayāz's Relationship

ʿAṭṭār narrates many stories about the homoerotic relationship between Sultan Maḥmūd and Ayāz. Although he adds a spiritual dimension to the stories, ʿAṭṭār's narratives of this relationship do not conform to the standards of the Sufi philosophy of "gazing at male beauty" and loving that beauty. The relationship in question can be considered a homoerotic affair in which one can expect sexual encounters and consummation. The fact that Ayāz was able to rise from Turkic servant to king of Lahore may indicate that he achieved this status because of his beauty and availability and resultant relationship with the sultan. This relationship violated the codes of the philosophy of *shāhidbāzī* because, as ʿAṭṭār portrays it, it was sexually charged, indiscreet, and reciprocated by the subject of affection; besides, the beloved was an adult man rather than an adolescent boy. What deserves attention here is that Ayāz and, particularly, Maḥmūd deconstruct their identities and emerge as new subjects due to their allegedly transgressive experiences in this relationship.

In many narratives, ʿAṭṭār depicts the sultan publicly expressing his love for Ayāz. One such narrative is the story of "The Beggar who Fell in Love with Ayāz" in *Muṣībat-nāma*. Here, ʿAṭṭār relates that Sultan Maḥmūd ordered a beggar who fell in love with Ayāz to forget him and go away because Ayāz is only for the sultan to love. The beggar replies to the sultan that if he claims Ayāz to be his, then he is not truly in love because love, selfishness, and possessiveness contradict one another. The beggar claims to love Ayāz sincerely because he has already annihilated his self through his love. He expresses that although the sultan may forbid him to see Ayāz, he cannot make the love he feels for Ayāz disappear from his heart (discourse 5, part 9). This narrative is a comment on sincere love that necessitates selflessness. The lover needs to lose his or her self in order to merge with the beloved other. The story reveals that a lover never stops loving the beloved even though external forces, such as the government, the community, or some other social institutions may threaten him. By placing the sultan and the beggar alongside each other as rivals, ʿAṭṭār invokes class as a category of desire, especially since it is being violated and transcended. Furthermore, ʿAṭṭār portrays the love between a human being and the divine as the apotheosis of love that crosses class and gender boundaries.

The violation of class and gender boundaries that result in the construction of subjectivity abounds in ʿAṭṭār's poetry. In the context of Maḥmūd and Ayāz's relationship, this type of violation appears in the following excerpt from *Ilāhī-nāma*, discourse 8, part 4:

> Every moment he increased his devotion to his master,
> for as he rubbed his feet he kissed them also.
> Said Maḥmūd to the silver-breasted Ayāz:
> "What is the purpose of thy kissing my feet?
> Of all the seven members why shouldst thou kiss the feet?
> Thou hast, alas, neglected the other members.
> When thou seest the value of the face,
> why dost thou prefer the humble foot?"
> Ayāz replied: "It is a strange matter.
> All mankind have their share of thy face,

For they all see thy moon-like countenance;
but none has access to thy feet.
Since here there is no one other than we,
our intimacy is greater, and this I must have for my own."

به خدمت هر دم افزون بود رایش
که می مالید و می بوسید پایش
ایاز سیمبر را گفت محمود
"ترا زین پای بوسیدن چه مقصود؟
ز هفت اعضا چرا بر پا دهی بوس
دگر اعضا رها کرده به افسوس
چو قدر روی می بینی که چون است
چرا میلت به پای سرنگون است؟"
ایازش گفت که "این کاری عجیب است
که خلقی را ز روی تو نصیب است
که می بینند رویت جمله چون ماه
نمی یابد به پای تو کسی راه
چو اینجا نیست غیری این باخلاص
بسی نزدیک تر این بایدم خاص."

To Ayāz, adoration of the sultan's feet represents the highest degree of intimacy between them. The acts of kissing and touching the body members of the beloved literally refer to the sensuality and physicality of the relationship. The sultan asks Ayāz why he kisses his feet only, perhaps indicating his own desire for further intimacy. Ayāz explains that kissing the sultan's feet is an act of deep intimacy, for he has access to what is inaccessible to others. This conversation depicts the desire for intimacy and privacy between them. The words "face" and "feet" are emphasized in this narrative; face as the body member visible to all, and feet as the body members visible only to a select few. Dihkhudā in *Lughat-nāma* defines *pā* (foot) as the foundation and main member of the body (*bun*, *bunyād*). This can serve as an indication of Ayāz's desire for a strong and foundational love relationship. It is also worthwhile to examine the vocabulary that the sultan uses with reference to Ayāz, one that is very sensual and mostly feminine. In reference to the description of Ayāz as silver-breasted (*sīmbar*), Dihkhudā's *Lughat-nāma* indicates that the adjective is applied to someone with a very white body and skin. This explains the sensual reference to Ayāz's body and his complexion.

In a spiritual context, ʻAṭṭār suggests through this story that the seeker desires to see what is veiled. This veil is the veil of imperfection, that of God's creations. God as the most perfect one is pitted against his imperfect creations. To reach the divine, the imperfect human should transcend the veil. This in itself creates "otherness," and if humans desire to view the Creator unveiled, they have to transcend the earthly constructed paradigms. Moreover, this desire to see the divine unveiled is the reason for the Sufi's transcendence. The Sufi wants to be intimate with the divine in a way that no ordinary person can be. She or he longs for intimacy that cannot be disrupted by earthly matters. In order to behold the divine unveiled, the Sufi has to move beyond the ordinary, annihilate the self, and become united with the divine. Hence the reason for Ayāz's desire to behold what is veiled from ordinary people's eyes; in this case, the sultan's feet.

This narrative also hints at the desire of the lover to be humbled in front of the beloved, and this is another instance demonstrating how love enables a lover to violate class hierarchies. ʿAṭṭār reveals how, for the sake of the unattainable love of the other, a lover violates socially constructed boundaries, which consequently results in his encounter with a world of possibilities, such as alternative ways of loving. This openness to alternative human forms and ways of loving, and the violation of socially and culturally constructed taboos, which was offered by ʿAṭṭār aptly enough in the medieval period, is what Foucault advocates for his contemporary readers as well. Violating sociocultural paradigms and breaking away from the barriers that the mind has constructed allows for the deconstruction and reshaping of subjectivities.

The desire to behold the beloved unveiled is illustrated by yet another story in which ʿAṭṭār portrays Maḥmūd and Ayāz's intimate affair in *Ilāhī-nāma*, discourse 11, part 6. Whereupon hearing that Ayāz has gone to the bath alone, Maḥmūd rushes there with a swollen heart,

> He beheld the face of that perī-like one
> which had set the walls of the bath in flames.
> From the reflection of his face the walls
> with the door and the roof were all set a-dancing

> بدید القصه روی آن پری وش
> وزو دیوار گرمابه درآتش
> زعکس صورتش دیوارحمام
> همه رقاص گشته از درو بام

The setting of the story in the bath and the imagery of the walls in flames add strong sensuality to the narrative. The flame serves as a metaphor for the fire of passion that Ayāz's beauty has set in the sultan's heart. In this narrative, the lover wants to behold the beloved in his entirety, rather than just an arm or a leg (Ritter 481). Gazing upon the lover's face ignites the sultan's heart but the sultan is not content. Furthermore, there are sexual overtones within ʿAṭṭār's language. When the sultan's passion is concerned, particularly important is the term *perī*, which refers to a beautiful female supernatural fairy in Persian mythology. The word used by ʿAṭṭār in the Persian text is *parīvash*, a name given to females. This might be a comment on Ayāz's feminine role in the relationship. When the sultan sees his beloved's beauty in its entirety, he gives up his entire soul to every part of Ayāz's body. This manifestation of surrender and humility by the sultan serves as a reference to the ability of the power of love to transform the sultan into a slave of love. In this narrative, ʿAṭṭār blurs the lines of the master-servant relationship of power by turning the sultan into a subordinate servant of his own slave. In this way, ʿAṭṭār comments on the construction of knowledge and maintenance of power by subversion of the dominant discourses in his poetry. The reference to burning and the flaming heart in the extract below signifies the fire of passion, which in the mystical context refers to the passionate longing of a Sufi to see the divine unveiled and be united with him. This also indicates that being the slave of the beloved is the highest status a human being can attain. In the same story in *Ilāhī-nāma,* discourse 11, part 6, bewildered, Ayāz asks about the reason for the sultan's sudden rapture:

> The king replied: "When I saw only thy face,
> my heart had no conception of each separate member.
> Now that all thy limbs have become visible to me,
> I am the slave of each of them as they are of thee.
> My heart was burning for love of thy face;
> now a hundred more fires have flared up.
> Since my heart is ravished by each and all of your members,
> to which shall I now give my love?"

شهش گفتا "چو رویت در نظر بود
ز یک یک بند تو دل بی خبر بود
کنون چون دیده آمد بند بندت
شدم چون بند بندت مستمندت
مرا از عشق رویت جان همی سوخت
کنون صد آتش دیگر برافروخت
چو یک یک بندت آمد دلنوازم
کنون من با کدامین عشق بازم؟"

ʿAṭṭār uses the word *naẓar* to denote the sultan's gaze upon Ayāz's body members, which refers to *shāhidbāzī* or *naẓarbāzī.* He also uses the Persian word *mustamand*, which is translated in English as a sense of neediness associated with pain and suffering. Maḥmūd, the lover, needs to see and enjoy his beloved in full. The lover and the beloved are always defined in light of each other. The lover is *mustamand* (needy), asking for the beloved's love and attention, and the beloved is always coy and coquettish. The theme of beholding the beloved in full as no one else can is invoked here again—a reference both to the sultan's earthly desire for intimacy and, on the metaphorical level, to the Sufi's desire to see the divine unveiled. This beholding of the beloved's beauty is a reference to the beloved's constant need for the lover's admiration and love.

Ayāz reciprocates the sultan's desire, which contradicts the principles of the philosophy of *shāhidbāzī*. This story shows the strong love and intimacy between the lover and the beloved, who lose themselves in each other. Both Maḥmūd and Ayāz want to observe their beloved in their totality, as no one else can. In that sense, in this love affair, it is not clear who is the lover and who is the beloved, who is the passive partner and who is the active partner. It seems that there is no sense of conformity to the standard rules here. Not only are gender boundaries being crossed, but also the dominant master-subordinate slave relationship is reversed. ʿAṭṭār seems to be suggesting that in a spiritual context, these demarcations lose meaning. All that matters is the love between the lover and the beloved, both in the earthly and the heavenly contexts; otherness is diminished. The limit has been superseded in order for the self and the other to merge with each other and transgress the law, as Foucault would say. Here, in addition to queering malehood, ʿAṭṭār introduces the possibility for new kinds of love and sexuality to arise and thrive. Through this narrative, ʿAṭṭār shows that boundaries exist in order for us to enjoy crossing them and experience Lacanian jouissance. Since we can never be limitless, except in our minds and hearts, boundaries help us to imagine what is impossible as what is prohibited. ʿAṭṭār's writing, however, provides us with the opportunity to imagine the impossible and transgress its boundaries. ʿAṭṭār encourages human beings to be free from the shackles of reason and filled with love so that they may be able to subvert worldly paradigms. This is where ʿAṭṭār's ideology and Foucault's theory converge; they both advocate losing logic and human consciousness, which maintain worldly demarcations and limit human beings, in order for individuals to be able to grow personally and, for ʿAṭṭār, spiritually as well. ʿAṭṭār's writing allows for the crossing of all impossible earthly boundaries created by human logic.

Although gender lines are blurred in almost every narrative about the sultan and his slave, the violation of class hierarchy is highlighted in many of them as well. One instance of class violation appears in *Ilāhī-nāma*, where Maḥmūd asks Ayāz to tell him who in the world has the greatest kingdom and is the greatest of kings. Ayāz responds that his kingdom is greater than the sultan's because although he is a sultan, he has lost his heart—the essence of humanity—to Ayāz. Therefore, Ayāz is the king, and because he has control over the sultan's heart, his kingdom is greater. Ayāz claims that for this reason even the heavens envy him. In *Ilāhī-nāma,* discourse 14, part 11, ʿAṭṭār ends the narrative with a comment on the significance of the human heart, which he describes as the empire of love:

> Since the essence of thee is thy heart and thou hast no heart,
> of what use is thy empire?

چو اصل تو دل است و دل نداری
بگو تا مملکت را بر چه کاری؟

This story reveals that the love of this beautiful man annuls all rules, reversing the master-slave power relationship. ʿAṭṭār uses the "heart" in this story as a literary metaphor for the sultan's kingdom. Whereas the sultan offers his kingdom to Ayāz willingly, Ayāz refuses to accept it because he has a better kingdom, which is the sultan's heart. As Hellmut Ritter writes, in Maḥmūd and Ayāz's narratives, "it is from the beloved slave that love's rules are to be learned and these are chiefly presented through the refined answers and instructions which [Ayāz] gives to his royal lover" (384). However, ʿAṭṭār does not intend to abolish the rules of the philosophy through this reversal of roles and liberate his lovers from all historically set limits. Rather, he attempts to unmake established narratives, encourage openness, and introduce alternatives by crossing socially constructed boundaries. ʿAṭṭār's final spiritual comment refers to the "heart" as the main and fundamental element in every human being, the lack of which signifies emptiness and the absence of spiritual origin. ʿAṭṭār highlights love as affirmative power in the process of transgression and construction of subjectivity for the sultan and Ayāz.

Regardless of Ayāz challenging Maḥmūd's authority at times, ʿAṭṭār portrays him as a loyal servant who resists the temptation to accept honors and prospects of advancement in order to remain with Maḥmūd. In *Ilāhī-nāma*, discourse 8, part 6, ʿAṭṭār relates that at his dying hour, Maḥmūd asks Ayāz secretly to stay faithful to him after his death and not serve any other master. Ayāz replies that if he were "an eater of carrion," he could not have hunted a better game than Maḥmūd. By this he means that if he meant to take advantage of the sultan, and were looking forward to his master's death so as to serve another master, he would not have fallen in the game of love with Maḥmūd:

Since I can bind Maḥmūd with a single hair of my head,
I have not the heart to gird my loins before another.
As long as Ayāz, thy intimate, is alive,
all will be well in the end

چو محمودی به مویی می توان بست
نیارم پیش غیراو میان بست
ایازخاص تا موجود باشد
مدامش عاقبت محمود باشد

They promise loyalty to each other even after death. Romantic language overflows the text. There are also references to hunting, the hunter, and the hunted as a reminder of the popular game of love, also a common trope in medieval European literature. Note also Ayāz's sensual comment that he can enslave the sultan by a single hair. In addition, the power relationship is again reversed as the sultan asks the servant to stay faithful to him, showing Ayāz's power over the sultan and his heart. Class hierarchies are challenged here through ʿAṭṭār's rewriting of the established scripts of the time in order to illustrate that these hierarchies only exist in the human mind.

As with all of his poetry, in this narrative ʿAṭṭār adds the importance of the spiritual dimension, and not just love, in transgressing worldly limits. On a spiritual level, ʿAṭṭār portrays Ayāz's devotion as the longing of the true seeker to be in union with the beloved rather than gaining any earthly advantages. At the end of this poem, ʿAṭṭār makes a reference to Iblīs (Satan), who in the Islamic tradition was cursed by God because after worshipping God for thousands of years and boasting about it, he refused to prostrate himself before Adam when God asked him to do so, since he desired to venerate only God. In Islamic Sufi tradition, Iblīs is therefore considered the monotheist lover that, cursed by God, accepts it as an honor. This analogy illustrates that like Iblīs, Ayāz prefers to be cursed but stay faithful to his beloved.

Subversion of class hierarchy, power relations, and gender lines is a recurrent theme in ʿAṭṭār's writings on Maḥmūd and Ayāz. In *Manṭiq al-ṭayr*, an anecdote relates that Maḥmūd handed the command over his army to Ayāz but that Ayāz had no interest in this and broke into tears. When asked why, he claimed that busying himself with the army would keep him away from his beloved sultan, and he would not be able to be as close to him as he was before (*Manṭiq al-ṭayr*, lines 3101–25). ʿAṭṭār portrays how earthly engagements can keep the seeker away from the truth, and how a real lover will avoid worldly desires in order to stay in the proximity of the beloved. What is more, as long as the proximity of the sacred signifies power and reality, the lover will long for this closeness. ʿAṭṭār reveals the true devotion of Ayāz in this narrative. A true servant of God and a true lover will never desire to be away from the divine beloved. Even if the sultan granted sovereignty over his kingdom to Ayāz, the latter would never leave the sultan because he feels wealthy and powerful through being around the sultan. Although Ayāz claims to be obedient to the sultan, he refuses the sultan's generosity, which is an act of resistance to authority and another moment of subversion of the class and power relationship. Through this resistance, ʿAṭṭār's Ayāz rewrites the prescribed narratives about power relations through the power of love.

Breaking away from the imposed limits of the mind through the violation of gender and class boundaries is a theme discussed in another story from *Ilāhī-nāma,* discourse 8, part 11. Here, Maḥmūd, as the king of the world, desires to grant a wish to each one of his great nobles. At the moment when all are being offered an opportunity to request what they desire, Ayāz expresses his wish to become the target for Maḥmūd's arrows since in that way he will always be in the sultan's sights. He explains his reasons for this choice:

> For first he must several times
> cast a glance at the target and then only shoot the arrow.
> Since that glance will come first
> how will it be difficult to bear the wound that comes afterwards?
> You see that wound upon its way,
> but I see only that glance bestowed by the king.
> If he first cast ten glances upon me,
> how shall I then flee in fear of one wound?

که اول بر نشانه چند ره شاه
نظر می افگند، پس تیر آنگاه
چو اول آن نظر در کار آید
در آخر زخم کی دشوار آید
شما این زخم می بینید در راه
ولی من آن نظر می بینم از شاه
چو باشد ده نظر از پیش رفته
به زخمی کی روم از خویش رفته

ʿAṭṭār uses the Persian word *naẓar* (gaze, glance) again when talking about Ayāz being in the sights of the sultan, which is another reference to the philosophy of gazing at male beauty. In this story, Ayāz himself asks to be the object of the sultan's desire and gaze. Ayāz admonishes the other courtiers for not wanting to be the target of the sultan's *naẓar* (gaze) only because of the pain they would experience as a result of his arrow hitting them. The wound he refers to may also mean the pain of social condemnation and marginalization for his unconventional love. After all, this love, with its transgressive nature concerning sexual matters (as well as heavenly love with its unorthodox nature), is considered an alienating factor which can stigmatize him. However, the same alienating factor can also make love seem sublime and exceptional. To Ayāz, a wound does not matter if it comes from the beloved. The romantic overtone of Ayāz's desire to be the target of the sultan's arrows is also a reminder of Cupid and his arrows. Although Cupid brings love into people's lives, the love is accompanied by pain—the pain of losing oneself in the beloved, annihilating the self, and merging with the other. The story also hints at the significance of the gaze which is typically aimed at a woman by a man. The desire to be the target of the sultan's gaze, therefore, refers to Ayāz's possible passivity. In the mystical context, on the other hand, a wound refers to "the concept of the union of lover and beloved (or the soul with God) and of the lover losing his identity in that of the beloved" (Hanaway, "The Concept of the Hunt" 31–32). The union of the lover and the beloved, the earthly and the heavenly, the breaking away from the barriers of the mind, the breaking of the self, the reconstruction of subjectivity, and the acceptance of the other are concepts reiterated here.

Losing oneself and emerging as a new subject in union with the beloved is also depicted in *Ilāhī-nāma*, discourse 7, part 17, where ʿAṭṭār relates how Maḥmūd once asks Ayāz to go hunting with him. Ayāz replies that he has already made a catch and hunted down his game. The king asks what Ayāz has caught, and Ayāz replies that he has caught game with his *kamand* (lasso). The king then asks Ayāz to show him his lasso. Ayāz lets his long hair fall down to his feet and explains:

> My lasso . . . consists of my restless locks and
> the king of the world is the game that they have caught

کمندم . . . زلف بیقرار است
شه عالم کمندم را شکاراست

Ayāz's words infuriate the sultan, who orders Ayāz to be bound from head to foot in his "lasso." Although Maḥmūd enchains Ayāz, his heart is secretly attached to him. After the punishment, Maḥmūd asks Ayāz who the game in the lasso is and Ayāz's response is the same. Still believing that Ayāz is the game, Maḥmūd asks for the reason. Ayāz tells the sultan that even if his body is tortured to death, his heart will remain in perfect union with the sultan; and he claims that the same is true for the sultan because he has also lost his heart to Ayāz. Then, in the same discourse 7, part 17, he speaks about the preeminence of the heart over the body:

The body is the branch and the heart the root.
I am in perfect union with thy pure heart.
If my body has fallen for a moment into thy snare,
thy heart has fallen into my snare for ever.
Since thy heart is always the game in my snare,
I have my game always there

غلامش گفت تن فرع است و دل اصل
تمام است از دل پاک توام وصل
اگر یک دم تنم در دامت افتاد
دلت در دام من ناکامت افتاد
چو پیوسته دلت باشد شکارم
شکار خویش دایم کرده دارم

This narrative shows that the lover and the beloved, the master and the servant are no longer two separate beings. It is extremely sensual and vivid in its romantic language, making it difficult to believe that the relationship is merely a spiritual and not a physical one. ʿAṭṭār employs expressive adjectives such as "silver-breasted" to refer to Ayāz, and affectionate expressions, such as the beauty of Ayāz's "lasso," to draw a picture of this relationship. He also uses the imagery of hunting again by introducing such terms as "lasso" or "locks" in reference to the seductive weapons of the beloved, reminiscent of medieval European literature. In *Lughat-nāma*, Dihkhudā defines "lasso" as a noose and "hunting" as the intention of killing a creature; the terms thus connote suffering and pain. As mentioned earlier, the pain suffered by the lover is to some extent due to the difficulties of losing oneself in the other. Without self-annihilation and the pain that accompanies it, there will be no union. The public exhibition of Maḥmūd and Ayāz's love affair and its indiscreetness is another violation of the philosophy of *shāhidbāzī*. While the relationship is public and indiscreet, ʿAṭṭār embraces it because Maḥmūd and Ayāz's transgressive love relationship opens up possibilities for alternative performances and identities. Consequently, this love allows for the construction of new subjectivities in harmony with the divine other as well as the sociocultural and sexual other. Many elements and notions from contemporary theoretical discourses, such as Foucault's, can be found in this poetry. These narratives help us dig deeper into medieval subjectivities which tell us about modern subjectivities as well. The sublime love between Maḥmūd and Ayāz crosses artificially constructed boundaries and reaches to the core of their beings where they lose themselves in each other.

The coalescence of the couple is described in *Muṣībat-nāma*. When Maḥmūd falls ill and lies unconscious for three days, Ayāz likewise falls unconscious at his side, because their lives and souls are so closely intertwined. When Maḥmūd regains consciousness, he asks Ayāz when he arrived there. Ayāz replies that he has just arrived; however, the sultan's vizier tells him that Ayāz is lying. The sultan is infuriated and asks for the reason for Ayāz's dishonesty. Ayāz responds that he has no existence without the sultan, therefore when the sultan was unconscious he lost his own consciousness, and when he gained it back, so did Ayāz (*Muṣībat-nāma,* discourse 31, part 4). The imagery of both falling unconscious at each other's side has sexual overtones. The literal message of the story might refer to the close relationship between the lovers; however, the mystical meaning refers to the existence of the seeker in the sole terms of the existence of God. Although power boundaries are not crossed in this story, those of gender or the passive-active relationship are pushed. Ayāz, who was the passive recipient and object of the sultan's gaze and desire in the earlier narrative, now becomes his active lover by making the sultan his own object of desire. This reversal of roles is a reminder of Kristeva's ideas that when "in love 'I' has been an *other* . . . a state of instability in which the individual is no longer indivisible and allows himself to become lost in the other, for the other" (*Tales of Love* 4). When the ego breaks, Maḥmūd and Ayāz lose themselves in each other; Ayāz's existence has no meaning without Maḥmūd's and vice versa. It is at this moment that the self and the other merge and become indivisible; this is also the Kristevan zenith of subjectivity. When the self is de- and reconstructed through the crossing of boundaries, it emerges as a new subject that is able to transcend the earthly and unite with the divine. Likewise, when Sufis transgress the earthly boundaries through their peculiar spirituality, despite violation of the status quo, their subjectivity becomes reshaped and they emerge as new subjects totally in submission to the will of God.

The disappearance of otherness between Maḥmūd and Ayāz is unraveled in *Manṭiq al-ṭayr* (lines 1145–46). ʿAṭṭār writes that one day Ayāz fell ill, and the sultan, who was overcome with immense sorrow, sent a messenger to inquire about him. However, although the messenger makes haste, he arrives to find Maḥmūd already there. The messenger is terrified, telling the sultan that he did not stop on his way to Ayāz. The sultan replies that he knows of a hidden path which took him to Ayāz faster,

> My soul is with him (though my flesh is here)
> And guards his bed solicitous with fear.

گر تنم دور اوفتاد از هم نفس
جان مشتاقم بدو نزدیک و بس
مانده ام مشتاق جانی ازتومن
نیستم غایب زمانی ازتومن

The absence (*ghāyib*) that the sultan refers to is meant to be physical if we consider the Persian word *tan* (body); however, he also refers to the closeness of his *jān* (soul) to Ayāz, which is spiritual. Dihkhudā defines *tan* as the physical body and *jān* as the spiritual element present in each and every human. The sultan's mind is overwhelmed with Ayāz's pain. When Ayāz is in pain, so is the sultan. Pain and suffering, however, refer in the mystical context to the suffering that Sufis undergo on their path to the union with the divine. The sultan's early arrival and his reference to the hidden path also refer to the mystical path and union with the divine, which is invariably a direct and personal experience hidden from the ordinary eye. It also refers to the proximity between lover and beloved in the earthly and heavenly sense alike. In this relationship, there is no otherness. The distance between "I" and "other" has been eliminated. To use Foucauldian language, the self and the other are interdependent, through which the other has already become known.

As these narratives illustrate, love empowers Maḥmūd and Ayāz and enables them to cross earthly constructed paradigms and the constructed barriers of their minds leading to annihilation of the self and the embrace of the other. Embracing the beloved other occurs in *Muṣībat-nāma*, when Maḥmūd visits Ayāz at night while he is sleeping. He uncovers Ayāz's foot, washes it with rosewater and tears, places his cheek against it, and kisses it until dawn. When Ayāz wakes up, he finds the sultan unconscious, lying on the floor with Ayāz's foot on his face. He, however, does not withdraw his foot, and this seems inappropriate to the sultan when he wakes up. Nevertheless, Ayāz explains that although the sultan came to Ayāz as a king, he has turned into a slave and rendered him a slave's service. Maḥmūd had become weary of being the master, which is why he gave in and became the slave. Ayāz bids him to stand up and be the king again, since being a slave does not suit Maḥmūd and is Ayāz's duty. Ayāz then explains to the sultan that he is the beloved and whatever he does seems right to Ayāz and therefore he would not have avoided or interfered with the sultan kissing his feet. He asserts that he is at the sultan's service and if the sultan kissed his feet, he kissed his own feet in reality (*Muṣībat-nāma*, discourse 32, part 5). Again, this story portrays the power of love to reverse the master-slave relationship. Maḥmūd and Ayāz become a single entity through love; the sultan becomes a servant and the slave becomes a king. Whereas in the earlier narrative it is Ayāz who humbles himself, admiring the sultan's feet, the roles are reversed here and the sultan desires to be humbled now. This is how class boundaries are crossed. ʿAṭṭār comments that annihilation of the self results in the reversal of all orders, and the seeker and the Creator are united through love. This reversal of the power dynamics becomes the main resource for the couple's inspiration to construct new subjectivities in ʿAṭṭār's poetry.

Reading ʿAṭṭār and Foucault contrapuntally, we encounter the narrow zone of the limit which "has its entire space in the line it crosses" that "incessantly crosses and recrosses [the] line which closes up behind it . . . and thus . . . return[s] once more right to the horizon of the uncrossable" (Foucault, "Preface" 34). Foucault's limit—that is, human logic or consciousness—is the narrow zone to which human beings return after every instance of transgression. Since the limit (human logic) seems uncrossable, the crossing of it brings humans back to the same limit over and over; this is how Foucault's boundary crossing is spiral and does not amount to full liberation. A similar moment of boundary crossing is available in ʿAṭṭār's poems. Maḥmūd and Ayāz cross the same line over and over and return to the limit of their minds, once more to cross it yet again. However, the truth is that the limit exists in order for it to be crossed; otherwise, there would be no limit at all. Boundaries are there to be transgressed and subversion offers alternatives and possibilities. Through this spiral boundary crossing, ʿAṭṭār's characters reach a point where they come to terms with the social or sexual other, deconstruct their selves, and emerge as new subjects.

Conclusion

In each narrative, ʿAṭṭār's depiction of the relationship between Maḥmūd and Ayāz, although encompassing some earthly elements, corresponds with the mystical longing of the Sufi to be united with the ultimate beloved. In each narrative, we read about not only sexual violations of standard norms of the day, but also the subversion of class, gender, and power hierarchies. ʿAṭṭār's inclusion of this earthly relationship and boundary crossing in his works illustrates that the heavenly can be sought even in the most transgressive (to some) types of earthly desires.

ʿAṭṭār shows that even though Maḥmūd and Ayāz's homoerotic love affair does not fit the philosophy of *shāhidbāzī*, it can nevertheless be a doorway to divine love. By writing a story of love between men, ʿAṭṭār supplies an instance of mutual desire instead of one-sided objectified desire, as in the philosophy. Thus ʿAṭṭār transgresses the standards of the philosophy and, to some extent, produces a new rhetoric for homoerotic desire. In fact, by writing stories about mutual desire between men, ʿAṭṭār creates opportunities for queering malehood, imagining alternative ways of loving, and transgressing the status quo. In addition, his rendering of a master-slave, dominant-subservient power relationship as something fluid and his blurring of the lines with regard to the traditional passive-active partnership seem to work as a critique of class and gender norms.

ʿAṭṭār explores the unacceptable, the impossible, and the unimaginable through crossing the limits of the human mind, simultaneously allowing space for his readers to cross and imagine the unimaginable. ʿAṭṭār also implies that the true love of God, as well as being a Sufi, is in itself transgressive; after all, it involves renouncing earthly, normative relations, such as marriage and procreation, very much the way a homoerotic relationship does. ʿAṭṭār undermines religious, moral, cultural, and social laws so as to open up venues for alternatives. He deconstructs the established narratives in order to offer possibilities and encourage embracing otherness, and he does so by employing the power of love. To ʿAṭṭār, love is a process of becoming oneself. The rhetoric of love for God's creation becomes one of the means of loving God rather than an elapsed phase to be forgone. Hence, he makes his point about Sufism, which aims at a more transcendental goal, that is, love of all creations of God as emanations of the divine. We observe the same in medieval European literature, where love empowers high-ranking clerics to cross the worldly constructed paradigms that define and dictate who is to be loved and who not.

Although it would be impossible to comprehend exactly what the world, its surroundings, and the crossing of its boundaries meant to ʿAṭṭār's medieval subjects, as we can see, looking at medieval conceptualizations of transgression and the limit, the self and the other, and the construction of subjectivity is beneficial for the production of knowledge in modern times. It is important for us as modern subjects to find out how we relate to the formative exemplars of these concepts located in a distant past. In order to be able to wrap our brains around the problem of how to account for the transgressive subjectivity of medieval individuals, a contrapuntal reading of subjectivity in these two periods is essential. Hence, although the medieval and the modern are two independent periods in history which have produced their own sociocultural, religious, and social schemes, their harmonic interdependence is undeniable. Additionally, looking at ʿAṭṭār's acceptance of Maḥmūd and Ayāz's violation of class, gender, and the sexual standards of the day makes us question our understanding of (alleged) modern transgressive subjects and their rights, which are still being violated.

Chapter 5

Majnūn and Lailā, and Lancelot and Guinevere

The Narrative Lines

The love story of Majnūn and Lailā is one of the most popular passionate romances in the Muslim world. Its fragmented episodes can be found in numerous literary works, including ʿAṭṭār's *Ilāhī-nāma*, *Muṣībat-nāma*, and *Manṭiq al-ṭayr*. Lailā's name refers to the word *layl*, meaning "night," which can be considered an allusion to the hidden, secret romance of the two. In a spiritual context, since she is the *shāhid* that Majnūn needs on the divine path, her name can also be a reference to the divine hidden from ordinary people. Similar impassioned love relationships can be found in European medieval courtly love stories such as *The Romance of Lancelot and Guinevere* by Chrétien de Troyes (late twelfth century). Although they belong to two different traditions and genres, both stories portray subversive love that breaks away from traditional conventions and crosses religious and social boundaries. The characters' transgressions in turn result in their reconstruction of their selves and shaping of a new subjectivity.

The story of Majnūn (or Qays) and Lailā tells us about the couple's passionate love that defies strict rules governing arranged marriages in the Muslim world. Majnūn and Lailā's indiscretion attracts public attention and they become cautious; however, Majnūn's impatience to be with the beloved leads to his erratic behavior. At times, he wanders around, ignoring everyone; at other times, he recites love poems for Lailā, being in a state of exhilaration. People think Majnūn mad because of his excessive emotions expressed through poetry dedicated to Lailā, which brings dishonor to her and her tribe. As a result of this shame and dishonor, Lailā's family confines her to her home and does not allow the lovers to see each other. This intensifies Majnūn's already disturbed behavior and he flees to the desert, occasionally returning to recite love poems for Lailā in front of her door. Majnūn's roaming in the desert, living with animals, being improperly clothed, and the whole of his erratic behavior convince Lailā's family that they need to protect her honor as well as their own. On the other hand, to save his son, Majnūn's father tries to arrange his marriage to Lailā, but Lailā's father does not agree to marry his daughter off to a madman. Ultimately, Lailā marries Ibn Salām but does not share a bed with him due to her love for Majnūn. When Lailā becomes ill, she requests to be buried wearing her bridal costume, to show that she is waiting for her beloved. Majnūn hears the news of Lailā's death and, even more deranged than before, rushes to her tomb, where he spends all his time reciting poems for her. After a while, people find Majnūn's dead body over Lailā's tomb and bury him alongside her. Later on, Lailā's cousin Zayd has a dream of Lailā and Majnūn united in paradise. In several Middle Eastern literary traditions, their story became the archetype for depicting lovers driven insane by the intensity of their passion.

The legendary story of Majnūn and Lailā's love is unauthenticated although it is furnished with historical facts. It first appeared in Arabic and did not have a coherent narrative. However, it also became known in Persian, Azeri, Turkish, Urdu, and Hindi literatures and cultures. The earliest written version of the legend is that of Ibn Qutayba (828–889). Later, Ibn Dāwūd (868–910) also included in his *Kitāb al-Zahrā* (*The Book of the Beautiful*) some poetic fragments ascribed to Majnūn. About a century later, Abū Faraj al-Iṣfahānī (897–967) included in his *Kitāb al-Aghānī* (*The Book of Songs*) numerous anecdotes and poetic fragments ascribed to Majnūn. These were the main sources of the legend before *Maṣāriʿ al-ʿushshāq* (*The Gates of Lovers*) of Sarrāj al-Qārī (ca. 1026–1106) (Khairallah 49). There are a series of reports and fragmented narratives about Majnūn's life and his love for Lailā, mostly repetitive and often contradictory. These episodic fragments had been collected from the late eighth century on, and their number increased continually during the medieval period. There are many narratives that were handed down separately and many others that were ascribed to Majnūn only because of their stylistic affinity to his poetry or because of references to Lailā. The romance of Majnūn reached its height of popularity during the Abbasid period. Majnūn and his passionate love story became the center of writers' attention; many verses were written about Majnūn, and his story was included in anthologies of love poetry. Because Majnūn's love madness was comparable to the Sufis' moments of rapture, Majnūn's story entered mystical works as well. Episodes of Majnūn and Lailā's love story appeared in Sufi works, including ʿAṭṭār's poetry.

The love story of Majnūn has multiple narrative lines in the Arabic versions. One narrative relates that Majnūn and Lailā were members of the same Bedouin tribe and grew up together tending the flocks of their families. Another one narrates that Majnūn met Lailā as an adult. Both accounts tell the story of his passionate love for Lailā. It is possible that Majnūn was modeled upon an Arab poet who might have lived in the late seventh century. Michael Dols suggests that the initiator of the Majnūn story was a young Umayyad (661–750) who used Majnūn as his pen name to relate his unhappy love for his cousin; however, there is no substantive evidence. Regarding the historical authentication of the story, Dols notes that the inclusion of Nawfal ibn Musāḥiq, who was the governor of Medina in the seventh century, adds a historical touch to the legend and suggests that the romance probably took shape in the late seventh or early eighth century. Majnūn and Lailā are believed to have lived on the Arabian Peninsula, in the newly emerging cities of Basra and Kufa. Another account records that the Majnūn legend is the result of the rivalry between the northern and southern Arabs in the early Islamic era. It is related that the southern Arabs had a well-formulated type of poetry that praised chaste love like that of the late medieval Western troubadours. This type of poetry was called ʿudhrī, and the most famous ʿudhrī poet was Jamīl al-ʿUdhrī (660–701), who was consumed with love for a woman from his own tribe called Buthayna. However, Buthayna's parents refused to accept him as their son-in-law and married Buthayna to someone else. Therefore, although Jamīl al-ʿUdhrī was distraught, he glorified pure love, worshipped his beloved, and believed in a lover's self-denial and suffering. Dols postulates that in response to Jamīl al-ʿUdhrī's poetry, the northern Arabs of the tribe of Amir ibn Ṣaʿṣaʿa fashioned a famous poet, Qays ibn al-Mulawwaḥ (late seventh century) or Majnūn, who was even more desperate than Jamīl in his love affair (Dols 320–21).

In Persian literature, it was the poet Nizāmī Ganjavī (1141–1209) who put the fragmented episodes of Majnūn's life together into a single narrative poem in 1188. Nizāmī changed some elements of the original Arabic story to suit the tastes of his Persian audience. For instance, he made use of garden imagery instead of the Bedouin desert that served as a setting in the early versions of the story. Nizāmī influenced later poets of the Islamic world, who adapted his work and imitated his narrative of Lailā and Majnūn. The narrative of Lailā and Majnūn reached its most accomplished mystical expression in Jāmī's allegorical work in 1484. In short, through these episodes, Majnūn became the epitome of a mystical lover and his beloved became the metaphorical divine. Although there are numerous different versions and narrative lines of this story, one definite thing is that there was an Arab tradition of courtly love, similar to that from the Western world, into which the romance of Majnūn and Lailā easily fits.

Despite their contextual differences, some affinities can be seen between the passionate love of Queen Guinevere and Lancelot and that of Majnūn. It is believed that Chrétien de Troyes composed *The Romance of Lancelot and Guinevere* at the request of Marie de Champagne (1145–98). It is a part of the cycle of Arthurian legend and, like the Majnūn legend, has different versions, including French and English. The main themes of this courtly love in both its French and English versions are the knights of the Arthurian Round Table, the quest for the Holy Grail, and the love triangle of King Arthur, Queen Guinevere, and Lancelot, particularly the disruption of conjugal harmony caused by the adulterous love affair between the queen and Lancelot. Lancelot is an important figure for his chivalric tale in the Arthurian legend. In the French version of the story, used in this chapter, Lancelot is even more important than Arthur himself. The French version also emphasizes the combination of earthly and spiritual love.

The plotline involves Lancelot embarking on a journey to rescue Queen Guinevere, who has been abducted by Meleagant, the son of King Badgemagus. On his way, Lancelot mounts a cart driven by a dwarf—an incongruous mode of transport for a hero, because at that time in Europe, criminals were taken to jail by carts. Lancelot's climbing up onto the cart could cause misunderstandings and bring him shame and dishonor. At first, he hesitates to travel on the cart, but seeing that there is no other option, he does so. Later, Guinevere is disgusted by Lancelot for doing so. Lancelot goes through various trials before he rescues the queen. He crosses the Sword Bridge, which consists of sharp blades from end to end, fights Melegant, and saves the queen's life. During the combats between Lancelot and Meleagant, Lancelot comes close to losing because he cannot stop gazing at Guinevere; however, he is able to collect himself in time. During the first battle, King Badgemagus, Meleagant's father, pleads with the queen to stop the fight to save his son's life. Later, Meleagant accuses the queen of sleeping with Kay, another knight, and forces Lancelot to fight again in order to defend the queen's honor. Again, the king pleads with Lancelot to free his son. Finally, Lancelot kills Meleagant in King Arthur's court. Lancelot's success is predicated upon his obedience to the queen and consistency in love; he idealizes his beloved and the beloved does the same in return. Lancelot and Guinevere's love cannot be physically consummated but can be glorified and idealized spiritually. As in Majnūn and Lailā's love narratives, although the erotic is present, the spiritual and elevated aspects of love rather than its erotic aspects are highlighted.

Like Majnūn and Lailā's love narratives, *The Romance of Lancelot and Guinevere* has been reworked throughout history. It first appeared in Chrétien de Troyes' *Cheavalier de la charrete* (*Knight of the Cart*) in 1177, and later in Sir Thomas Malory's (ca. 1415–1471) *Morte d'Arthur* (*The Death of Arthur*) in 1470. Lord Alfred Tennyson (1809–1892), Dante Gabriel Rossetti (1828–1882), and William Morris (1834–1896) also reworked it in the nineteenth century. The thematic and stylistic affinities are many between the love stories of Majnūn and Lailā and Lancelot and Guinevere. In fact, there are arguments that the European courtly love genre might have been impacted by Islamic love story traditions. According to William Farina, the European courtly love ethos was most likely impacted by the Islamic literary traditions of Spain. He writes, "Although Chrétien certainly imposed a powerful stamp of originality upon [*The Romance of Lancelot and Guinevere*]," textual evidence suggests that he probably reworked a "pre-existing, popular story" from ancient times and beyond Europe "and embellished it." For instance, Farina refers to the game of chess that appears in Chrétien's work; chess originated in the Middle East long before its introduction into Europe. He credits the eleventh-century Andalusian Ibn Ḥazm's *The Neck-Ring of the Dove* as being the forerunner for transmitting the courtly love style to Western literature (19–27). Whether the Islamic literary traditions influenced the European courtly love tradition or vice-versa is of secondary importance here since we have already discussed the many intellectual interactions between the Middle East and the West in the first chapter. What is of more significance in this chapter is that both of these romances center thematically upon passionate love which defies moral, religious, and social constraints and helps in construction of the characters' subjectivities.

A difference between the two traditions is that, unlike the European tradition of courtly love, although passionate love was considered a sin in Muslim mysticism, it was not a heresy or an independent doctrine outside of or in opposition to orthodoxy. For instance, in ʿAṭṭār's poetry, according to Leonard Lewisohn, the philosophy of love expresses both an ascetic and an aesthetic theology. In Sufism, the lover contemplates divine beauty and love through human beauty in the physical world. Thus, ʿAṭṭār's erotic Sufi lyrics are similar to the *fin'amors* (refined, purified love) of medieval Provençal courtly love tradition, which violated the social ethos doubly. In this love tradition, the lady must be married and her lover must be inferior to her in terms of social status. Eros in medieval Europe broke social and religious taboos; this love was adulterous and illicit. So was the Sufi ideal of love. It was transgressive in both a social sense and a religious sense, although it was not necessarily adulterous or illicit (Lewisohn, "Sufi Symbolism" 292). The demented lover, Majnūn, who contemplates Lailā constantly, became the model for transgressing limits and transcending earthly constructed paradigms through Sufi love. Likewise, Lancelot, who is consumed by the queen's love, gets caught up in the middle of an adulterous love affair.

This chapter explores these violations in the context of ʿAṭṭār's portrayal of Majnūn's passionate love for Lailā. ʿAṭṭār's narratives of this love story illustrate that it was adjudged forbidden not only because it was excessive and regarded as love madness, but also because it violated the traditional Islamic right of fathers or guardians to decide on the marriages of their children. Majnūn's obsessive behavior brought shame and dishonor to Lailā and her family. Majnūn's constant visits to Lailā's home and his recital of love poems to her were among the ways in which Majnūn displayed his emotions for Lailā publicly. Such a public declaration and display went against the arranged marriage conventions in Islamic culture.

Arranged marriages became common after the emergence of Islam in the Arabian Peninsula. At this time, people began to follow a patrilineal, polygynous, patriarchal marriage system, with men controlling women's sexuality. Although the region was already familiar with male control over women and female seclusion and exclusion from the public sphere, Islam imparted special value and recognition to the preeminence of paternity and vested in the male proprietary rights to female sexuality. Islam reformulated the nexus of sexuality and power between the sexes. The reformulation of the marriage institution affected women's position in society and imposed limitations on them (Ahmed 45–46). In this way, the conventions of pre-Islamic Arabia, where women were active participants in the affairs of their community, were forgotten (62). If the Majnūn legend took shape in the late seventh and early eighth centuries, our couple would have been bound by the conventions of the father-guardian law for their marriage. However, we see that Majnūn broke away from the arranged marriage tradition and violated the law. Majnūn's renunciation of all social and material values also represents his rejection of established intellectual, social, and psychological limitations and symbolizes the basic yearning of the "I" to be at one with the "other." Majnūn's quest for self-purification and annihilation of the ego in order to be in union with the societal other and the divine other is a "spiral curve, gradually transcending the limitations of ego, society, and material world" (Khairallah 2).

In this chapter, I examine their violation of the laws pertaining to the institution of marriage and explore Lancelot's idealization of his unattainable object of love and breaking the law for love's sake. As opposed to Majnūn's demise for recitation of love poems, the importance of a lover's eloquence in expressing his love as a means of acquiring love is emphasized in Lancelot's expression of love, which is in line with European codes also noted in Andreas Capellanus's *Andreas Capellanus On Love* (*De Amore*). According to Capellanus, "The adorned language of a lover usually unleashes love's darts; it creates a good impression about the speaker's moral worth" (45). Capellanus's treatise on love is a highly scholastic work on the doctrine of love and marriage in a feudal society.

This chapter also asserts that, contrary to many other Islamic theologians and thinkers of the time who condemned Majnūn's passionate love and saw it as insanity, ʿAṭṭār regards Majnūn's love for Lailā as the threshold upon which divine love is found. This subversive love allows Majnūn to de- and reconstruct himself in order to emerge as a new individual in full union with the divine. ʿAṭṭār's inclusion of Majnūn's story in his mystical works shows his belief that a lover should be insanely and truly in love in order to forget all worldly considerations, such as humiliation, suffering, rejection, and isolation, and be able to cross social and moral boundaries and transcend normative concepts. ʿAṭṭār's invitation of his characters to cross the constructed sociocultural barriers of their mind places him alongside Foucault and other modern theorists who view transgression of the limit as a means toward the construction of subjectivity. ʿAṭṭār's nonjudgmental treatment of Majnūn's love madness further highlights his openness towards alternative possibilities. This chapter also reads Chrétien de Troyes's *The Romance of Lancelot and Guinevere* alongside ʿAṭṭār's poems about Majnūn and Lailā. In reference to the acceptance of these couples' loves, I will also engage in discussions of the condemnation of love madness by Muslim writers and explorations of medieval European codes of chivalry and courtly love in Andreas Capellanus's *Andreas Capellanus on Love.*

Condemnation of Love Madness

Muslim writers have had differing views on profane, excessive love. Authors with a positive view, such as ʿAṭṭār, considered passionate love as a complicated and extremely interesting phenomenon which was at the same time an uncannily human experience. The positive view of passionate love complied with the Neoplatonic notion of love—a philosophical and religious system that both rivaled and influenced Christianity from the third to the sixth century and was derived from the works of the Greek philosopher Plato—with the addition of elements of oriental mysticism where the fusion of an individual soul with the absolute is highlighted. Others, however, glorified chaste love rather than passionate love. Hence, chaste love became a subtle ideal from the ninth century onwards in Baghdad. In addition, the negative view considered all love as lust and condemned it as a moral transgression which could end tragically. Love was seen as a liability to Arab male pride. Writers with a negative view of love such as Ibn al-Jawzī (1116–1201) believed that unregulated earthly desires should not replace the preeminence of God in a believer's heart. The intention of these writers was to define acceptable behavior according to scriptures and eradicate the perceived indulgences of the Sufis (Dols 314–15).

Similarly, in medieval Europe there were works about chivalric codes and courtly love in a moral framework to maintain control over social violence and exploitation. Through these chivalric codes, the strong were morally mandated to protect, and not to exploit, the weak. This was true about feminine beauty, and loving and courting women as well. In a society where women had few rights, men were taught to approach and court women through certain coded rituals. Capellanus's *Andreas Capellanus On Love* (*De Amore*) is one such product of twelfth-century Europe that discusses the notion of courtly love and its codes. He includes dialogues, letters, and love cases, and condemns this type of love, which he believes goes against scriptures (Scattergood 64). Capellanus's text is an intellectual work, completely aware of classical literature such as Ovid's works and the poetry of the troubadours. The most significant accomplishment of this text is that it opens up to discussion questions on love that are not readily answerable or suggestive of a solution. The work focuses on both secular and religious aspects of love. One might wonder why Capellanus felt the need to write a book full of instructions for proper behavior. Was it because he (as a monk) was trying to regulate an existing sexual practice such as adultery (in courtly love) by introducing proper codes of conduct? Or were there other reasons? Whatever the reason, the book was written to constrain unbridled passion—much like the works with a negative view of passionate love in the Islamic discourse were—and whose purpose was to regulate deviations in matters of love.

Capellanus's counterpart in the Muslim world was Ibn al-Jawzī, the Hanbalite scripturalist who strongly believed in morality and had the most inimical view on profane love. In his *Dhamm al-hawā* (*Vilifying Love*), he elaborates on the dangers and evils of intense earthly longing and unrestrained sexual yearning. He argues that passionate love drives humans to madness, suicide, incest, and lust. Ibn al-Jawzī was against the secular and Neoplatonic Sufis' explanations of love. Writing on love, Ibn al-Jawzī equates passionate love with madness (see Bell, "Selection and Organization"). In so doing, Ibn al-Jawzī seems to be referring to Ibn Sīnā's discussion of love in his book *Qānūn* (*The Canon of Medicine*), where he considers love as a hallucinatory disease, like melancholia. The main argument is that by gazing (*naẓar*) at the beloved and by listening to erotic poetry, the two lovers are attracted to each other. However, this passionate love goes beyond the confines of attraction and chaste love because it dominates human reasoning and causes the lovers to act unwisely. Therefore, it is reproachable and should be avoided by a discreet person (Rouhi, "A Decade of Studying"). In this way, passionate, profane love was simultaneously seen as a "moral issue, a religious goal, a social ideal, and a medical problem" (Dols

318–19). It was often viewed as a type of insanity, and romantic love and free association with women and their seduction were to be avoided (318–19). This is why the notion of a mad poet-lover did not fit easily into the refined style, or *adab* (literary canon), of the period. Nonetheless, by the tenth century, the notion of obsessive, melancholic profane love (love madness) became a major theme in Islamic Sufi literature, and the popular romance of Majnūn and Lailā was incorporated into Arabic and Persian belles lettres.

As the sacred and profane appeared alongside one another in Sufi works, so did the themes of a mad lover and a disturbed holy fool. Schimmel considers the teachings of the Sufis and their literature responsible for this development. The mystical interpretation of a holy fool was especially influential in enriching the status of illiterate and unrefined saints whose conduct seemed inappropriate to many. However, there was no evidence that those men were not genuinely mad, and as long as they stayed harmless, they enjoyed absolute freedom without being subjected to social derision or religious constraints (Schimmel, *Mystical Dimensions* 19–20, 105). Sufi writers called those "mad" men "friends of God" who could freely express themselves, make imprudent comments about God and the world order, or even speak to him with a higher presumption than common people (Ritter 171). They were treated with reverence and consideration because of the special relationship they had with God, who, for most ordinary people, is unattainable and unintelligible.

This class of holy fools plays a significant role in ʿAṭṭār's works, and its application to Majnūn is only one such example. ʿAṭṭār applies the term *dīwāna* (madman) to anyone who deviates from social and moral norms. However, these men are not treated with abhorrence in ʿAṭṭār's poetry. Under the guise of their madness, they are free to do and say things that would be taboo for an ordinary person. Most significantly, they are frequently portrayed as austere and bitter critics of rulers and hypocrites—something that ʿAṭṭār was as well (Ritter 172). In some of his works, ʿAṭṭār depicts these demented figures as leaving all orthodox rules of their faith and questioning even the divine. For instance, in a narrative in *Ilāhī-nāma*, ʿAṭṭār illustrates the way a madman reproaches others for being concerned with worldly matters. The madman (holy fool) not only criticizes others for their worldliness, but also gives them sound advice (discourse 7, part 13). We might not expect advice from a madman; however, due to his closeness to the divine and his ability to comprehend beyond the worldly, the madman is a good counselor and one of the "friends of God." Reading ʿAṭṭār's works, we find these traits in Majnūn. Whereas his passionate, excessive love for Lailā causes him to lose his senses, appear a madman, and cross social-tribal boundaries, in ʿAṭṭār's mystical poetry, he is one of the "friends of God" and is in fact saner than most people around him.

Idealization of Lailā's Beauty

In ʿAṭṭār's works, Lailā's beauty and Majnūn's love for her become the means through which Majnūn transgresses earthly boundaries, constructs his subjectivity, and reaches divine love and beauty. Although scholars have mentioned that Lailā has not been described as particularly beautiful, to Majnūn, who loses his senses because of her, she is the exemplar of beauty. Comparing Lailā's beauty to the divine breath at the time of Adam's creation, Schimmel writes, "The eye of intelligence cannot recognize true beauty hidden behind outward form, as the Divine Breath was hidden behind the form of Adam; it fits Majnūn, the man demented by love, to see the unique beauty of Leylā behind a form which looks completely unexciting to loveless, intelligent, hence inhuman, people" (*The Triumphal Sun* 255). In ʿAṭṭār's poetry, we see that the chains and shackles of an intellect that is prone to assess outward appearance no longer have the power to imprison Majnūn. Much like Foucault's advocacy for breaking away from the shackles of human logic, Majnūn's love for Lailā is portrayed as surpassing human reasoning and as the embodiment of divine love put in the perspective of love in Sufism. Majnūn, completely engrossed in his love for Lailā, becomes a representative of the rhetoric of contemplating the divine in the form of an earthly woman in Persian literature. His idealization of Lailā and his loss of intellect replaced with rapture are typical mystical experiences. Like Foucault, ʿAṭṭār encourages individuals to free themselves from the shackles of reason, which limit humans, and replace it with love in order to be able to shape their subjectivity anew.

Majnūn's idealization of Lailā and his abandonment of the limitations imposed by human intellect are portrayed in a narrative in *Muṣībat-nāma*. In this story, the caliph tells Majnūn that there are thousands of women in the world who are more beautiful than Lailā; however, to Majnūn, Lailā is the absolute beauty. Majnūn's eye of the intellect is blind, he only sees one beauty, and it is the beauty of the beloved. As in Sufism, the eye of the intellect is incapable of registering and observing divine beauty. It is only through love that a Sufi can see divine beauty. ʿAṭṭār relates that the caliph summons Majnūn, questioning him about his blind love for Lailā. He offers Majnūn many other beautiful women in order for him to forget Lailā. However, Majnūn responds that Lailā's love has deep roots in his heart and soul, and if he decides to consider someone else to love, he will in fact be committing suicide unconsciously (*Muṣībat-nāma*, discourse 31, part 2). Of course, this death in its mystical context would mean being cut off from the divine beloved by replacing love for him with love for someone else. The caliph's interrogation of Majnūn and his attempts to convince him to consider another love is evidence of the social anxiety surrounding Majnūn's nonconformity to hegemonic stereotypes of Arab maleness regarding passionate love as detrimental. An Arab male is supposed to demonstrate his ability to resist the excesses of female beauty and seduction, but Majnūn is incapable of showing such resistance to Lailā's beauty. In the final lines of this narrative, ʿAṭṭār refers to the popular quranic (and biblical) story of Zulaikhā's love for Yūsuf. Similar to Lailā, Yūsuf has frequently been referred to as an earthly beauty, *shāhid* in mystical love poetry. Like Lailā, Yūsuf becomes the *shāhid* that the excessive lover, Zulaikhā, needs in order to be able to see divine beauty and love. Both Yūsuf and Lailā are inaccessible, they are idealized, and they serve as mirrors aiding their lovers to purify their souls and see the divine beloved unveiled. They both become catalysts for their lovers to reconstruct their identities before they can fully unite with the divine.

The lover's refusal to adore anyone but the beloved can also be found in the European courtly love tradition. As Capellanus notes, "There is another merit in love worthy of no passing praise. Love adorns a man with what is almost the virtue of chastity, because he who is aglow with the light of one love can scarcely contemplate the embrace of another, however beautiful. In his eyes the appearance of any other woman is rough and inelegant whilst all his thoughts are on his love" (39). And this is what we witness in Lancelot's love for Guinevere as well. Despite Majnūn's emphasis on Lailā's physical beauty, which is an agent that provokes changes in him, Ali Asghar Seyed-Gohrab points out that it is her moral beauty that has been the focus of many mystics since the ninth century (216). In other words, Lailā's physical attributes together with her moral qualities make her an earthly portrayal of divine beauty and love; that is, a mystical *shāhid*. Thus, although the beloved's physical beauty is glorified, it is the superiority of the moral beauty of the beloved that dominates these stories. This is an indication of the preeminence of spirituality in ʿAṭṭār's poetry.

In his doctrine on love, Capellanus also emphasizes the beloved's moral beauty and honesty of character over her outward physical beauty (45). Majnūn and Lancelot stay faithful to their beloveds and refuse to love other women. For Lancelot, this is revealed when he is forced to lie in the same bed as a young lady because of his pledge in return for her hospitality. Chrétien narrates,

> The knight had only one heart, and it was no longer his; he had entrusted it to another so that he could bestow it nowhere else. Love, who governs all hearts, made it stay in one place. All hearts? No, but only those he values. The man whom love designs to govern ought to esteem himself the more. Love held the knight's heart in such high regard that he governed it above all, and bestowed on it such supreme pride that I am not inclined to blame him if he loathes what Love forbids and concentrates all his attention on Love's will. (185)

This obvious preference of chaste love over passionate love and morality over physicality is also testimony to society's anxiety over deviations from social and moral norms.

In Persian lyrical poetry, in addition to moral and physical beauty, the beloved's sweet scent is also highlighted, since it causes the lover to faint and lose his senses as if affected by mystical rapture. According to Seyed-Gohrab, compounds such as "the soul's scent" (*bū-yi jān*) and "the fragrance of love" (*bū-yi ʿishq*) abound, communicating the acute discernment of a person in love. Majnūn is extremely sensitive to his beloved's sweet scent and smells it either figuratively or literally. Therefore, Lailā's scent also became a topos in love poetry (260). Similarly, in ʿAṭṭār's poetry, we observe Majnūn using sensual vocabulary and sensory language to illustrate the power of love that ultimately leads to the sacred. This is exemplified in *Muṣībat-*

nāma, where ʿAṭṭār relates that Majnūn runs hysterically towards the graveyard when he hears about Lailā's death. When someone offers to show him her grave, Majnūn replies that he can find it by smelling Lailā's scent (discourse 30, part 7). Finding the beloved by the scent of her body is a powerful image. The fact that the lover can recognize the beloved through sensory apparatuses also draws on the Sufi idea of the perception of the divine through the senses. The divine beloved is veiled, and a Sufi can only feel him through the senses. The lover idealizes everything about the unattainable beloved, ranging from facial beauty to sweet scent. This unattainability and idealization of the beloved enables the lover to refine the mirror of his or her own heart.

The concept of the idealization of the beloved resulting in the refining of the lover's soul is also discussed by Lacan in the context of European courtly love. Lacan writes, "courtly love was . . . a poetic exercise, a way of playing with a number of conventional, idealizing themes, which couldn't have any real concrete equivalent. Nevertheless, these ideals, first among which is that of the Lady, are to be found in subsequent periods, down to our own" (*The Seminar Book VII* 148). He adds that central to this idealization is the inaccessibility of a feminine object, the lady. The lady, according to Lacan, is the inaccessible object which stimulates desire and is sublimated; using Freud's terminology, Lacan calls her *das Ding* or the thing. Hence the depersonalized, idealized lady or the thing who has no real equivalent is an abstract character, sublimated only by the lover in love poems. She is therefore an "inhuman partner" who might sometimes function as a machine. She is never characterized and has no concrete virtues. Lacan adds that the lady functions as a mirror upon which the subject-lover projects his ideals and fantasies; however, this mirror also fulfills "a role as limit," which "cannot be crossed." The subject-lover cannot move beyond the mirror (Lacan, *The Seminar Book VII* 149–51). The lady is inaccessible; she is the absolute other, the thing.

ʿAṭṭār's Majnūn is also passionately in love with his inaccessible beloved. Lailā functions as a mirror for Majnūn to de- and reconstruct himself, but she is also beyond access with certain limits. Her depersonalization and inaccessibility makes her an "inhuman partner" who is sublimated by Majnūn but is probably not real. In a metaphysical context, Lailā refers to the inaccessible divine. Since the mirror in mysticism is a signifier for reaching perfection and seeing the divine, we can also interpret Lailā as the mirror—or the *shāhid* in Islamic Sufism—through which the lover purifies his soul and discovers divine love. Thus, it is through the unattainable earthly beloved that our lover is empowered to transgress the barriers of his mind, transcend earthly constructed paradigms, and reshape his subjectivity. In his discussions of transgression and the limit, Foucault suggests that construction of subjectivity occurs by moving beyond the obstacles in one's mind. The lover reconstructs his identity through the violation of worldly constructed laws, which are in reality only in his mind. In Majnūn's case, he first falls in love with the unattainable beloved who requires him to transgress the earthly limits in order to be able to emerge as a new subject. ʿAṭṭār emphasizes the element of unattainable sublime love in this discourse, and highlights the significance of reshaping subjectivity through the violation of worldly boundaries and taboos.

Violation of the Law and Social Marginalization

In addition to breaking away from arranged marriage customs, Majnūn's act of fleeing to the wilderness and his relationship with animals is also socially transgressive. Majnūn is not only portrayed as melancholic and depressed, but is also depicted as a solitary barefoot and bareheaded wanderer in the wilderness. Living in the wilderness, Majnūn makes friends with the animals and when he purifies his soul, they all begin surrendering to him. In Sufism, every creature is believed to be praising the divine in his or her own way. In the mystical context, Majnūn's friendship with animals might be considered his way of praising the divine, and the animals' surrender to him might be their way of submitting to the divine as well.

In terms of social etiquette in the medieval Muslim world, a man's style of dress clearly indicated his social status. Esteemed Muslim men were expected to wear shoes at all times, be well dressed, and wear a distinguishable headdress. Majnūn breaks away from all of these standards. His isolation also defies the strong ties that were expected to bind an individual and his family in Islamic societies. His given name, Qays, is changed to Majnūn, which can be seen as another sign of his rejection of his family and social identity. At that time in the Muslim world, men were expected to live among their fellow men, marry, have children, and lead a life of assimilation in the society (Dols 333–35). However, we see that Majnūn renounces all of this and lives in the wilderness with animals, which is considered a further rejection of society and his own humanity. Schimmel comments on this type of renunciation, suggesting that "it was easy for the ascetic to renounce things declared doubtful by Muslim law; but the tendency to renounce even things considered lawful by the community of the faithful sometimes reached absurd degrees" (*Mystical Dimensions* 111). Of course, this is not to say that Majnūn is solely responsible for this isolation; society plays a significant role in his marginalization as well. An instance of society affirming and deepening Majnūn's isolation is when Lailā's father does not accept him as his son-in-law. By writing about Majnūn's transgressions and consequent marginalization in society, ʿAṭṭār demonstrates the ways that society can stigmatize those who break away from the status quo, and the impact that the separation from the beloved can have on the lover.

Society's part, particularly the part played by Lailā's family, in Majnūn becoming a social pariah is depicted in one of the narratives in *Manṭiq al-ṭayr* (lines 3390–95). ʿAṭṭār writes that since Lailā's family forbids her to leave home and see Majnūn and prohibits Majnūn from coming close to Lailā, Majnūn disguises himself as a sheep so as to go near Lailā and to smell her scent:

> When Leili's tribe refused Majnūn, he found
> They would not let him near their camping ground.

Distraught with love, he met a shepherd there
And asked him for a sheepskin he could wear,
And then, beneath the skin, began to creep
On hands and knees as if he were a sheep.
"Now lead your flock," he cried, "past Leili's tent;
It may be I shall catch her lovely scent
And hidden by this matted fleece receive
From untold misery one hour's reprieve."

اهل لیلی نیز مجنون را دمی
در قبیله ره ندادندی همی
داشت چوپانی در آن صحرا نشست
پوستی بستد ازو مجنون مست
سرنگون شد پوست اندر سر فکند
خویشتن را کرد همچون گوسفند
آن شبان را گفت "بهر کردگار
در میان گوسفندانم گذار
سوی لیلی ران رمه، من در میان
تا بیابم بوی لیلی یک زمان
تا نهان از دوست، زیر پوست من
بهره گیرم ساعتی از دوست من."

Wearing sheepskin and hiding among animals, Majnūn breaks traditional expectations that he should be well clad and socialize with his fellow men. Majnūn contravenes all social and cultural norms, and in so doing, he makes a fool of himself for the sake of his beloved. This is an instance where ʿAṭṭār affirms the breaking of shackles of reason for the sake of love. Majnūn's nonconformity is reflected through several of his transgressions. He is not concerned about being criticized or ridiculed by people. ʿAṭṭār presents Majnūn as a lover who accepts social marginalization and all the associated suffering for the sake of his beloved. In order to be united with his beloved, he is willing to transgress all limits. When Majnūn is asked about his clothing and outward appearance, he confidently replies that these worldly matters lose significance when all that the lover is concerned about is to be close to the beloved. His fellows try to talk him into wearing proper clothes, but he replies that in the proximity of the beloved a "wool skin" garment is sufficient (*Manṭiq al-ṭayr* lines 3403–09).

When one said: "What a tattered fleece defends
Your body from the cold; but trust in me
I'll bring you all you need immediately."
Majnūn replied: "No garment's worthy of
Dear Leili, but I wear this skin for love –
I know how fortune favours me, and I
Burn true to turn away the Evil Eye."

The fleece for him was silk and rare brocade;
With what else should a lover be arrayed?
I too have known love scent the passing air—
What other finer garment could I wear?
If you would scour yourself of each defect,
Let passion wean you from the intellect—

یک تن از قومش به مجنون گفت باز
"بس برهنه مانده ای ای سرفراز
جامه ای کان دوستر داری و بس
گر بگویی من بیارم این نفس."
گفت "هر جامه سزای دوست نیست
هیچ جامه بهترم از پوست نیست
پوستی خواهم از آن گوسفند
چشم بد را نیز می سوزم سپند
اطلس و اکسون مجنون پوست است
پوست خواهد هر که لیلی دوست است
برده ام در پوست بوی دوست من
کی ستانم جامه ای جز پوست من
دل خبر از پوست یافت از دوستی
چون ندارم مغز، باری پوستی!"

Majnūn goes on commenting on the materiality and worldliness of the people around him, saying that garments made of satin and silk are not worthy of the one willing to be close to the beloved. He adds that it is only under the wool garment that he was able to smell the scent of the beloved. Literally, this "wool skin" garment refers to the sheepskin that he wears in order to go near Lailā in disguise; however, it also alludes to the clothing made of wool, worn by Sufis to experience pain and suffering on the divine path. The word used for this wool garment is also believed to be the root for the word Sufi in Arabic and Persian. Of course, the beloved that these lines refer to is not only the earthly beloved, but also the heavenly beloved. It is only by wearing the Sufi wool garment and enduring pain and suffering on the divine path that the lover can feel the proximity of the beloved through his or her senses. Here, we can see the lover's desire to be in the proximity of his beloved without anything worldly, even if that means losing his senses and being free from the shackles of his logic. In this way, in ʿAṭṭār's world, spirituality and love rather than logic occupy center stage. ʿAṭṭār shows how Majnūn touches upon the mystical significance of the story by renouncing worldly concerns such as clothing. He refers to the woolen coat as the best clothing for anyone who longs to be admitted to the beloved's proximity. If Lailā represents the *shāhid*, then Majnūn's woolen coat refers to the Sufis' woolen coat (*khirqih*). ʿAṭṭār also comments on the importance of love and the way it transforms people if they abandon trivial earthly concerns. Sacred and erotic language is used interchangeably when ʿAṭṭār draws on sensual imagery to illustrate Majnūn's loss of senses and his breaking into tears, making references to "fire" to depict excessive passion. ʿAṭṭār exposes the transformative power of love in the extract below (*Manṭiq al-ṭayr* lines 3398–3401):

And so Majnūn, disguised beneath the skin,
Drew near his love unnoticed by her kin—
Joy welled in him and in its wild excess
The frenzied lover lost all consciousness;
Love's fire had dried the fluids of his brain—
He fainted and lay stretched out on the plain;
The shepherd bore him to a shaded place
And splashed cold water on his burning face.

عاقبت مجنون چو زیر پوست شد
در رمه پنهان به کوی دوست شد
خوش خوشی برخاست اول جوش ازو
پس به آخر گشت زایل هوش ازو
چون درآمد عشق و آب از سرگذشت
برگرفتش آن شبان بردش به دشت
آب زد بر روی آن مست خراب
تا دمی بنشست آن آتش ز آب.

Majnūn violates several social norms here. He does so by wandering among the flock of sheep, wearing sheepskin and, most significantly, going near the forbidden beloved. This story also invokes the notion of humility which is embraced by the lover. Majnūn humbles himself by being among animals for the sake of his beloved. Not only does he push the boundaries of social etiquette, but he also crosses the lines of class hierarchy by appearing among animals and wearing wool skin. At the end of the narrative, ʿAṭṭār articulates his mystical interpretation through Majnūn's words that it is only true love that can free the lover from earthly desires and transform the earthly into the heavenly. ʿAṭṭār adds that the smallest step a Sufi takes toward annihilation of the self will turn the seeker into a lover of the beloved. If a Sufi longs for true glory, she or he should walk on the path of love sincerely, because losing the intellect and annihilating the self on this path is not an easy endeavor (*Manṭiq al-ṭayr* lines 3410–12):

To leave such toys and sacrifice the soul
Is still the first small step towards our goal
Begin, if you can set aside all shame—
To risk your life is not some childish game.

عشق باید کز خرد بستاندت
پس صفات تو بدل گرداندت
کمترین چیزیت در محو صفات
بخشش جان است و ترک ترهات
پای در نه گر سرافرازی چنین
زان که بازی نیست جانبازی چنین.

Majnūn's withdrawal into the desert is an expression of the rejection of social and conventional standards. However, society's reaction to this withdrawal shows that Majnūn is viewed as a threat to the social hegemony. Majnūn is presented as a violator of social and moral expectations. As Foucault argues, this kind of transgression is not aimed at opposing "one thing to another, nor does it achieve its purpose through mockery or by upsetting the solidity of foundations; it does not transform the other side of the mirror, beyond an invisible and uncrossable line, into a glittering expanse" ("Preface" 35). For Foucault, the relationship between transgression and the limit is not an absolute one which allows the negation of one in favor of the other. Foucault's transgression of the limit does not lead to the breaking of all historically constructed paradigms nor does it transform what is beyond the limit. However, it does allow for breaking away from the shackles of human logic, the construction of identities, and the possibility of various alternatives. Foucault's transgression is relative; it moves beyond a simple black and white dichotomy. Majnūn's transgression is similarly neither negative nor positive; it does affirm "limited being," "division," the invisible on the other side of the mirror, and the uncrossable line, yet it is not an approval of separation. Although Majnūn's transgression is aimed at the "uncrossable line" which is inaccessible and beyond the limit, it retains in itself the existence of differences. The limit Majnūn encounters is not a confining force. It rather allows space for growth. Through Majnūn's nonconformity, ʿAṭṭār illustrates the existence of possibilities and invites societies to acknowledge differences. ʿAṭṭār offers an instance of the construction of the self for Majnūn. He allows Majnūn to transgress social-tribal (and logical) boundaries in order to reach this point of breaking his ego.

The concept of love taking the hero on an intense emotional journey during which he loses control of reason is also found in the European courtly love tradition. Reason and passion are always at war with each other; however, "the irrationality born of great love can inspire the greatest deeds of prowess in war or single combat, or the single-handed undertaking of great adventure" (Sanders 47). Lancelot's willingness to undergo humiliation when Queen Guinevere orders him to refrain from fighting Meleagant upon Meleagant's father's request in one instance, and the queen telling him how to fight at the tournament at Noauz in another exemplifies the conflict between the beloved's desire and society's expectation of a knight. The fallout from Lancelot's violation of society's expectations in order to attain the beloved's approval shows how the lover can become the target of social derision and criticism for this type of behavior. Lancelot's traveling on the cart to rescue the queen is another instance of him appearing insane. Although he hesitates momentarily, Lancelot is not concerned with social norms or society's reproach. As Chrétien comments, "It is impossible to assert that any act inspired by Love deserves reproach. Any act a man may perform for his beloved is a sign of love and courtesy" (223). In the Sword Bridge episode, Lancelot picks the most dangerous path to rescue Guinevere: "at the foot of this treacherous bridge [ran] the menacing water, black and roaring, dense and swift. . . . The bridge across the cold water consisted of only a brightly polished sword, though the sword, the length of two lances, was strong and stiff. . . . [Lancelot]

. . . believed two lions or two leopards were tied to a rock at the other end of the bridge" (207). Guided and later healed by love, Lancelot crosses this bridge only to realize at the end that the lions and leopards were illusory. Hence, our mad lover gladly accepts social criticism and even considers it a blessing. As Corinne Saunders argues, "In Lancelot, love-madness rather than reason underpins high chivalric achievements" (47). Similar to Majnūn's story, in European courtly love, love takes the hero on an intense emotional journey where he loses control of reason. Both Majnūn and Lancelot accept social derision and humility for the sake of the beloved.

Society criticizes and derides Majnūn for deviating from its accepted standards, and yet he longs for his beloved's satisfaction (or perhaps for his own), even if it means that she might well reproach him, or that he will become subject to derision by others. The sheepskin narrative explores social expectations and norms constructed through moral and social scripts which have little meaning for Majnūn, whose goal is to be united with the beloved and for whom being criticized by the beloved or by others does not matter. Regarding the beloved's reproaches and criticism, Helmut Ritter notes that the easiest thing for the lover to bear is the words of abuse from the beloved, which the lover regards as concealed secret affection (403). The importance of this kind of love, the consequent pain of being reproached for it, and the lover's preference to be reproached by the beloved rather than praised by others is illustrated in the following narrative from *Manṭiq al-ṭayr* (lines 4209–11). Majnūn asserts that being criticized by Lailā is a much better reward than being praised by the entire world. ʿAṭṭār writes,

Think of Majnūn, who said: "If all the earth
Should every passing moment praise my worth,
I would prefer abuse from Leili's heart
To all creation's eulogizing art—
The world's praise cannot equal Leili's blame;
Both worlds are less to me than Leili's name."

گفت مجنون "گر همه روی زمین
هرزمان برمن کنندی آفرین
من نخواهم آفرین هیچ کس
مدح من دشنام لیلی باد وبس
خوشتر ازصد مدح یک دشنام او
بهتر ازملک دوعالم نام او."

Although Majnūn is separated from the beloved, her words of abuse are enough for him to feel her presence. ʿAṭṭār uses the imagery of a moth burning around the fire to which it is drawn, which is commonly used in Persian poetry to express the true love and loyalty of the lover to the beloved, who is undaunted by burning in its fire, that is, in its pain. The same story appears in al-Ḥallāj's works, where he describes the fate of the moth that burns in the fire but realizes the reality. The use of the term "fire," which is a reference to the fire of Majnūn's passionate love, is also noteworthy, since "fire" is usually reminder of passion and excessive love. The moth, symbolizing Majnūn, endures the pain of this suffering without any complaints (*Manṭiq al-ṭayr* lines 4216–18):

> They answered him: "How can a moth flee fire
> When fire contains its ultimate desire?
> And if we do not join Him, yet we'll burn,
> And it is this for which our spirits yearn—
> It is not union for which we hope;
> We know that goal remains beyond our scope."

"کی شود پروانه از آتش نفور؟
زان که او را هست در آتش حضور
گرچه ما را دست ندهد وصل یار
سوختن ما را دهد دست، اینت کار!
گررسیدن سوی آن دلخواه نیست
پاک برسیدن جز اینجا راه نیست."

ʿAṭṭār articulates that the moth never leaves the fire because it is only through the fire that the soul is purified, the beloved is unveiled, and the moth-lover can feel the presence of the beloved. The fire therefore cleanses the lover from all impurity, physical, mental, and spiritual, and transforms the lover into a true seeker of love who stays with the beloved at any cost. It is at this moment that the beloved reveals her or his face to the lover. This process of the soul's purification is similar to the process of the lover breaking himself in order to be one with the beloved. The allegory of the moth also speaks about the fate of the true lover of the divine. In this poem, ʿAṭṭār also refers to the divine beloved and the difficulties of entering God's kingdom and witnessing his unveiling. ʿAṭṭār comments that after the annihilation of the ego through his reproaching, the lover reaches divine proximity, upon which the heavenly beloved might unveil himself. However, since the divine path is full of pain and suffering, the lover might become frustrated and hopeless. Even so, ʿAṭṭār believes that the lover should endure the hardships and accept the reproaches. Once again, we can see ʿAṭṭār's emphasis on love on this divine path. It is through this unrelenting love that the lover can move beyond the earthly limits, purify his or her soul, and construct his or her identity, as the moth does. Through the beloved's criticism, Majnūn's soul is cleansed and his love is sublimated and glorified; he is now ready for merging with the other, for the zenith of subjectivity.

Another narrative depicting the lover being criticized by the beloved can be found in *Ilāhī-nāma,* discourse 18, part 11, where ʿAṭṭār recounts how Lailā asks Majnūn to tell her about his worldly possessions. Then, she criticizes him for owning an earthly thing, even though it is only a needle. Majnūn's sole possession in the world is this needle which he uses to extract the thorns that prick his feet when he wanders in the desert seeking Lailā. However, to the beloved, even this tiny connection to the world of earthly matters seems unnecessary on the path of love. ʿAṭṭār is saying here that on the path of love, the lover should be sincere and not seek the easiest way to reach the beloved. If the lover is faithful, he will endure the pain of a thorn on the path because that thorn leads the lover to union with the beloved; hence, there should be no need for a needle to extract the thorns. The lover should suffer silently and consider the thorn a blessing. ʿAṭṭār compares the lover's suffering and pain on the path with the suffering of a rosebush aspiring to see a rose. He reminds the reader that human beings are more sublime than a rosebush; thus, they should show a higher degree of endurance in their search for the divine beloved. He writes that trials and difficulties on the path toward God should not discourage the seeker from his or her goal because those are better than any worldly comfort. The seeker should not look for worldly things and material possessions to replace or soothe the pain on the path toward the heavenly beloved:

Art thou inferior to the rose-bush
which endures the thorn for a year in hopes for the rose?
A thorn in thy foot on account of Lailā
is better than a hundred roses woven into a garland by another.

{کمی تو از درخت گل درین کار
که سالی بر امید گل کشد خار؟}
زلیلی خاردر پایت شکسته
به از صد گل ز غیری دسته دسته

In addition to being reproached by the beloved, Majnūn often gets criticized by the society that regards his passionate love as lust and the cause of his crossing the boundaries of social decency. The rigidity of accepted social norms becomes exposed in ʿAṭṭār's narratives about Majnūn. In these works, people's disparate reactions to Majnūn's love madness seem to stem from social anxiety over his forbidden, passionate love. ʿAṭṭār's inclusive language, inviting and accepting everyone, however, does not show derision for Majnūn's love madness and his transgressions. His affirmative perspective advocates the acceptance and love of those who are different from us. Similar to Foucault, ʿAṭṭār encourages the lover to surpass the barriers of his own mind and to merge with the other in order to reconstruct his subjectivity. Society's anxiety over passionate love transpires similarly in its attitude towards Sufis' love of the divine and the mystical raptures which cause them to be marginalized and misunderstood by ordinary people. No one would be able to comprehend the pains and afflictions that a Sufi wayfarer experiences on his or her spiritual journey unless they had endured the same kind of pain. In his poems, ʿAṭṭār emphasizes the power of love which enables a Sufi, too, to endure suffering and resist social norms. Consequently, an individual who has not suffered the same afflictions will not be able to understand what Majnūn endures. When ʿAṭṭār shows Majnūn comparing himself to a feeble and worn out donkey that carries the same heavy load every day in a story in *Ilāhī-nāma* (discourse 14, part 23), this might appear quite absurd, as Ritter points out, to someone who has never experienced sorrow himself and only known a life of comfort and indulgence. In this narrative, ʿAṭṭār addresses those who have experienced grief and mourned (138). In fact, ʿAṭṭār refers to the pain and sorrow of love that Majnūn carries in his heart every day. He appeals to those who have had the same experience of pain and sorrow. He points out that in order to experience and understand this pain, lovers should break themselves, humble themselves, and emerge as new individuals. The lover should exist in the beloved. He explains that those who have not suffered know nothing of true love, its pains, and its sacrifices. Ritter notes, "suffering does not have to emanate directly from the beloved. It can be suffering which is through the beloved, but for his [or her] sake and the sake of love" (413). In ʿAṭṭār's portrayal of Majnūn, for the sake of Lailā's love, Majnūn endures social criticism, considering the whole situation fair, proper, and emblematic of love. To him, it is a sacrifice on the path of love; and his only desire is his beloved's awareness of his suffering. This process is, however, only possible through the empowerment that love provides Majnūn to cross social and moral boundaries and endure all suffering for the sake of his beloved. The suffering of the lover for his beloved is also a common motif in European courtly love narratives.

Like Majnūn, Lancelot is presented as suffering many death-dealing actions, particularly on the Sword Bridge and during his battle with Meleagant, but he defeats all and survives. Drawing a vivid picture of Lancelot's painful adventures for love, Chrétien narrates, "In deep pain and distress, [Lancelot] managed to make the crossing. His hands, knees, and feet were bloodied. But Love, his leader and guide, offered him relief and medication; for this reason, his suffering was sweet. On his hands, knees, and feet he succeeded in reaching the other bank" (208). Like Majnūn, Lancelot undergoes many trials on the path of love. Love empowers Lancelot and Majnūn to cross social and moral boundaries and endure the sufferings for their beloveds. In return, all they ask for is the beloved's acknowledgement of this suffering.

The Transformative Power of Love

Through suffering, the lover reaches the point where he must renounce his worldly desires, negate his ego, and then merge with the beloved. ʿAṭṭār portrays how the magnificence of love transforms the lover gradually as Majnūn begins his journey toward the heavenly beloved. It is this magnificent love that allows the lover to endure all pain on the path. In the following poem from *Ilāhī-nāma*, discourse 3, part 9, ʿAṭṭār shows how Majnūn first loses himself in his earthly love, Lailā; then annihilates the self; and finally begins measuring his age with an unworldly yardstick. He counts the years he has lived from the moment he saw Lailā's face. The moment of seeing his beloved's face has more significance for him than his forty years of life without the beloved, which he considers futile. Majnūn equates the moment of unveiling to a thousand years. ʿAṭṭār adds that this unveiling signifies the lover's proximity to the divine, too. In this proximity, a thousand years are like one moment; the seeker ceases to exist in this closeness, and worldly losses lead to heavenly profit,

Majnūn replied: "There was once a supreme moment
when Lailā showed me her face.
I have lived forty years, and all of this is loss,
but that moment is equal to a thousand years.
Since during those forty years I was by myself
I was poor in the coin of my life.
But that one moment was equal to a thousand years,
for together with Lailā I had time without measure."

پس او گفتا "بسی سر وقت بوده ست
که لیلی یک نفس رویم نموده ست
چهل عمر من است و این زیان است
و لیکن از هزاران یک زمان است
چو این چل سال من با خویش بودم
ز نقد عمر خود درویش بودم
ولی آن یک زمان سالی هزار است
که با لیلی مرا خود بی شمار است."

In a mystical context, the physical beauty of the earthly beloved is seen as the veil concealing God's absolute beauty. However, worldly beauty serves the purpose of making the lover's eye accustomed to the magnificent beauty of the divine, so that later the lover can endure divine magnificence in God's presence (Ritter 451–52). To see God's face is all that the lover desires in the hereafter; it is the only reward in paradise. However, the lover should embody a seeing eye to be able to behold God's perfection. He must be prepared and capable of seeing God. The lover's earthly eye cannot serve this purpose; it will not be able to stand the absolute radiance of God's beauty; therefore, his eye should be accustomed to beauty through the earthly representations of absolute beauty (588–89). In ʿAṭṭār poems, Lailā's beautiful face functions as the catalyst that prepares Majnūn for the divine unveiling and beauty. Like Lailā, the divine is unattainable. To reach him, Majnūn must lose himself in order to be able to merge with the divine other, and this is possible only through moving beyond earthly limits. If Majnūn longs to be in his proximity, he should stay prepared, so that when he is admitted and God's grace falls on him, he will be ready to enter God's kingdom. Since Lailā is the earthly representation of the divine, ʿAṭṭār shows how Majnūn ceases to exist in her presence and proximity. He loses himself and is ready to become one with the societal other and the divine other. In proximity to Lailā, Majnūn is overcome with the beauty of the beloved and is absorbed in her grandeur; this is made obvious even by his external appearance and conduct, such as the pale color of his face and his hair standing on end. As Furūzānfar states, modesty that balances external conduct and outward appearance and allows the lover to pay attention to the inward qualities of the beloved is essential in love (*Sharḥ-i Aḥvāl* 155). In *Ilāhī-nāma*, discourse 6, part 6, ʿAṭṭār writes that Majnūn loses himself every time he approaches Lailā's dwelling:

Whenever Majnūn saw Lailā's door
he could not endure the sight and would run away.
The colour of his face would become like saffron,
and his hair would become from end to end like so many lances.
All his limbs would fall a-trembling
like a fox that beholds a fierce lion.

چو مجنون درگه لیلی بدیدی
نبودی تاب آنش می دویدی
شدی چون زعفران آن رنگ رویش
سنان گشتی ز سر تا پای مویش
فتادی بر همه اعضاش لرزه
چو روباهی که بیند شیرشرزه

The glory and magnificence of love have been emphasized in this story. ʿAṭṭār refers to the power of love which makes the courageous man of the wilderness tremble in front of the beloved. Majnūn's outward appearance and loss of control over his conduct highlight his humiliation in front of the beloved. Love gradually transforms him. If the sight of the earthly beloved affects Majnūn in this way, what could the proximity and unveiling of the heavenly beloved do?

Similar comments on the power of love are found in Capellanus's doctrine on love, where he refers to love which transforms a powerful and arrogant person into a humble one:

> Love makes the hirsute barbarian as handsome as can be: it can even enrich the lowest-born with nobility of manners: usually it even endows with humility the arrogant. A person in love grows to the practice of performing numerous services becomingly to all. What a remarkable thing is love, for it invests a man with such shining virtues, and there is no-one whom it does not instruct to have these great and good habits in plenty! (39)

Both ʿAṭṭār and Capellanus touch upon the sublime notion of love, which is above and beyond all earthly matters. The proximity of the beloved makes the lover more sensitive and causes him to concentrate solely on the beloved. This concentration in turn creates a secret communion between the lover and the beloved in a way that, for the lover, makes everything seem somehow connected to the beloved; even the beloved's name acquires special status and is viewed with reverence. With the mind full of thoughts of the beloved, the lover stays in the everlasting presence of the beloved, even though the beloved may not be physically present. In ʿAṭṭār's narratives, Majnūn experiences this union with Lailā. He senses Lailā's closeness everywhere without Lailā being physically present. This condition is so overpowering that the only way to communicate with Majnūn is by saying Lailā's name; and he is only capable of intelligible speech when he speaks of her (Ritter 419–21). For Majnūn, Lailā is omnipresent. He can feel her through his sensory system. Majnūn is undergoing a process of self-annihilation; a process at the end of which the lover will no longer exist separately, but be one with the beloved other. This is the moment when the self and the other merge into oneness through the spiral construction and reconstruction of the lover's identity, as Foucault suggests.

In the same manner, Lancelot's consciousness is filled with thoughts of his beloved. On his way to save Queen Guinevere, Lancelot is so lost in thoughts of her that he is almost defeated by a knight guarding a ford. He also falls into rapture over Guinevere's comb and a few strands of her hair, which he finds on the way. Chrétien writes, "like one powerless and defenseless against Love's control, the knight of the cart fell into such thoughts that he lost thought of himself. . . . He thought so much about her alone that he heard, saw, understood nothing" (179). The lover's concentration on the beloved results in his glorification of all things that are pertinent to the beloved.

Commenting on the union of the lover with the heavenly beloved, Bihruz Sirvatian writes that those who suffer from love madness in *Ilāhī-nāma* contemplate the divine and know nothing but God. They have renounced all worldly matters. At a moment of history when hypocrisy, greed, and tyranny pervade Iranian society, they deny everything for the sake of their union with God. To them, God's existence is a necessity. God's name is their key to every locked door. This belief transpires even in their earthly love affairs and the name of their beloved gives life and hope to them (Sirvatian 33). In *Ilāhī-nāma,* discourse 7, part 14, we read how Lailā's name becomes the key to all locked doors for Majnūn. It becomes essential to mention Lailā's name in order to communicate with him:

> If anyone began to pronounce the name of Lailā
> in front of Majnūn, he would recover his reason.
> And if they spoke aught else than the name of Lailā
> he would go mad and utter cries.

کسی کو نام لیلی کردی آغاز
برمجنون همی عاقل شدی باز
وگرجزنام لیلی یاد کردی
شدی دیوانه و فریاد کردی

ʿAṭṭār examines how Majnūn's concentration on Lailā is the result of his self-annihilation. In the same discourse (7, part 14), ʿAṭṭār suggests that on the path towards the union with the divine, only the seeker who has lost himself or herself can think of God; otherwise, all else is self-love:

> If thou art conscious of the loss of self
> it is right to think of him,
> But whilst there is still the wall of self before thee,
> if thou thinkest of him, thou wilt think only of thyself.

اگر گم بودن خود یاد داری
روا باشد که ازوی یاد آری
ولی تا ازخودی سدیت پیش است
اگریادش کنی آن یاد خویش است

Majnūn gives up himself. To reach the inaccessible beloved, he transgresses the earthly, surpasses the limit, and thus purifies his soul. He becomes one with the other. When the loving soul gives up on otherness and submits to union with the one, it loses itself: "The blending-love with the One is the elimination of otherness" (Kristeva, *Tales of Love* 120). When the self is negated, the divine other will reveal himself and there will be union. ʿAṭṭār portrays Lailā as the divine beauty in the form of a woman whose love transforms Majnūn. However, Majnūn must first move beyond the earthly in order to become one with the divine other. He therefore breaks the limit, which in turn allows him to transcend the artificially constructed notions of this world, and deconstruct himself. He reconstructs his identity and finally unites with the societal other and the divine other. When Majnūn becomes one with Lailā, otherness is eliminated. This is the moment when he becomes ready for the union with the heavenly beloved. Through embracing his earthly other, he submits to the divine.

Union with the Heavenly Beloved

By abandoning the self, Majnūn is enabled to focus on the heavenly beloved and fill his consciousness with a sole concern—union with him. Majnūn experiences the so-called "presence and absence" defined as "presence near God and absence from oneself" (Schimmel, *Mystical Dimensions* 129). Therefore, the only path to true union with the beloved is self-identification of the lover with the beloved. When the lover becomes one with the beloved in all respects, his consciousness is filled with only one idea, and that is the beloved (Ritter 425). The highest reward for the lover is to be in union with the beloved. He counts the days of his life based on the time spent in the beloved's presence (430). This state is vividly depicted in the narrative from *Muṣībat-nāma*, where Lailā comments on Majnūn's love for her. She claims that a true lover should not be wandering in the desert or be able to sleep peacefully for a minute; a true lover should lose himself in his beloved. Majnūn is ultimately absorbed in Lailā's love and loses himself completely in her, so that all he can talk about is Lailā. Lailā becomes his word of prayer, his food for sustenance, and his only concern. This is when Lailā's physical presence becomes intolerable for Majnūn. When Lailā is informed about Majnūn's state, she says that now he can be called a true lover since the only thing he minds is Lailā, whereas before that he was attached to material possessions and had other concerns besides Lailā. ʿAṭṭār comments that a Sufi should be like Majnūn, abandoning all worldly thoughts and attachments in order to contemplate the divine and be in harmony with him (*Muṣībat-nāma,* discourse 1, part 4). This self-identification with the beloved is so extremely important for Majnūn that Lailā's physical closeness loses its significance.

Majnūn's idealization and glorification of Lailā gradually leads him to self-identification with her, and, ultimately, to absolute separation from her; he no longer desires to see Lailā because her physical presence distracts him from the purity of his heart's vision. Majnūn now longs to surpass the earthly by contemplating the heavenly. In this way, ʿAṭṭār portrays Majnūn's spiritual transformation; he becomes the Sufi lover of the divine who observes the divine beloved everywhere. Majnūn finds God in the inmost corner of his heart, not in the outside world (Schimmel, *Mystical Dimensions* 432). The external presence of Lailā becomes agitating for Majnūn. Complete internalization of love is the first step for him to move forward on the path toward the pure love of God. Majnūn becomes the mad lover of the divine. This self-identification leads him to reconstruct his identity as his lustful, passionate love for Lailā gives way to a spiritual one. Thus, it is self-identification with the supreme ideal that guides Majnūn to annihilate himself and "the lustful body." This is the sublimation of love; "love is sublime only if it remembers divinity—that is perfection" (see Kristeva, *Tales of Love* 66–67). Majnūn expresses his total self-identification with Lailā in the following narrative from *Ilāhī-nāma,* discourse 22, part 8, where someone sees him sitting happily in front of Lailā's painting and comments that he has never seen Majnūn and Lailā together in one place. Majnūn responds furiously that there has never been a separation between him and Lailā. On the path toward the beloved, Majnūn merges with his beloved and does not recognize himself as a separate being. This is when the lover ceases to exist and only the beloved is left. ʿAṭṭār shows this unity in a narrative where Majnūn claims to have overcome the duality and reached unity; he explains how he and Lailā are no longer two separate beings but a single individual. Majnūn replies:

> That is now over,
> for Majnūn is now Lailā and Lailā, Majnūn.
> Duality has disappeared;
> all is now Lailā and Majnūn is no more.

جوابش داد که "آن بگذشت اکنون
که مجنون لیلی و لیلی ست مجنون
دویی برخاست اکنون ازمیانه
همه لیلی ست و مجنون برکرانه."

Majnūn reaches a status so sublime that he no longer exists without the divine (*Ilāhī-nāma,* discourse 20, part 12):

> The foundations of the union between us
> were firmly laid before the creation of the two worlds.

میان ما و او پیش از دو عالم
اساس اتحاد افتاد محکم

The contemplation of the earthly love and beauty of Lailā transforms Majnūn. After this spiritual transformation, he becomes the Sufi lover who exists only in the divine. He reaches the state of not-being which enables him to become the mystical lover of the divine. The powerful love of the earthly beloved has led Majnūn to a union with the other. He transgresses social boundaries, breaks away from the barriers of his mind, loses himself and his logic, reconstructs his subjectivity, and becomes united with the societal other and the divine other. Similarly, through all the trials and tribulations and violations of the moral and social codes of his day, for the sake of Queen Guinevere, Lancelot breaks away from manmade barriers, breaks his ego, and loses himself in the beloved.

Conclusion

In ʿAṭṭār's works, lovers like Majnūn not only anticipate with patience the moment of entering the divine beloved's presence, but also actively seek this closeness. They are driven by intense longing, they wander throughout the world to find the inaccessible hidden divinity; that is, the primeval ground of all being (Ritter 357). The merits that empower these seekers of God to continue on their formidable path to reach proximity with God are their high aspirations and perseverance. They yearn to enter the primordial ground of being and become united with the Supreme Being. This is a power which is more effective than any other effort at overcoming restraints and hindrances; it is a power which can travel a day's distance in minutes and lead to great achievements where all other efforts fail. It is the power of love. It provides a Sufi with assistance to attain his or her goal, to reach God, and to achieve union with him. The intensity of the lover's feelings is stronger, his capacity for suffering and enduring is greater, and his happiness because of his proximity to God is more enhanced than those of world-renouncing ascetics and saints who see the purpose of their existence in acts of obedience (358–59).

Majnūn seeks divine love and proximity with patience. His love exceeds such standard concepts as good and evil; he focuses on his beloved. He loses his reasoning because it is through insanity and excessive love that he will be able to endure dishonor, suffer humiliation, and bear isolation. This insanity is the sign of Majnūn's perfection as a true Sufi. Similarly, Lancelot goes beyond worldly concerns and social humiliation in his attempts to please Guinevere. He accepts criticism from the beloved and society, and at times seems insane; however, it is through this insanity in love that he proves his sincerity in love.

ʿAṭṭār shows how Majnūn is unwilling to negotiate and will not avoid love's ultimate demand even if it leads him to liminality. It is the power of love that allows Majnūn to transgress social boundaries. Ultimately, he abandons his former self and becomes one with the divine. Throughout this journey that ends in union, he de- and reconstructs himself; this time, to long solely for the divine beloved. Through this love story, ʿAṭṭār rewrites the established narrative about human logic, love madness, transgression, and construction of identities.

Investigating how subjectivity is encoded in a wide variety of ʿAṭṭār's poems, this chapter brought to bear on medieval poetry a body of theory which supports the necessity for medieval literary texts to be read alongside modern theory so that medieval texts may be considered living entities. To say that ʿAṭṭār's medieval insight on transgression, the law, and subjectivity is one that contemporary theory is just gaining might be an overstatement, but, to an extent, it is true. It seems that various medieval writers, including ʿAṭṭār, had already answered the questions posed about the self, the other, and subjectivity, which have been the focus of modern theorists' attention over the past few decades. Considering subjectivity as open to active exploration for individuals to seek and understand themselves in reaction to boundaries, taboos, and laws provides us with the recognition of diversity of subjectivities, traditions, cultures, and discourses that inform the past as well as the present. Through this contrapuntal reading, we observe that a simple human right, such as being accepted in spite of hailing from a different class or a different culture, which was addressed by ʿAṭṭār in medieval Iran, is still a topic of discussion today.

Chapter 6

Shaykh Ṣanʿān and the Christian Girl, and Abelard and Heloise

Reciprocity and Self-Transformation

One of the most emblematic love narratives that appear in ʿAṭṭār's *Manṭiq al-ṭayr* is the story of the love of Shaykh Ṣanʿān, Ṣamʿān in some manuscripts, for a Christian girl. This story is told at an important moment in the larger narrative when birds are uncertain about the right course on the journey towards the *sīmurgh* and the hoopoe uses the story, among other examples, to teach the birds about spirituality. Whether Shaykh Ṣanʿān's story is mere fiction or there is some truth behind it is unknown, although there have been numerous attempts to identify Shaykh Ṣanʿān and prove that he was not a fictitious character. Some scholars argue that Shaykh Ṣanʿān's name is a reference to a shaykh named Ibn-Saqā who lived in Baghdad in the twelfth century. Others suggest that the story of Ibn-Saghā was popular at the time, and having heard it, ʿAṭṭār would have used it but not have changed the name of the main character, particularly because Ṣanʿān and Saghā rhyme. Another speculation is that ʿAṭṭār was probably aware of and had read a similar story about an individual called ʿAbd al-Razzāq Ṣanʿān in Muḥammad al-Ghazzālī's *Tuḥfat al-mulūk* (*Masterpieces of the Saints*) who lived in Yemen (Maleki 99–109). Despite numerous attempts to learn about Shaykh Ṣanʿān's identity, there is no definite information about his life, personality, and spirituality to this day; what has been preserved, however, is the story of his unconventional love for a Christian girl.

The ambiguities regarding Shaykh Ṣanʿān's identity and the attempts to uncover it touch upon concerns regarding a medieval author's forging of relationships between readers, authors, and texts, common also to medieval Europe. Like reading and writing, literary activity in the late medieval period has frequently been described as gendered—a sexually charged experience. Literary production focused not only on the author, reader, and text, but also on social relations and the human body. In the Middle Ages, stretched animal skins were used for writing and drawing on, which created a figurative identification between the human or the animal body and text. Writing was also regarded as a means for displacing, establishing, and undermining political authority. Textual processes were linked to political ideologies contemporary with the texts themselves and seen as portents of potential subversiveness (see Dinshaw, *Chaucer's Sexual Poetics*; Campbell, "Sexual Poetics"; Scala, "Desire in the Canterbury Tales").

The significance of this argument for the present study lies in the process of textual transmission and literary production, the fact that narratives are usually taken from cultural examples and can be distorted but, nonetheless, help us to interpret our lives. It is important to see how cultural examples can be shared and used to educate and how narratives can be at stake. In this case, although we are not certain whether Shaykh Ṣan'ān and the Christian girl were real people or allegorical representations, 'Aṭṭār portrays them as individuals who embody psychological dimensions, demonstrate a capacity to make choices, and have a certain interiority, which speaks to their subjectivity. Thus, viewing them as cultural examples of subjectivity can help us better understand medieval subjectivity as well as modern subjectivity.

'Aṭṭār's Shaykh Ṣan'ān is an eminent ascetic who spent fifty years practicing abstinence and penance with his four hundred disciples. He never transgressed any of the Islamic traditional moral codes and laws until he embarked on a journey from Mecca to Rūm after having had a dream. He subsequently falls in love with a Christian girl, converts to Christianity, burns the Quran, and begins drinking wine, going to taverns, wearing the *zunnār*, and herding swine. He transgresses all the moral and religious boundaries of Islam. Wearing the *zunnār*, the belt worn by unbelievers (mostly Christians and Zoroastrians) who paid tribute in the Islamic regions to be differentiated from Muslims, was an act of subversion by the shaykh. Although the Christian girl lived in Rūm (which was not an Islamic region) where the belt might not have had this significance, it can, nevertheless, be read in this story as an indicator of the shaykh's non-Muslimness. What Shaykh Ṣan'ān did was considered blasphemous. This was an absolute rebellion on his behalf; but, eventually, due to the prayers of one of his most loyal disciples and the intercession of Prophet Muḥammad, he regains his senses, converts back to Islam, and returns to Mecca. At this point in the story, the Christian girl who fell in love with the shaykh sees in her dream that she must follow the shaykh to Mecca. She meets him in a desert on the way, converts to Islam, and dies immediately.

By the end of the story, both Shaykh Ṣan'ān and the Christian girl have undergone outward and inward transformations. The girl, who is portrayed as an earthly love object at the beginning of the story, and whose only desire is to satisfy her own worldly urges, by the end of the story turns into a symbol of heavenly love and helps her lover purify his soul of worldly desires. This is an example of earthly love functioning as a bridge that the lover has to cross to reach divine love. The Christian girl becomes the *shāhid*—the earthly manifestation of divine beauty in human form—that leads the ascetic Shaykh Ṣan'ān to the pure love of the divine. However, in this process, she is transformed too.

A similar impassioned story in medieval Europe is the love story of Heloise (1101–1164) and Abelard (1079–1142), though their story is believed to be real. Even after nine hundred years, the teacher-student love affair of Abelard and Heloise, Canon Fulbert's niece, inspires us. Their love story has been passed down to us through their correspondences, after they took monastic vows, in the form of a book titled *The Letters of Abelard and Heloise*. Abelard was an innovative philosopher and popular teacher at Montagne Sainte-Geneviève, which became the University of Paris. His teachings were controversial and he was charged with heresy several times. He was at the pinnacle of his career when Canon Fulbert recruited him to teach his niece. Heloise was well educated and intellectually gifted. She strove for knowledge and the Truth; she looked for an answer to the question of human existence. Although Heloise was almost twenty years younger than Abelard, he very soon became fascinated by her intelligence. The couple soon found themselves so attached to each other that neither could withstand their spiritual and physical desires. They both knew that the religious laws of the time prohibited premarital sexual intercourse and clerical marriage, and, therefore, their unorthodox relationship. Heloise became pregnant, and to avoid scandal and to be safe, they ran away to Brittany and stayed with Abelard's sister. To protect Heloise's dignity, her uncle arranged a secret marriage between them. It was only after they married that they realized the marriage was a plot to ruin Abelard. Heloise took refuge in the convent at Argenteuil whereas, Abelard was attacked and castrated in Paris. After this humiliating punishment, and as a way out of an impossible amorous relationship, Abelard and Heloise took holy orders as monk and nun. Heloise became the prioress of a convent which was under Abelard's jurisdiction. After many years, Abelard broke the silence and sent Heloise a copy of his autobiographical account, which included stories of their love, titled *The Story of His Misfortunes*. Notwithstanding their separation, they continued to correspond in letters regularly and their love endured.

This chapter explores the rigid policies that resulted in religious and sexual repression in medieval Middle Eastern and European societies. The story of the love and religious transgressions of Shaykh Ṣan'ān and the Christian girl and Abelard and Heloise speak about their understanding of religious laws in medieval societies and about the power of love. In medieval Europe, most clerics who were assigned high-ranking positions of teaching in the church remained celibate so that they would not have social or familial concerns. Abelard and Heloise's love is so strong that they transgress the law. Not only do they engage in premarital sexual intercourse, but they also commit the sin in the sacred space of the convent and during the period of Lent and the passion when such intercourse is forbidden even for married couples. Likewise, medieval Iranian society, although egalitarian to a great extent, was not accepting of such subversive acts as Shaykh Ṣan'ān's conversion to Christianity and burning of the Quran.

Advancing with a critical analysis of the story about Shaykh Ṣan'ān and the Christian girl, we can see that Shaykh Ṣan'ān faces the Christian other, falls in love with her, and subsequently transgresses the laws of Islam. In the meantime, considering that the mystical relationship is embedded in the earthly, suspicion of conversion, as well as conversion itself, is crucial on the score of identity, expression seeking, allegiance, self-transformation, and psychology. Hence, the shaykh is provided with an opportunity to acquire an alternative spirituality and identity. Violation of the religious law creates the opportunity for the shaykh to accept the religious other and, in the meantime, to construct his subjectivity. In Abelard's case, too, violation of the religious laws makes it possible for him to face the other that threatens his clerical status. Consequently, these encounters open up the possibility for both Abelard and Heloise to de- and reconstruct their subjectivities and attain spiritual growth.

In this chapter, we can also point to ʿAṭṭār's boldness in narrating the story of Shaykh Ṣanʿān's love. Since ʿAṭṭār believes that love is the reason for the shaykh's aberration, the latter is shown as one who deserves forgiveness from the divine. ʿAṭṭār portrays the shaykh as an individual who is connected to reality but is simultaneously an exceptional phenomenon. He appears to be like everyone else in this world but at the same time he is different and alien. He is ordinary enough, in Fradenburg's words, so as not to be cut off from the real altogether, but he possesses a transgressive and mystifying energy as well ("Sovereign Love" 69). ʿAṭṭār is accepting of Shaykh Ṣanʿān's transgression because, as a true Sufi, he believes that any kind of love, even the most ordinary, can be a doorway to divine union. For ʿAṭṭār, a lover does not think about whether what she or he does is good or evil. ʿAṭṭār shows that a lover's only desire is to please the beloved—earthly and heavenly—regardless of any worldly considerations. This beloved can be loved as carnal as long as she or he is inaccessible and alien; and the love is derived from the jouissance of the taboo and the distance. This is what Fradenburg calls "sovereign love," the love that allows the subject to be connected to the sovereign in order to reshape desire. Through "mutuality of lack and fulfillment," this sovereign love allows the subject to feel simultaneously with and free of power. It allows space for reciprocity and transformation (71). Through this love, the shaykh's being is made and unmade; his subjectivity is deconstructed and reshaped; and his and his beloved's mutual transformation occurs.

By including Shaykh Ṣanʿān's story in his works, ʿAṭṭār, on the one hand, shows his acceptance of religious transgression, and, on the other hand, by adding the Christian girl's conversion to Islam, warrants the shaykh's temporary conversion to Christianity. ʿAṭṭār illustrates the religious taboos which hinder individual growth and which he suggests should be broken. ʿAṭṭār's justification for the violation of these taboos (the law) is love. In this chapter, I will look again at ʿAṭṭār's poetry and Foucault's notions contrapuntally to explore the ways the shaykh and the Christian girl break the barriers constructed in their minds in regard to the religious other, and are consequently directed towards a whole new world of possibilities through which they de- and reconstruct their subjectivities.

Medieval Religious Paradigms

During the first centuries of the spread of Islam, Muslims encountered members of other religions, such as Christians, in large numbers. Between 610 and 750,

Christians who lived under Islamic rule in the Arabian Peninsula were considered minorities, although they constituted the majority in numbers. The encounter between the new Muslim religion and society and the ancient societies and cultures generated hopes of freedom in some and fear and awe in others. From a religious perspective, the new changes had two principal features. On the one hand, Muslim rulers tried to declare the testimony of faith in Islam and in Muḥammad throughout the land and impose the "rule of right belief" on all of their subjects, although they had initially allowed most of the Christian and Jewish minorities to retain their own religion. This freedom of faith was allowable because the Quran stated that the faith of Jews and Christians was valid to some extent, although certain beliefs and practices of these two religions were substantially criticized. On the other hand, however, there was a campaign by Muslim rulers to eradicate all public exhibits of Christian symbols, especially the sign of the cross. Members of the minority population living under Muslim rulers were expected to pay a special poll tax (*al-jizyah*), which they believed, based on the Quran, was required of the people of the book. This shows that Christians and other non-Muslims were tolerated within certain limits. In addition to paying the tax, non-Muslims could not engage in certain professions. There was also a policy which promoted the equality of all Muslims, be they Arabs or new converts. Socially speaking, for the Christians living under the caliphs, these circumstances made conversion to Islam an attractive option. Beginning in the eighth and continuing into the ninth century, conversion to Islam accelerated due to the hardships non-Muslims faced as second-class citizens under Islamic rule. Gradually, economic hardships became as important as ideological ones (Griffith 6–22). With the emergence of the Abbasids and the transfer of the government from Syria to Mesopotamia, the attitudes of Arabs towards Christians changed for the better to some extent. However, due to the war against Byzantium, during the reign of Hārūn al-Rashīd (r. 763–809), Christians once again became suspicious in the eyes of the rulers. The tenth century, however, was a turning point for Christians living under Muslim rule. They managed to reinforce their position by fostering close links to the authorities of the time. They also continued to hold important positions until the end of the reign of the last Abbasid caliph (Khanbaghi 33–44).

Although Muslims and Christians had coexisted since the beginning of the Arab conquests, neither religion was tolerant of those who abandoned their original faith and converted to the other; this is true even to this day. In a world where Muslims were expending considerable effort on spreading Islam and making religious minorities aware of what they considered the flaws of their faiths, someone like Shaykh Ṣan'ān who abandoned Islam for the love of a Christian girl and burned the Quran was viewed as subversive, and what he did was an act of apostasy. Shaykh Ṣan'ān might have been a fictitious character; however, the mere fact that this fictitious character, his infatuation with a Christian girl, his conversion to Christianity, and ultimately the trope of the Christian child (*tarsā-bachcha*) entered the literature of the period attests to the existence of such unorthodox relationships in real life as well.

The Christian Child or the *Tarsā-Bachcha*

In Sufi literature, a Christian child (girl or boy) is regarded as the earthly manifestation of divine love in human form, the love of whom is the first step on the divine path for the wayfarer. Learning to love a Christian child and finding one's way back to Islam are two of the hurdles that the wayfarer must overcome in order to perceive divine love and be united with the divine. Dihkhudā's *Lughat-nāma* defines *tarsā shudan* and *tarsā gardīdan* as conversion to Christianity. The noun *tarsā* (pl. *tarsāyān*) derives from the Persian verb *tarsīdan*, which means one who fears or dreads. However, it is a Middle Persian term which commonly refers to a Christian. Franklin Lewis argues that although the term *tarsā* was employed sociolinguistically in the Middle Persian period, it seems to have had a negative connotation referring to those who were seen as *kāfir*s (nonbelievers) even though they were people of the book (Lewis, "Sexual Occidentation" 713–14). ʿAṭṭār refers to the Christian girl as *tarsā*, reminding us of that sociolinguistically negative connotation, which is one more reason to observe the shaykh's interaction with this nonbeliever as transgressive.

In Persian literature in the eleventh century, Nāṣir Khusraw identified *tarsāyān* as Christian Trinitarians in his *Jāmiʿal-ḥikmatayn* (*The Reconciliation of Philosophy and Religion*). In it, he writes that they are a category of Christians "who say that God is three and all three are one" (qtd. in Lewis, "Sexual Occidentation" 714). The word *tarsā* also appears in the works of tenth-century poets like Kasāʾī and Firdawsī. The Christian child or *tarsā-bachcha* acquired a symbolic Sufi meaning, as Maḥmūd Shabistarī (1288–1340) describes in his *Gulshan-i rāz* (*Garden of Mystery*). Shabistarī uses various mystical terms such as the ruined taverns of the *kharābāt*, the *sāqī*-cupbearer, the *shāhid*-ephebe, the *zunnār*-belt, and the Christianness of *tarsāʾī*. The symbolic Christian child emanates light and serves as both singer and wine server; nonetheless, she or he is also the one who reveals and destroys the pretentiousness of the ascetics, the Sufis, the mosque goers, the *fuqahā*, and all those on the path of religion. She or he transforms everyone's world, converting some to believers, others to infidels. This Christian child is the figure that helps an infidel to save the corrupt soul. She or he awakens a worshipper from the sleep of negligence and purifies his or her soul. Through the Christian child, the worshipper in *Gulshan-i rāz* discovers his ultimate identity and reality (Shabistarī 112–16). Regarding the theme of overturning power, the discussion about the Christian child is also a reminder of the nativity stories and of Christ as child.

The Christian child is one of the most important symbols in ʿAṭṭār's poetry as well. According to Husayn Ilahi-Ghomshei, this enigmatic Christian child "who appears as a 'Vintner,' 'Barmaid,' 'Cupbearer' or 'Bartender' hawking wine to Muslims—is a kind of archetypal *puer aeternus* [eternal boy or eternally young child-god] within the Persian poetic imagination personifying the epiphany of God to the heart of the spiritual aspirant" (44). Conforming to the same rhetoric, the Christian girl who leads Shaykh Ṣanʿān away from his conventional asceticism and entrances him with her beauty is the same one who initiates him into the higher religion of love (Ilahi-Ghomshei 43). Through the image of the Christian girl, ʿAṭṭār illustrates how this same earthly manifestation of divine beauty, being both the "idol" and the "Christian child," seduces the shaykh and transforms him into an unconventional Sufi master who contemplates divine beauty in female form. Before meeting the Christian girl, Shaykh Ṣanʿān was a pious ascetic; however, after his encounter with her, he becomes a real devotee of the religion of love. ʿAṭṭār shows how the Christian girl helps the shaykh to convert from his "'illusory Islam' (*islām-i majāzī*) to 'real infidelity' (*kufr-i haqīqī*)" (Ilahi-Ghomshei 47). As Lewisohn comments, in ʿAṭṭār's works, "Love's great act of subversion was, both erotically and religiously . . . with the divinity or icon of the Divine appearing to the Sufi lover in a Christian or Zoroastrian form" ("Sufi Symbolism" 292). The question of whether or not the Christian girl is an allegorical, rhetorical, or actual person echoes patristic exegesis, such as that of the *Song of Songs*, which always tries to insist that the meanings present in the text are purely allegorical and have nothing to do with actually loving black beauties or Christian girls. However, the truth is that it is not possible to control the associations set in train by such comparisons. The body is always a template for metaphor, but that does not mean that metaphors do not refer back to the body (see Lakoff and Johnson, *Metaphors*).

The Christian girl's love empowers the shaykh. He breaks away from formalistic Islam, converts to Christianity, and perceives the sacred love of the divine through the earthly manifestation of the Christian girl. In this love story, the hierarchy of believer and infidel is subverted. Religious, social, and traditional taboos are violated. Conventional piety surrenders to the universal and unconventional power of love. This story also depicts a Foucauldian moment of transgressing the limit, which offers alternatives and, through liminal experiences, reshapes established cultural and religious boundaries. The violation of the law allows the shaykh's self to face the Christian other, and through reconstruction of subjectivities, dismantles the binaries of self and other, believer and infidel, Muslim and Christian, and eventually leads to the shaykh's union with the divine other. ʿAṭṭār shows that it is through love that the shaykh is enabled to violate all the established laws of his faith. This in turn allows the shaykh to reconstruct his subjectivity and emerge as a person who is accepting of religious others. ʿAṭṭār advocates the transgression of this limit because it not only rewrites the established narratives of the time about religious others, but also leads to the reconstruction of the shaykh's and the Christian girl's subjectivity.

From Asceticism to Mysticism

Comparing asceticism with mysticism, Jalal Sattari writes that asceticism without love causes arrogance and vanity, and creates an illusion of union with the divine. Being infatuated with pretentious asceticism is the result of self-conceit, which is itself the consequence of egoism, and egoism is the worst kind of idolatry. Contrary to pretentious asceticism, love annihilates the ego and guides the wayfarer towards perfection (Sattari 75–77). This reading of asceticism presumes that a true lover is free from worldly matters, social concerns, egoism, and self-conceit. To be a true lover, the wayfarer has to move beyond asceticism. Although it might seem that an ascetic turns into a selfless human through self-discipline, the truth is that an ascetic's lower self, that is, his or her ego, is looking for a good opportunity to reappear and imprison an ascetic's soul. Therefore, mere piety and asceticism do not refine the wayfarer's soul and do not annihilate the ego. It is only through the trials and pains of love that an ascetic can truly and completely polish the mirror of his or her heart. This is the process that Shaykh Ṣanʿān must undergo to transform from an egotistical ascetic into a love mystic. It is important to note that the shaykh's self should be broken in order for him to merge with the other, and for this union to occur, the shaykh has to break taboos; but from the very beginning of the poem ʿAṭṭār emphasizes that this is possible only through love.

The juxtaposition of asceticism and mysticism is echoed in the very first lines of the poem. In *Manṭiq al-ṭayr* (lines 1191–94), ʿAṭṭār begins the narrative by relating that Shaykh Ṣanʿān has reached perfection in asceticism, practices mortification day and night, and has mysterious skills and abilities to heal people:

Ṣanʿān was once the first man of his time.
Whatever praise can be expressed in rhyme
Belonged to him: for fifty years this sheikh
Kept Mecca's holy place, and for his sake
Four hundred pupils entered learning's way.
He mortified his body night and day,
Knew theory, practice, mysteries of great age,
And fifty times had made the Pilgrimage.

شیخ صنعان پیر عهد خویش بود
در کمال از هر چه گویم بیش بود
شیخ بود او در حرم پنجاه سال
با مریدی چارصد صاحب کمال
هر مریدی کان او بود ای عجب
می نیاسود از ریاضت روز و شب
هم عمل هم علم با هم یار داشت
هم عیان هم کشف هم اسرار داشت

Although he has reached perfection in mortification and asceticism, the shaykh has never experienced love, particularly earthly human love. Love of the Christian girl is sent to him from the divine as a trial on his spiritual path. Since Shaykh Ṣanʿān is an ascetic, the Christian girl—his beloved object—should indeed repulse him. As an ascetic, he should avoid associating with women; as a Muslim shaykh, he should not be attracted to a Christian girl. Schimmel argues that the frenzy of love is beyond all religious and social boundaries; it defies logic and puts the shaykh in a state that he himself would have never anticipated. ʿAṭṭār illustrates how divine beauty reveals itself in the form of a woman, and how the love of this woman, being so deep, can change the entire orthodox life of a shaykh into an unconventional Sufi life when he surrenders to love (Schimmel, *Mystical Dimensions* 432). The Christian girl becomes the *shāhid*—the earthly manifestation of divine beauty and love—through whom the shaykh can contemplate the divine presence on earth. Hence, Shaykh Ṣan'ān owes his conversion from asceticism to mysticism to his encounter with the Christian other and to the subversive love of her, which leads him to transgress worldly constructed paradigms, to transcend the earthly, and to reconstruct his subjectivity. The shaykh's frenzied love of the Christian other empowers him to move beyond all earthly boundaries; however, this only happens when the shaykh frees himself from the chains of logic, as proposed by Foucault.

Regarding this frenzy of love, 'Aṭṭār narrates that when the shaykh meets the girl and she lifts her veil, fire erupts in the joints of his limbs. When the shaykh sees the girl's face, he falls in love with that "idol's face" and loses control completely. He falls unconscious because of the intense fire of love (*Manṭiq al-ṭayr* lines 1232–35):

> The Christian turned, the dark veil was removed,
> A flare flashed through the old man's joints—he loved!
> One hair converted hundreds; how could he
> Resist that idol's face shown openly?
> He did not know himself; in sudden fire
> He knelt abjectly as the flames beat higher;
> In that sad instant all he had been fled
> And passion's smoke obscured his heart and head.

دختر ترسا چو برقع برگرفت
بندبند شیخ آتش در گرفت
چون نمود از زیر برقع روی خویش
بست صد زنارش از یک موی خویش
گر چه شیخ آنجا نظر در پیش کرد
عشق آن بت رو کار خویش کرد
شد بکل از دست و در پای اوفتاد
جای آتش بود و بر جای اوفتاد

'Aṭṭār uses the word "veil" in this narrative to explicate the two different layers of the poem. First, it refers to the veil that the girl is wearing, the removal of which has a sexual undertone; in the next line, 'Aṭṭār refers to the maiden's unveiled hair which can enslave the shaykh. Although the shaykh tries to avoid being tempted by this seductress, he is caught in a flash of fire and passion, loses control, and falls. Second, if the girl is an earthly manifestation of the divine in human form, then the veil is that of ignorance—the veil that hides the divine from ordinary people's eyes. The earthly love of the Christian girl sets fire to the shaykh's heart after the unveiling occurs. This is similar to the process a Sufi undergoes on the divine path. When the divine unveils himself, He sets the Sufi on fire and the Sufi falls unconscious and bewildered. In Shaykh Ṣan'ān's case, the unveiling of the Christian girl brings bewilderment and then awareness to him and leads him away from his disciplined asceticism to love mysticism. The Christian girl as the *tarsā-bachcha* functions as both the one who leads the shaykh astray and the one who ultimately enlightens him.

Although in Persian poetry, the term "idol" is typically used to refer to the beloved who is worthy of worship and praise because they are the image of the divine, ʿAṭṭār's reference to the Christian girl's "idol face" resonates with Emmanuel Lévinas's ideas about the other's face. Lévinas's "face of the other" refers to "a living presence; . . . [an] expression. . . . [a] face [that] speaks"; it is the first encounter of the "I" with the living presence of another person (*Totality* 66). As Lévinas explains, this "living presence" is exposed to the "I" and expresses himself or herself by being there as an undeniable reality which cannot be reduced to ideas or images in the mind. The impossibility of capturing this other conceptually indicates the other's irreducibility to a finite entity over which the "I" can have power. It shows the "infinity" of the other and questions the self's freedom. Although the other is expressed in various ways through actions, thoughts, gestures, and so on, the most expressive aspect of the other's presence is the face, because "the face resists possession, resists my powers" and it is "present in its refusal to be contained" (194–97). The face breaks through the form that delimits it and "speaks to me and thereby invites me to a relation" (198). This relation is incommensurate with a power exercised, be it enjoyment or knowledge. It is through this face that "the other expresses his eminence, the dimension of height and divinity from which he descends" (262). When the face of the other enters the self's world and crosses the boundaries that his or her mind has delineated, the other becomes a party to the construction of the self as well. However, this is only the construction of the self's mind; the other can never be the self's "same" because it transcends the self's attempts to apprehend it. Lévinas writes, "The other (*L'Autre*) thus presents itself as a human Other; it shows a face and opens the dimension of height, that is to say, it infinitely overflows the bounds of knowledge" (Lévinas, *Emmanuel* 12). These bounds of knowledge are the framework for the reality that the self constructs in his or her mind. The other exists outside this frame because she or he rises above the boundaries constructed by the self. It is because of this transcendence that the other is sacred for Lévinas (*Totality* 195). In this way, the other becomes the one for whom the "I" allows space for growth, evolvement, and transcendence.

In Shaykh Ṣanʿān's narrative, the Christian girl can be viewed as Lévinas' "living presence" who is exposed to the shaykh's "I" and expresses herself by being present as an undeniable reality that cannot be reduced to ideas or images in his mind. She is real, but she resists possession and refuses to be confined. The shaykh's "I" cannot have power over her; his freedom is questioned. As with Lévinas's face of the other, when the shaykh sees the Christian girl's face unveiled, he falls in love, surrenders his faith (his asceticism), and exchanges it for Christianity (mystical love). By breaking through the limits, her face invites the shaykh into a relation which is incompatible with the dictates of power and the law. The Christian girl's face expresses eminence and the divinity from which she descends and invites the shaykh to transcend the worldly. Thus, the shaykh becomes unconcerned about losing his good name and fame, and ultimately falls into social and religious degradation. Since the Christian girl exists outside of the shaykh's boundaries of knowledge, the shaykh has to cross those boundaries which his mind has constructed. Because of this transgression, the shaykh's Christian other becomes the *shāhid* that leads him to spiritual transformation, personal growth, and ultimate union with the divine. In consequence, the shaykh also allows space for the Christian girl's growth and transcendence by admitting her into Islam by the end of the story.

Yet, since the Christian other exists outside the framework of the barriers and structures inside the shaykh's mind, loving her is a difficult task (*Manṭiq al-ṭayr* lines 1237–40):

> Love sacked his heart; the girl's bewitching hair
> Twined round his faith impiety's smooth snare.
> The sheikh exchanged religion's wealth for shame,
> A hopeless heart submitted to love's fame.
> "I have no faith," he cried. "The heart I gave
> Is useless now; I am the Christian's slave."

عشق دختر کرد غارت جان او
کفر ریخت از زلف بر ایمان او
شیخ ایمان داد و ترسایی خرید
عافیت بفروخت رسوایی خرید
عشق بر جان و دل او چیر گشت
تا ز دل نومید وز جان سیر گشت
گفت "چون دین رفت چه جای دل است
عشق ترسازاده کاری مشکل است."

The shaykh's journey toward spiritual perfection is a real trial. It is the path from asceticism to mysticism; however, it is also a reference to the social stigma and marginalization that the shaykh endures for his subversive love of the Christian girl and his abandonment of Islam. This difficult trial also refers to the encounter of the shaykh's "I" with the Lévinasian other's face, the merging of his self with the other, and the reconstruction of reality in his mind.

The shaykh's actions and thoughts are surrounded by cultural and religious metaphors that structure his perception of his surroundings. The same concepts that govern his mind also govern his everyday functioning. They structure what he perceives and how he relates to others. These metaphorical concepts, which are highly dependent on the shaykh's cultural experiences and contexts, play a significant role in defining the reality he lives in. The shaykh should therefore be willing to transgress these prohibitions, which reinforce the fact that under normal circumstances, these actions and transgressions would seem horrible, even to the readers. The shaykh's transgression of these metaphoric hurdles, which are the constructed barriers of his mind, and his encounter with the other help him to restructure the way he defines his reality. But this also means that if the shaykh's mind has its own constructed barriers, then the Christian girl is his unattainable love object for whose love the shaykh must rise above these barriers in his mind (see Lakoff and Johnson, *Metaphors*). ʿAṭṭār's sublimation of love becomes even further discernible here when the shaykh cuts across the barriers of his own mind with the help of the Christian girl's love.

Regarding the reconstruction of realities and fascination with faces, Fatemeh Keshavarz also discusses ʿAṭṭār's use of the sun metaphor for the Christian girl's face and complexion in the story. Although ʿAṭṭār uses the metaphorical sun to portray the bright complexion of the Christian girl, the rays of the sun also highlight the most significant moments of the story (Keshavarz, "Flight of the Birds" 123). For instance, when the shaykh first meets the girl and she unveils herself, he compares her beauty to the sun and confides that both the sun and he himself appear to drown in envy and in the fire of her beauty (*Manṭiq al-ṭayr* lines 1213–16):

There sat a girl, a Christian girl who knew
The secrets of her faith's theology.
A fairer child no man could hope to see—
In beauty's mansion she was like a sun
That never set—indeed the spoils she won
Were headed by the sun himself, whose face
Was pale with jealousy and sour disgrace.

از قضا را بود عالی منظری
بر سر منظر نشسته دختری
دختری ترسا و روحانی صفت
در ره روح اللهش صد معرفت
بر سپهر حسن در برج جمال
آفتابی بود اما بی زوال
آفتاب از رشک عکس روی او
زردتر از عاشقان در کوی او

The light emanating from the Christian girl represents the earthly manifestation of the divine light. Through this light, the shaykh is ultimately led to spiritual insight and perfection. Although initially she leads the shaykh astray, the Christian girl emanates light and illuminates the Shaykh's heart. She is the means of the shaykh's transformation. She is the mirror through which the shaykh sees his own true heart. The sun resurfaces yet again in the dream of the shaykh's disciple, featuring the radiant face of Prophet Muḥammad. Similarly, it reappears in the Christian girl's dream to guide the girl in her pursuit of the shaykh and her final transformation. Thus, when she wakes up, it is a real awakening symbolized by the rise of a second sun. It is the sun which guides her to the shaykh in the desert, where she can find salvation (*Manṭiq al-ṭayr* lines 1547–48):

And then the Christian girl whom he had loved
Dreamed in her sleep; a shaft of sunlight moved

Before her eyes, and from the dazzling ray
A voice said: "Rise, follow your lost sheikh's way."

دید از آن پس دختر ترسا به خواب
کاو فتادی در کنارش آفتاب
آفتاب آنگاه بگشادی زبان
کزپی شیخت روان شو این زمان

According to Keshavarz, the first sun in the story represents the radiant face of the girl; however, the second rising of the sun illuminates her heart. This time, the shaykh becomes the earthly emanation of divine light to guide the Christian girl on the right path. The sun appears again when the girl dies and it slips under the cloud to signify her departure. The metaphorical sun represents the moments of yearning, struggle, joy, and union. Keshavarz writes, "Through this reappearing meta-sign, we have come to appreciate the interconnected nature of various events in the story and the various levels of human experience. 'Aṭṭār is aware that such capsulated poetic signs can deliver messages that would otherwise require pages of explanation" ("Flight of Birds" 123–24). This metaphorical sun representing "the face of the other" is what opens up possibilities for new human experiences for the shaykh, the experiences of acceptance, growth, and transcendence.

Whereas the beauty of the face and the light complexion of the Christian girl fascinate Shaykh Ṣan'ān, Abelard is intrigued by Heloise's wit and intelligence. Abelard is attracted to Heloise's erudition, and Heloise is seduced by Abelard's teaching reputation. The teacher-student relationship facilitates Abelard and Heloise's love relationship. As Jo Keroes argues, "The teaching occasion not only affords the opportunity for acceptable intimacy between pupil and teacher but also permits, even encourages, their relation to become explicitly erotic" (17). The teacher-student relationship provides them with the privacy required for an intimate relationship. It is a relationship which, in Kristeva's words, might seem abject because of the existing differences which make it desirable but foreign. It is the uncanny and abject relationship which embodies love, affection, and reciprocity. And these attractions are the prerequisites to their love story, as, in *The Story of His Misfortunes*, Abelard writes, "Her studies allowed us to withdraw in private, as love desired, and then with our books open before us, more words of love than of our reading passed between us, and more kissing than teaching" (Radice 67). It is in this relationship that subjectivities are shaped and identities are reconstructed. And interestingly, it is Heloise's studies of religion that leads them to their earthly love and the process of identity shaping.

We observe a similar transformation from the carnal to the spiritual through love in Abelard and Heloise's relationship as well, though mostly for Abelard and less for Heloise. When Heloise receives Abelard's autobiographical accounts after many years of silence and separation, in her first letter she demands that Abelard return to her life by visiting the nunnery, advising the sisters, or corresponding more regularly. Despite their mutual agreement on the indissolubility of their marriage, they disagree about the relationship between religion and marital affection. Abelard renounces earthly marriage by accepting a heavenly one. Heloise brings up the matter of obligations that Abelard should feel towards her as his wife. She then begins an argument on true love and its characteristics, which surpass selfishness (Radice 109–14). Heloise tries to persuade him to profess his love and return to her. Abelard instead offers lessons on the mercy of God, which aids them to avoid temptation. He turns to his Christian teachings and refers to God's love, which transcends every human being's carnal love; therefore, he argues, Heloise should concentrate on divine love rather than earthly love such as his (73–74). Yet, according to W. G. East, in *The Story of His Misfortunes*, Abelard uses love songs as an acceptable medium to express his love for Heloise: "This channel for the expression of his love had now been cut off, but another had been opened up. He could now express a love for her, as ardent as before, but now refined, sublimated, subsumed in their common love for Christ" (50–51). On the one hand, Abelard's writings show that he has developed a true religious vocation, whereas Heloise remains unremorseful, feels betrayed, and is sexually frustrated. On the other hand, while Heloise remains cloistered until the end of her life, Abelard returns to his teaching in the outside world. In this way, their erotic love transforms to a religious tutorial relationship in their correspondences.

While both these stories portray the process of the couples' spiritual growth, by the end of Shaykh Ṣanʿān's story the reader is left wondering if the Christian girl is only a means for the shaykh's transformation. This is suggested by the fact that the Christian girl dies after her conversion to Islam; her sudden exit implies that she was merely used to help the shaykh emerge from his trials victoriously. This way of reading the story leads to the conclusion that the Christian girl is the means through which the shaykh reaches spiritual perfection. Although this might attest to her instrumental utilization, it is also a testimony to her higher spiritual status as an initiator of spirituality. It is also significant that, in this function, she is provided with an equal opportunity for self-seeking and self-expression, through which she benefits from a reciprocal relationship with the shaykh and from their mutual transformation. However, much like the shaykh, she should also cross the earthly boundaries and aim at the unattainable, which is outside the framework of her mind and its constructed realities. The encounter with the unattainable, that is, the religious other, functions as an opportunity for self-seeking and self-expression due to which both the shaykh and the Christian girl emerge as new subjects. On the one hand, we observe this transcendence and growth in the character of the Christian girl. On the other hand, we see that the shaykh's love for the Christian girl is so intense that it has the power to transform both of them. Jalal Sattari believes that it is because of experiencing earthly love that the shaykh emerges out of his trials victoriously. Therefore, the best way to treat the Christian girl's character is to grant her martyrdom in love (Sattari 112). It is through love that the Christian girl is rewarded with liberation, particularly spiritual liberation. ʿAṭṭār portrays the Christian girl as remorseful for her conduct at the moment of her death. She repents and asks the shaykh to admit her into Islam (*Manṭiq al-ṭayr* lines 1583–85):

She knelt before him, took his hands and said:
"The shame I brought on your respected head
Burns me with shame; how long must I remain
Behind this veil of ignorance? Make plain
The mysteries of Islam to me here,
And I shall tread its highway without fear."

دیده بر عهد وفای او فکند
خویشتن در دست و پای او فکند
گفت "از تشویر تو جانم بسوخت
بیش ازین در پرده نتوانم بسوخت
برفکندم پرده تا آگه شوم
عرضه کن اسلام تا با ره شوم."

In this moment, ʿAṭṭār employs the word "veil" again when he refers to the Christian girl's spiritual desire to be acquainted with the mysteries of the divine. ʿAṭṭār shows how the girl confesses that her soul is burning outside the veil and she cannot bear being outside any longer. She wants to be in the proximity of the divine; she wants to see him unveiled because the proximity of the divine offers efficacy and power. Therefore, she converts to Islam and dies immediately. It can be interpreted that the joy from the proximity of the divine is so intense for the girl that she cannot endure his unveiling and dies. The union of the shaykh and the girl represents not only the spiritual marriage of true minds, but also the transformation of both. The girl who initially was an idol and seduced the shaykh has transformed him so that she now needs him for her own transformation. It seems that each is the *shāhid* for the other. In short, since the sacred supplants the profane, the Christian girl is subsequently left out of the story through conversion to Islam and martyrdom. After her death, adding her mystical commentary, ʿAṭṭār reminds us that this can happen to everyone and that she was a drop that returned to the great sea of the truth (*Manṭiq al-ṭayr* lines 1595–96):

She was a drop returned to Truth's great sea;
She left this world, and so, like wind, must we.

قطره ای بود او درین بحر مجاز
سوی دریای حقیقت رفت باز
جمله چون بادی ز عالم می رویم
رفت او و ما همه هم می رویم

ʿAṭṭār comments that this is the destiny of every human being. Human beings are drops in the sea of fantasy, that is, this world; but they all return to the sea of reality, to the Truth. So it is better to return with awareness. He advises the reader that what happened to the Christian girl is every human's destiny. As in the case with the Christian girl, the time of our death will approach too, and it is fast like a breeze. Our life on this earth is short and transient, and we will soon be called back to the Creator, to our origin. Thus, it is better for us to be aware of and distinguish between the illusory and the real. ʿAṭṭār combines the earthly love of the shaykh and the Christian girl with the heavenly in order to paint a picture of the journey that each wayfarer takes on the divine path. The sacred and the profane come together to manifest divine love in the form of a woman, a Christian girl. The transgression of the religious law allows space for the shaykh and the Christian girl to grow spiritually and personally.

Subversive Love and the Violation of Religious Laws

According to ʿAṭṭār, the most sublime form of love is the one that gives up all selfish desires for the sake of the beloved. In his works, he shows how on the lower level of love, the lover frequently demands something, while on the higher level of love, the lover is willing to sacrifice everything to fulfill the beloved's desire. The lover simply agrees to perform enormous, sometimes impossible, tasks: "The lover's high aspiration also consists in not directing his love to a lowly object but rather to a high, even an unattainable object" (Ritter 398). One of ʿAṭṭār's most subversive lovers, Shaykh Ṣanʿān, gives up all selfish desires, wishing nothing but the beloved's satisfaction. His beloved is unattainable. The beloved asks him to perform impossible tasks and the shaykh does not shrink from the challenges brought upon him by the Christian girl. This is true on the spiritual level, too. The divine beloved is unattainable and the divine path is full of trials, but the wayfarer must confront and defy challenges in order to reach spiritual maturity.

Shaykh Ṣanʿān abandons his honor, fame, reputation, and religion for the sake of his Christian beloved. Religion and faith become unimportant in the face of his sublime love. Since the beloved is unattainable, the shaykh not only has to sacrifice religion and his good name, but he also has to experience a great deal of suffering on the divine path. At first, the beloved rejects the shaykh; she is cold and harsh. As a result, the shaykh chooses seclusion; he stops communicating with his disciples and spends his time in front of the beloved's door, hoping that she will take pity on him. He prays with his rosary. For a month, he sleeps at her doorstep until finally she feels sympathy for him (*Manṭiq al–ṭayr* lines 1310–14):

> The world lay drowned in sparkling light, and dawn
> Disclosed the sheikh, still wretched and forlorn,
> Disputing with stray dogs the place before
> His unattainable beloved's door.
> There in the dust he knelt, till constant prayers
> Made him resemble one of her dark hairs;
> A patient month he waited day and night
> To glimpse the radiance of her beauty's light.
> At last fatigue and sorrow made him ill—
> Her street became his bed and he lay still.

شیخ خلوت ساز کوی یار شد
با سگان کوی او در کار شد
معتکف بنشست بر خاک رهش
همچو مویی شد ز روی چون مهش
قرب ماهی روز و شب در کوی او
صبر کرد از آفتاب روی او
عاقبت بیمار شد بی دلستان
هیچ بر نگرفت سر زان آستان
بود خاک کوی آن بت بسترش
بود بالین آستان آن درش

The shaykh laments the force of love. His disciples gather around him, each one offering advice, all of which the shaykh rejects. The shaykh does not dread adversities on the path of love. He is not concerned with social criticism or his disciples' condemnations. The disciples desert him. He does not succumb to external pressures. It is the shaykh's duty to put up with the beloved's cruelty with patience and tolerate isolation, and so he does. These social forces are incapable of limiting the shaykh. He lies before the door of the girl's house until at last she puts forward four conditions for accepting his love (*Manṭiq al-ṭayr* lines 1349–50):

There are four things you must
Perform to show that you deserve my trust:
Burn the Quran, drink wine, seal up faith's eye,
Bow down to images.

گفت دختر گر تو هستی مرد کار
چار کارت کرد باید اختیار:
سجده کن پیش بت و قرآن بسوز
خمر نوش و دیده از ایمان بدوز

At first, the shaykh only acquiesces to drink wine (violating the religious law of Islam which forbids it), but as a result of his intoxication, he becomes an even more ardent lover and assents to the rest of the girl's demands. The Christians take him to a monastery where he converts to Christianity and dons a *zunnār*. Since the shaykh is in a Christian region, he becomes a minority and therefore subject to the Christian girl and her demands. He is treated as minority, yet he prefers that slavery to shaykhhood. In a spiritual context, he becomes intoxicated with divine love and prefers mysticism to asceticism; in other words, he becomes a true slave of the divine through love. Love is such a strong force that the most disciplined of all individuals might well fall into its trap. Overwhelmed with love for the Christian girl and intoxicated with wine, the shaykh loses self-control and agrees to all that the beloved demands. In fact, exhilarated by these two powerful forces, he seems to experience a mystical rapture (*Manṭiq al-ṭayr* line 1383):

The abject sheikh had sunk to such a state
That he could not resist his wretched fate. . . .

اين زمان چون شيخ عاشق گشت مست
اوفتاد از پای و کلی شد ز دست

However, the Christian girl has even more requests. This time, she requires that the shaykh herd her swine for a year as payment of her bride price. Finally, the shaykh complies with all of her conditions. Herding the Christian girl's swine is an act of subversion for the shaykh. Muslims abstain from consuming pork because, religiously, it is considered *ḥarām* (taboo). Following Judaic tradition, Muslims divide all living things into the categories of pure and polluted. The animals which have cloven hooves and chew cud, such as sheep and goats, are considered "pure" and therefore edible. Animals with claws, such as lions, dogs, cats, and pigs, are considered "impure" and therefore are forbidden. The Old Testament also excludes pigs since they have cloven hooves but do not chew cud. Although in this context, the shaykh is not directly said to be consuming pork, herding the Christian girl's swine might mean that it is also their means of sustenance.

The shaykh's subversiveness parallels the transgression of the Foucauldian "limit" which "opens violently onto the limitless, finds itself suddenly carried away by the content it had rejected and [is] fulfilled by this alien plentitude which invades it to the core of its being" ("Preface" 34). According to Foucault, in a world where the sacred has lost its meaning, human logic has become God, the limit. Now, if there is no sacred reference and no transcendental justification, Foucault encourages us to question: What is the limit for transgression? Where does one draw the line? The death of God has denied us the limit of the limitless. Without God, there is nothing to refer our transgressions to, nothing to provide us with a rationale for exercising it, nothing to liberate us. This is how Foucault critiques the humanist argument, suggesting that human reason has enslaved rather than liberated human beings. Foucault posits that in this secular world, sexuality is the only source of differentiation; hence, the reason for sexuality being the central limit.

Reading Foucault alongside ʿAṭṭār, we see that the shaykh's consciousness and logic, which limit him, have caused him to resist the girl's temptations up to a certain point. However, when he becomes intoxicated, indicating the loss of logic, and surrenders to her demands, the limit falls away, and all that had been rejected so far comes rushing in. Having crossed the limit, the shaykh, who had never before experienced love and had always conformed to formalistic Islam, faces the alien content that he had previously rejected and is carried away to the core of his being. Through this liberation from the limits of his own mind, the shaykh de- and reconstructs his identity and emerges as a new subject. Although he transgresses formalistic Islam (his old self), he emerges as a true mystic of love. The shaykh's crossing of religious boundaries is an act of transgression of formalistic Islamic law, but at the same time it is an act of surrender to the will of the divine; after all, these trials were originally sent to him by the divine. The shaykh's subversiveness, the process of making and unmaking his being, and his final submission to the divine represent the zenith of subjectivity, where he simultaneously transgresses and submits to the divine law and concurrently reconstructs his subjectivity.

After the shaykh agrees to herd the Christian girls' swine, ʿAṭṭār warns the readers to be careful about their inner swine because there is a swine inside every human being's psyche (ego) that cannot coexist with love (*Manṭiq al-ṭayr* line 1428–34):

This reverend sheikh kept swine—but who does not
Keep something swinish in his nature's plot?
Do not imagine only he could fall;
This hidden danger lurks within us all,
Rearing its bestial head when we begin
To tread salvation's path—if you think sin
Has no place in your nature, you can stay
Content at home; you are excused the Way.
But if you start our journey you will find
That countless swine and idols tease the mind—
Destroy these hindrances to love or you
Must suffer that disgrace the sad sheikh knew.

رفت پیر کعبه و شیخ کبار
خوک وانی کرد سالی اختیار
در نهاد هر کسی صد خوک هست
خوک باید سوخت یا زنار بست
تو چنان ظن می بری ای هیچ کس
کاین خطر آن پیر را افتاد و بس
در درون هر کسی هست این خطر
سر برون آرد چو آید در سفر
تو ز خوک خویش اگر آگه نه ای
سخت معذوری که مرد ره نه ای
گر قدم در ره نهی چون مرد کار
هم بت و هم خوک بینی صد هزار
خوک کش ، بت سوز، در صحرای عشق
ورنه همچون شیخ شو رسوای عشق

ʿAṭṭār advises the reader to exterminate his or her inner swine. This inner swine that always looks for the best possible moment to resurface and imprison the wayfarer's soul is the wayfarer's ego. It is capable of dragging even the most disciplined of all the ascetics into degradation. No one is immune from this swine; that is, the lower self (*nafs*). Although ʿAṭṭār cautions his readers against egoism, he does not judge or condemn Shaykh Ṣanʿān or his conduct. He warns everyone, regardless of religious status and rank. He believes that such falls and degradation can happen to anyone. He is forgiving of transgressors who break away from conventions for the sake of love. ʿAṭṭār embraces Shaykh Ṣanʿān's subversive conduct because it brings the self and the other together. Shaykh Ṣanʿān's transgression seems to be even more acceptable to ʿAṭṭār because it is aimed at the unattainable, the inaccessible. The shaykh crosses religious boundaries because the beloved is unattainable and his responsibilities are enormous. After all, is it not in the nature of most humans to aim for the unattainable—for that which is lost forever, as Lacan puts it? Do we not yearn for the most sublime? Is it not because of this desire for perfection that humans endeavor to reach beyond the veil and almost never feel fully satisfied?

Shaykh Ṣanʿān's love is unattainable because it rests upon the incompatibility of idealization and the law. When there is incompatibility between the object of desire and the law that forbids it, the superego needs to comply with the law. Naturally, the lover desires his or her love to be legitimate. Law is powerful and attractive. However, when it is enforced, the lover sees its tyrannical facet. Shaykh Ṣanʿān's idealization of the Christian girl is incompatible with the law. This loving couple is outside the law; it is the Kristevan "impossible couple" that transcends cultural laws for the sake of intimacy (*Tales of Love* 209). Regardless of the incompatibility of his love with the law, the shaykh aspires to direct his love at a high object, an unattainable one. Not only does he aim for the unattainable himself, he also guides his beloved towards the unattainable. However, since the shaykh desires the unattainable, the impossible, he has to cut across earthly paradigms. To reach the sublime, he needs to surpass his ego, which has imprisoned him with profane and worldly concerns and urges. Only after he breaks the chains of his logic and self-slavery and crosses the lines of pretentious asceticism does the shaykh truly realize that the most important element on the divine path is love.

Abelard and Heloise's love relationship is equally unattainable and incompatible with the law, and therefore impossible; however, the couple transcends the boundaries of the law and breaks away from traditions. In Heloise and Abelard's account, we notice demands similar to the Christian girl's. In her first letter, Heloise pleads for Abelard's return to her life; she argues that he ought to acknowledge his obligations, not only to her as his wife but also to the nuns at the nunnery, of whom he is their advisor (Radice 109). John R. Wallace argues that Heloise "uses this occasion to initiate correspondence with [Abelard], addressing her first letter in a manner that recalls the many ways they are bound to one another, a theme that will form the core of her arguments" (119). For instance, in the first letter, Heloise addresses Abelard as "master, or rather her father, husband, or rather her brother," and herself as Abelard's "handmaid, or rather his daughter, wife, or rather sister" (Radice 109). Regarding Abelard's responsibilities towards her, Heloise writes, "you must know that you are bound to me by an obligation which is all the greater for the further close tie of the marriage sacrament uniting us, and are the deeper in my debt because of the love I have always borne for you, as everyone knows, a love which is beyond all bounds" (113). Her demands of Abelard at this point in his life are equally as impossible as the Christian girl's demands of the shaykh.

Heloise then argues that her love is selfless as opposed to Abelard's. Wallace contends that she idealizes love: "to her, love should be absolute; it should be founded on pure, unselfish intentions that are supported with binding obligations" (127). We can see this, as Heloise writes, "God is my witness that if Augustus, emperor of the whole world, thought fit to honor me with marriage and conferred all the earth on me to possess forever, it would be dearer and more honorable to me to be called not his Empress but your whore" (Radice 114). She employs emotional and sometimes erotic language to entice Abelard into agreeing with her. This is similar to the flirtatious wiles that the Christian girl employs to attract the shaykh.

Abelard, however, responds by reminding her of the blasphemies they have committed. Having transformed into a true religious figure, Abelard talks remorsefully of their subversive acts that violated the sanctity of the convent and Heloise's wearing a nun's garb to disguise her pregnancy. He writes that what happened between them was mere lust and not love. Now that he has repented and replaced that profane love with the sacred love of Christ, he encourages Heloise to do so as well. While discussing their marriage, they both agree that it is indivisible, permanent, and not a matter of economic or sexual needs. However, whereas Heloise believes that marriage is an intellectual and emotional relationship, Abelard regards it as subject to divine will. Abelard renounces earthly marriage by accepting a heavenly one (Keros 73–74).

Abelard's change of mind and heart is obvious even in his writing style. Abelard and Heloise's letters portray a pedagogical method which was much contested in medieval Europe. Abelard was popular for his unorthodox teaching and for favoring *disputatio* (disputes, debating) over the more traditional *lectio* (lecturing). In *disputatio* teaching methodology, students and the teacher engage in dialogue with one another, while in *lectio*, the teacher conveys his knowledge to the students by lecturing and the students accept it without questioning. Thus, in *lectio*, the student-teacher relationship is asymmetrical, whereas in *disputatio*, there is more reciprocity and, more often than not, a nurturing of love, affection, and respect. Heloise and Abelard's student-teacher relationship in Heloise's letters abide by the rules of *disputatio*, allowing eroticism to lurk, while Abelard's refusal to profess his love for Heloise makes the relationship appear as a distanced and contained one, and thus follows the rules of *lectio*. Questioning Abelard in terms of his responsibilities regarding their marriage bond, Heloise is the subversive student, upsetting the subordinate-dominant or pupil-teacher relationship; however, to resolve this issue, Abelard resorts to *lectio*, by setting out the rules based on which cloistered nuns should abide (Keros 22–23).

Abelard and Heloise introduce a new age through their love—the age of courage to transgress the existing laws. As Joseph Campbell argues, Abelard and Heloise's love relationship highlights the anxiety of "the great theme that was in time to become a characteristic signal of our culture: courage, namely, to affirm against tradition whatever knowledge stands confirmed in one's own controlled experience," and that the couple's love accentuated "the majesty of love against the supernatural utilitarianism of the sacramental system of the Church" (54–55). Abelard and Heloise subverted the religious laws governing the society of the era. Like Shaykh Ṣan'ān and the Christian girl, they are the Kristevan "impossible couple." Violating the laws, crossing the uncrossable, they reconcile the self with the other and diminish the boundaries reigning over social interactions. They are great souls trapped in the clash between passion and conscience, another binary.

Violating the laws, crossing the uncrossable, the shaykh and the Christian girl and Abelard and Heloise reconcile their selves with their respective others and push the boundaries restraining social interactions. Their innermost selves long for a fusion with the other; they desire the disappearance of all these binaries. The couples' conflicting demands for various relationships and desires illustrate the incompatibility of representations which strikingly "are both reviled and desired" (Stallybrass and White 4). Feelings of "repugnance and fascination are the twin poles of the process . . . [through which the top] reject[s] and eliminate[s] the debasing 'low' conflicts powerfully and unpredictably with a desire for this Other" (4–5). Thus, despite the dominance of the law which rejects the transgressive other, there is abject fascination with this other which leads those involved in this process of repugnance and fascination to the construction of subjectivity through "a mobile, conflictual fusion of power, fear, and desire" (5). In consequence, it is because of these conflicting desires that the peripheral is frequently situated in the center. The shaykh and Abelard transgress and are rejected by their community; however, they are simultaneously at the center of social attention and criticism. In the meantime, what seems to be repugnant and forbidden at first attracts both men in the end. The Christian girl who seems a threat to the Muslim shaykh is reviled and desired at the same time. The young Heloise who endangers the high clerical position of Abelard is both rejected and loved. These couples cross the lines between two opposite poles and create a fusion that enables them to defy fear and reconstruct their identities. Crossing this line grants the shaykh and the Christian girl and Abelard and Heloise the power to accept the other.

Master-Disciple Subversion of Performativity

Conflicting demands and desires are present in other relationships narrated in the shaykh's story as well. Shaykh Ṣanʿān is not the only transgressive character that faces conflicting demands and desires in ʿAṭṭār's *Manṭiq al-ṭayr*. ʿAṭṭār depicts how the shaykh's disciples, who are expected to follow him unquestioningly, criticize, question, ridicule, and counsel him when they find out about his fascination with the Christian girl. Without luck, they try to persuade him to satisfy their demands (*Manṭiq al-ṭayr* lines 1243–45):

> Their remonstrations fell on deafened ears;
> Advice has no effect when no one hears.
> In turn the sheikh's disciples had their say
> Love has no cure, and he could not obey.
> (When did a lover listen to advice?
> When did a nostrum cool love's flames to ice?)

پند دادندش بسی سودی نبود
بودنی چون بود بهبودی نبود
هر که پندش داد فرمان می نبرد

زان که دردش هیچ درمان می نبرد
عاشق آشفته فرمان کی برد؟
درد درمان سوز درمان کی برد؟

The master-disciple or dominant-subservient power relationship is subverted here. The disciples challenge the shaykh's authority by not following him. Although serving the master is one of the highest honors for a disciple, the shaykh's disciples fail in their initial test to prove their willingness and ability to undergo the hardships on the divine path. Hurmuz Maleki refers to the debate between the shaykh and his disciples as a representation of two different philosophies of Sufism in ʿAṭṭār's day: asceticism and mysticism. On the one hand, there is the afflicted lover who sees the beloved wherever he looks; on the other hand, there is the society (the community) for whom love has no particular significance. It is also the debate between love and reason. It emphasizes the distinction between *ʿirfān-i ʿāshiqāna* (love mysticism) and *ʿirfān-i ʿābidāna* (asceticism)—praising God out of fear of hell and hope for paradise (Maleki 65–66). The debate between love and reason reminds us of the debate between the heart and the head at the time of the Enlightenment. It also points to Foucault's antihumanist tendencies, whereby he questions the Western foundation of human reason. Whereas ʿAṭṭār seems to be challenging a similar foundation, albeit in Islamic Sufism, what differentiates ʿAṭṭār from Foucault is his emphasis on love. Both ʿAṭṭār and Foucault consider liberation from logic essential for growth and transcendence, though one proposes it through centralizing love and the other through centralizing sexuality. They both advocate breaking the ego, merging with the unfamiliar other, and cutting across barriers as ways to reshape subjectivities and emerge as a new person. Although the shaykh was himself an ascetic, after being introduced to love, he despises rational counsel. However, as a shaykh, it is his duty to introduce and guide his disciples to love mysticism as well. It is also the disciples' duty to conform to their shaykh's authority under any circumstance, without question. Hence, both the shaykh and the disciples forget their duties and deviate from what is expected of them. The shaykh's infidel disciples symbolize all the feeble wayfarers on the divine path who waver and are at times insincere.

When the disciples travel back to the Kaʿba in Mecca, they meet one of the most loyal disciples who had not gone on the journey to Rūm with them. Upon hearing the news about the shaykh's degradation, he admonishes the other disciples for their weakness and disobedience. He explains that they have committed an act of absolute rebellion against their shaykh. He asserts that even if the shaykh converted to Christianity and wore a *zunnār*, they had to follow him and remain loyal. The loyal disciple represents the wayfarers on the divine path who are sincere and aim for union with the beloved, regardless of all hardship and suffering. It is only at times of adversity that true "friends" (also a reference to the "friends of God" in Sufism) are revealed. Abandoning the shaykh in his time of hardship and trial attests to the disciples' infidelity (*Manṭiq al-ṭayr* lines 1477–83):

"O criminals!" he cried. "O frailer than
Weak women in your faith—when does a man
Need faithful friends but in adversity?
You should be there, not prattling here to me.
Is this devoted love? Shame on you all,
Fair-weather friends who run when great men fall.
He put on Christian garments—so should you;
He took their faith—what else had you to do?
This was no friendship, to forsake your friend,
To promise your support and at the end
Abandon him—this was sheer treachery.
Friend follows friend to hell and blasphemy—
When sorrows come a man's true friends are found;
In times of joy ten thousand gather round.
Our sheikh is savaged by some shark—you race
To separate yourselves from his disgrace."

شرمتان باد! آخر این یاری بود؟
حق گزاری و وفاداری بود؟
چون نهاد آن شیخ بر زنار دست
جمله را زنار می بایست بست
ازبرش عمدا نمی بایست شد
جمله را ترسا همی بایست شد
این نه یاری و موافق بودن است
کانچه کردید از منافق بودن است
هر که یار خویش را یاور شود
یار باید بود اگر کافر شود
وقت ناکامی توان دانست یار
خود بود در کامرانی صد هزار
شیخ چون افتاد در کام نهنگ
جمله زو بگریختند از نام و ننگ

Leading them back to Rūm, the loyal disciple begins praying and asking for the shaykh's salvation. Ultimately, the Prophet, who promises to free the shaykh from his obsession with the Christian girl, answers the loyal disciple's prayers. When they arrive in Rūm, they find that the shaykh has regained his senses, has cast aside the *zunnār*, and is remorseful; after all, wearing the *zunnār* is another way of conforming to religious law. Hence, the shaykh has to free himself from all limits, including the ones that the Christian girl had imposed. After encountering much ostracization and castigation as part of his transformative process, the shaykh converts back to Islam (in reality, he is just initiated into love mysticism) and returns with his disciples to Mecca.

Like Shaykh Ṣanʿān, who was criticized by his disciples, Abelard was also subject to derision and belittlement, having been attacked and castrated in Paris.

Later, when he took the vow to lead a monastic life, he was still rebuked for his relationship with Heloise, as we read in *The Story of His Misfortunes*: "God is my witness that I never heard that an assembly of ecclesiastics had met without thinking this was convened to condemn me. I waited like one in terror of being struck by lightning to be brought before a council or synod and charged with heresy or profanity" (Radice 93). He was not only condemned by his colleagues, but also was questioned by Heloise and the community that demanded he pay visits to the sisters in the nunnery. However, he was even judged for visiting the nuns while he was, in fact, only doing his duty. This is how he puts it:

> all the people in the neighbourhood began attacking me violently for doing less than I could and should to minister to the needs of the women, as (they said) I was certainly well able to do, if only through my preaching; so I started to visit them more often to see how I could help them. This provoked malicious insinuations, and my detractors, with their usual perverseness, had the effrontery to accuse me of doing what genuine charity prompted because I was still a slave to the pleasures of carnal desire and could rarely or never bear the absence of the woman I had once loved. (Radice 97–98)

The community and Canon Fulbert similarly belittle Abelard at the beginning, then Heloise questions him in regard to his obligations. His colleagues in the church also reproach him. However, like Shaykh Ṣanʿān, he does not recoil and, finally, finds love in Christ and returns to his theological teaching.

Conclusion

ʿAṭṭār's story of Shaykh Ṣanʿān's love has found its way into world literature, including Kashmiri and Malay literatures. Shaykh Ṣanʿān's name can be found in Turkish and Sindhi mystical literature, too. Ṣanʿān became an emblem of true love and surrender regardless of religious and social boundaries. From the shaykh's metaphorical death to his return to Islam, the story is full of spiritual symbols and messages. Through love, the Christian girl aids the shaykh to free himself from the shackles of the self. He breaks away from all customs and chains of earthly slavery. The Christian girl, who is referred to as an idol, helps the shaykh to defeat the real idol inside himself, his ego. These idols—the self and the Christian girl—cannot be fought with logic. The only way to defeat these idols is through love; the only way to reconcile the self with the other is through love. The shaykh annihilates his ego in order to achieve union with his beloved. This is the moment of Shaykh Ṣanʿān's awakening and enlightenment, the moment of his liberation from asceticism and initiation into mysticism. It is through profane love that the possibility of union with the divine opens up for the shaykh. Love rather than reason advances the prospect of liberation from all worldly regulations and dualities in this story. The same is true for Abelard. Through earthly love and its tribulations, he refines his soul and attains spiritual maturity. He realizes that his and Heloise's experience has been an earthly urge, which changes and transforms him into a lover of Christ.

Shaykh Ṣan'ān violates religious laws, offends the theological community of his day, and is criticized for this violation. He is not concerned about social criticism or his disciples' reprimands, however. He endures all degrees of degradation, hoping to be united with the Christian girl. For 'Aṭṭār, Shaykh Ṣan'ān's love for the sake of union with the beloved is sublime (*Manṭiq al-ṭayr* lines 1409–10):

Hope for that moment justifies my pain;
Have all my troubles been endured in vain?

چون بنای وصل تو بر اصل بود
هر چه کردم بر امید وصل بود
وصل خواهم و آشنایی یافتن
چند سوزم در جدایی یافتن

Shaykh Ṣan'ān sacrifices his fame, reputation, and faith for the love of his beloved. Drinking wine, herding swine, wearing the *zunnār*, praising idols, burning the Quran, and wearing his Sufi cloak are all tokens of love's strong influence on him.

The return of his disciples out of sympathy for him underscores that disciples should follow their master in any circumstance, whether good or evil, and help him to navigate his way through spiritual hardships on the path to true love. The Christian girl's faith manifests the impact of the Truth. 'Aṭṭār draws attention to the centrality and power of love. In addition to the descriptions of love and its influence, he also talks about hardships, suffering, and pain on the path of love. He shows that no one should take pride in his or her faith because no one knows what destiny has in store for them (Furūzānfar, *Sharḥ-i Aḥvāl* 262–63). Despite Shaykh Ṣan'ān's rebellion against his religion, Islam, 'Aṭṭār does not chastise him. It is the shaykh's true love for the Christian girl that allows him to transgress all religious boundaries, and love for 'Aṭṭār is sublime.

Love is such a powerful force that it is impossible to resist. It can scandalize anyone and any community at any time. It subverts all laws and undermines all binaries. Love is the only sublimated element in these stories, allowing the characters to be extraordinary, transgress religious boundaries in order to emerge with new subjectivity, and realize that the essence of human existence is in fact love. Our couples' stories also reinforce the fact that mystical experiences are embedded in intersubjectivity and aimed at the unattainable, the inaccessible. These stories show that mystical experiences can reconcile the self with the other, make and unmake identities. They allow for the crossing of earthly boundaries and provide opportunities for de- and reconstruction of subjectivities.

Through the contrapuntal reading of Foucault and 'Aṭṭār regarding Shaykh Ṣan'ān and the Christian girl's story, we can argue that a person's subjectivity is a site through which various conscious and unconscious forces pass, and therefore these forces constantly construct and shape an individual's subjectivity. The shaykh and the Christian girl are not free agents of their lives unless they break away from their own constructed discursive web in which they are caught up. Although the conception of subjectivity as a person's identity is culturally specific and historically contingent, through a reading of Abelard and Heloise's story, this chapter also posits that no matter where and when, all people are subject to their particular cultural environments, and all subjectivity is constructed via an interaction with multiple external forces. While the concept of subjectivity as we know it today might not have existed in the medieval period, it can possibly be claimed that the medieval period saw the emergence of the kind of subjectivity that we are aware of today. Therefore, even though the concept and experience of subjectivity as it was for Shaykh Ṣanʿān and the Christian girl might have been different and changed over time, the understanding of their experience helps us to fathom modern subjectivity better. It also helps us to realize that while breaking away from religious dogma and prejudices was thinkable in the medieval period, it is still considered unthinkable in our modern world. Considering modern subjectivity as nonexistent in medieval times will only lead us to read ʿAṭṭār's characters as essentially fictional characters rather than real individuals with personal experiences like us. After all, are characters in literature not oftentimes inspired by and derived from real life experiences? Furthermore, though the medieval and modern periods, with all their intricate cultural and social interactions, are different from each other, they are simultaneously interdependent and useful for understanding the human experience.

Conclusion

Human Diversity and Inclusiveness

ʿAṭṭār's works explore divine love, with its peculiar qualities revealed through earthly love and the love of God's creations. Worldly love stories in ʿAṭṭār's works are presented in various ways and involve diverse individuals. His love narratives are allegorical representations enhanced with literary values. These narratives focus on various aspects of love. Some are explicitly sensual while others are spiritual. In the previous chapters, we explored four sets of unconventional love narratives in ʿAṭṭār's works, examining the convergence of profane and sacred love, the self and the other, inclusion and exclusion presented by ʿAṭṭār's treatment of transgressors, social pariahs, outcasts, and underrepresented individuals. I read these narratives alongside medieval European literature and in light of modern theory, and looked at the ways that modern theory, specifically Foucault's writings, and ʿAṭṭār's works encourage humans to transgress worldly constructed limits in order to reconstruct their identities. I initiated a conversation between Foucault and ʿAṭṭār in the hopes of illustrating that modern theoretical discourses on transgression and the limit can help us better understand medieval subjectivity, and that medieval literature can shed light on modern conceptions of transgression, the limit, and the construction of subjectivity.

Throughout, I examined love narratives which depicted the love of a beautiful person both as an earthly pleasure and as a spiritual phenomenon through which the absolute beauty of God is manifested. These narratives included the direct relationship of a woman with the divine (Rābiʿa al-ʿAdawiyya), opposite-sex relationships (Majnūn and Laylā, and Shaykh Ṣanʿān and the Christian girl) and same-sex relationships (Sultan Maḥmūd and Ayāz). In these narratives, loving a beautiful person, whether of the same or opposite sex, acquires a deeper meaning than that associated with an exclusively earthly relationship. I discussed the ways in which ʿAṭṭār parallels the love of a person with the love of God, and showed how this leads to spiritualization and the elevation of love above all other worldly emotions. ʿAṭṭār portrays this glorified emotion as one that cannot be experienced by ordinary ascetics or law-revering and pious worshippers, but only by the true lover.

I explored ʿAṭṭār's tendency to accept and embrace human diversity at a time when such diversity, although thinkable, was rare.

The Middle Ages are often characterized as a period when social and religious tolerance was low and minority groups faced violence, ranging from mass murders to verbal assaults. This was so both in Europe and in the Middle East. Nonetheless, ʿAṭṭār's works and the medieval European works examined here indicate that various communities and societies demonstrated a certain degree of social inclusiveness at that time as well. Sexual, racial, religious, and other minorities have always been subject to marginalization by groups that shape and construct the dominant discourses. However, regardless of the ongoing violence and exclusion of minorities, there have always been competing groups that contested prevailing ideologies. Societies and communities confronted with the unknown, which challenges their sense of self, attempt to find a way to mitigate this threat. In the medieval period, members of minority groups that were considered deviant were pushed to the margins, considered less than human, and subject to punishment by the mainstream. However, many literary works testifying to a certain degree of tolerance towards and acceptance of these minorities and transgressors have survived. One such example is, of course, ʿAṭṭār's works in the medieval Muslim world.

ʿAṭṭār's characters are representatives of the groups that do not conform to the dominant ideology. Looking at ʿAṭṭār's works such as *Ilāhī-nāma*, *Muṣībat-nāma*, and *Manṭiq al-ṭayr*, and his only prose work *Tadhkirat al-awlīyā*, I notice a preference for including marginalized members of society, such as women, homosexuals, religious, and social transgressors. ʿAṭṭār's acknowledgement of a female Sufi is reflected in his *Tadhkirat al-awlīyā* through Rābiʿa's life. His acceptance of sexual diversity is crystallized in the narratives about Maḥmūd and Ayāz. His openness towards religious transgression is demonstrated by the story of the love of Shaykh Ṣanʿān for the Christian girl. His inclusion of stories about a mad lover such as Majnūn illustrates his nonjudgmental treatment of social pariahs. In each chapter, I also explored ʿAṭṭār's openness with regard to embracing class and gender differences. ʿAṭṭār wrote many stories about slaves and masters where slaves are not depicted as oppressed outsiders; one such case is portrayed in Maḥmūd and Ayāz's relationship.

ʿAṭṭār shows that the law has always been there to be transgressed; this is nothing new. In addition, it exists because it was violated in the first place. Therefore, the relationship between the law and transgression is one of interdependence. As Foucault argues, "The limit and transgression depend on each other for whatever density of being they possess: a limit could not exist if it were absolutely uncrossable and, reciprocally, transgression would be pointless if it merely crossed a limit composed of illusions and shadows" ("Preface" 34). Hence, limits and laws are there to be crossed; otherwise, there would be nothing to call the law.

Oftentimes, ʿAṭṭār goes even further by including stories in which infidels, sinners, fools, and members of despised professions are presented as behavioral models for believers. In his works, even the outcast Satan, who refused to bow down before and worship Adam, becomes the most loyal servant and lover of God and proves his monotheism. ʿAṭṭār tries to integrate the transgressors and outcasts into society by including them in his works, regardless of the dominant sociocultural discourses aimed at regulating deviations and transgressors. Hence, like his characters, ʿAṭṭār himself might be seen as a transgressor due to his performative acts of transgression. The message of ʿAṭṭār's writing is that it is only after breaking away from the norm, crossing worldly constructed barriers, and accepting others that one is able to reconstruct his or her subjectivity.

Yet while this analysis praises ʿAṭṭār's work for teaching via transgression, it also cultivates a deeper understanding of how these works must be read today. ʿAṭṭār's performativity of identities recalls Judith Butler's argument that social reality is created through language, gestures, and symbolic social signs. Butler suggests that through speech acts we enact the conventions and ideologies of the world around us. In the performative act of speaking, we enact the reality with our bodies, but the reality remains a social construction. By performing conventions, by enacting them, we make them seem natural, real. Butler argues, "One is not simply a body, but, in some very key sense, one does one's body, and, indeed, one does one's body differently from one's contemporaries and from one's embodied predecessors and successors as well" ("Performative Acts" 122). Performing the conventions, which govern our perception of the world around us, creates our sense of subjectivity; however, this subjectivity is similarly socially constructed (122). Butler contends that there is an entire history beyond the subject that enacts these social conventions. What this subject does or performs is what was performed long before the subject even existed. Thus, these acts are being repeated like a script. This repetition is required for the hegemony of heteronormative standards to maintain power. Butler believes that even the most personal of our acts are scripted by this hegemony and its social ideologies. She emphasizes the significance of this construction in order to be able to fight for the rights of the unrepresented, for those identities that do not conform to the hegemony. Since these social ideologies are historical and are rehearsed repeatedly by the subjects' enactments, Butler believes that they can be equally challenged through alternative enactments and performances.

While Butler proposes these alternative performances in the context of sexuality and gender discourse for this day and age, we see that through an alternative enactment of his own, ʿAṭṭār challenges the social conventions and ideologies of his time, although they have deep roots in history. He tries not to repeat the social scripts about culture, class, religion, and sexuality by conforming to social hegemony. Instead, ʿAṭṭār allows members of marginalized groups to teach lessons of sincerity and piety to the followers of religion by referring to God's acceptance of all. In doing so, he attempts to integrate the so-called sociocultural outcasts, regardless of dominant discourses regulating deviations. Hence, like his characters, ʿAṭṭār himself is a transgressor due to his performative acts of nonconformity. Although he is not the only medieval author who is transgressive, he deserves attention for his storytelling, his diction, and his unique characterization. ʿAṭṭār constructed his "literary" body differently from his predecessors and contemporaries by adding delicate nuances which had a great impact on his successors, such as Rūmī. He did not conform to the ideological hegemony of his culture, and thus he not only created queer (transgressor) characters and queered the medieval period through disturbing the status quo, but also became queer himself.

Using "queer" here, I am situating myself in a discourse prevalent in medieval European literary scholarship. There has been significant scholarships devoted to "queering" the medieval period in European literature. One such work is the edited volume by Glenn Burger and Steven Kruger, *Queering the Middle Ages*. The book presents works which queer stabilized conceptions of sexuality in medieval Europe and allow readers to see the Middle Ages and its systems of sexuality in an off-center way. Using the term "queer," I illustrate how ʿAṭṭār disturbs the status quo and explores non-normative desire, which threatens the stability of dominant norms. Using a modern concept such as "queer," the medieval and modern, the present and the past, and literature and theory come together and converge.

ʿAṭṭār's openness to gender and sexual equality is highlighted in many of his works, in which narratives about diverse human forms are predominant. Previously, I discussed this openness in the context of couples; here, I look at noncouples as well. In *Ilāhī-nāma*, discourse 2, part 2, ʿAṭṭār narrates the story of an ʿAlīd (a descendant of ʿAlī ibn Abī Ṭālib, Prophet Muḥammad's son-in-law), a religious scholar, and a catamite (*mukhannas̱*), who are attacked by infidels on their way to Rūm and ordered to worship idols. To save their lives, the ʿAlid and the scholar ask their ancestors for help and appeal to their authority. The catamite, on the other hand, claims that since he is already considered to be lost and helpless, he has nothing to fear; therefore, he will not agree to worship idols even though the infidels will cut off his head. In the final lines of this narrative, ʿAṭṭār comments:

> When those two preferred life
> the catamite in such a situation behaved like a man.
> A strange thing that at the time of testing
> it is the catamite who is to be praised for manliness!
> When Qanuns go naked along this road,
> loins seek the protection of ants.
> If thou art less than a catamite in thy love of what thou desirest,
> thou art surely not less than an ant upon this road.

چو جان آن هر دو را در خورد آمد
چنین جایی مخنث مرد آمد
عجب کارا که وقت آزمایش
مخنث را ست در مردی ستایش
چو قارونان درین ره عور آیند
هزبران در پناه مور آیند
زحیزی گر کمی در عشق دلخواه
نه ای آخر ز موری کم دراین راه

ʿAṭṭār seems surprised that at the time of trial it is the catamite who represents the ideal of Sufi manliness and shows a higher degree of spirituality, but he admires him for being sincere and advises the reader not to be less than a catamite in loving on the path of divine love. The catamite, a classic example of a sexual transgressor in medieval Muslim societies, appears as the behavioral model for the faithful and is the more preferable character in the poem. The catamite's sexual transgression has provided him with an opportunity to accept all possibilities, even death; hence, the catamite, though sexually a minority, embodies a certain spiritual and transcendental quality.

The preference of sexual minorities appears again in a narrative in *Manṭiq al-ṭayr* (lines 1947-49), where ʿAṭṭār tells the story of Shiblī, who disappears for a while and is found later in a house of transvestites, among the unchaste. When asked what he is doing in such a "wretched" place, he answers that since the transvestites are neither men nor women, he feels like he belongs there. He likens himself to them, explaining that he is lost in his womanliness and ashamed of his lack of manliness because he loves public praise more than divine admiration. He says:

Devotion is the crown of all mankind;
Leave Uzza and such idols far behind
You seem a Sufi to the common folk
But hide a hundred idols with your cloak—
If you're a eunuch underneath, don't dress
In clothes of high heroic manliness!

بندگی کن بیش ازین دعوی مجوی
مرد حق شو، عزت از عزی مجوی
چون تو را صد بت بود در زیر دلق
چون نمایی خویش را صوفی به خلق
ای مخنث جامه مردان مدار
خویش را زین بیش سرگردان مدار.

ʿAṭṭār advises the reader (and Shiblī) to be aware of the self that can hold one back from slavery to God. Under a dervish's cloak a Sufi in his pride may hide hundreds of idols such as the idol of the self that desires self-praise. Unless a Sufi can be a faithful on the divine path, he is no different from the transvestites, who are considered here, metaphorically, to be the undecided. However, ʿAṭṭār is in fact inviting the transvestites and the Sufi to be sincere and not disguise themselves with false identities. He encourages them to be true to themselves. Thus, ʿAṭṭār recognizes gender and sexual differences, but does not criticize or ridicule those who are different. ʿAṭṭār accepts all human forms if they are true to themselves, which speaks to the significance of identity and subjectivity for ʿAṭṭār.

ʿAṭṭār's works demonstrate the kind of openness that was rare in medieval times; they adopt a standpoint and an attitude that encourage the discussion of human diversity and the treatment of the other. In *Ilāhī-nāma*, discourse 9, part 12, ʿAṭṭār portrays a sinner reading the book of his life on the day of judgment; he finds nothing but blackness and sin. Frustrated, hopeless, and believing that he is heading for hell, the sinner turns the book over and finds the final record of his deeds on its back. It is a record of his repentance, which has caused God to forgive all his sins. He reads that for each sin, he was allowed ten good deeds; and when he repented, ten good acts replaced each sin. Exhilarated, he feels like a freed slave. Ashamed of his wretchedness, he tells God that he has committed more sins than are recorded and asks the Prophet to provide him with another opportunity to clear his sins with good acts. He claims that although he died a sinner, God in his grace has forgiven him. ʿAṭṭār ends this narrative with the following words:

> If thou learnest the secret that is within the pure soul,
> thou art in danger of destruction.
> Who knows what this wondrous secret is or
> to what wonders this secret gives rise?
> But all the difficulties which lie before thee are placed there
> because thou art nothing.
> They were placed in thy pathway in order that thou mightest,
> if possible, become aware of thyself.

ز سری کان میان خاک و پاک است
اگر آگه شوی بیم هلاک است
که می داند که این سر عجب چیست
چنان سری عجایب را سبب چیست؟
ترا در پیش چندین پیچ پیچی
ازان آمد که یعنی هیچ هیچی
بلی این جمله زان افتاد در راه
که تا جانت شود زان راز آگاه

ʿAṭṭār warns the readers about the dangers of the secret within their soul and the wondrous things it can do. He explains that the secret exists in order to teach human beings about their ego and God's grace. The secret is placed in their pathway in order for them to become aware of themselves. Hence, the secret ʿAṭṭār is referring to is the human self (ego) which leads humans astray. In this narrative, ʿAṭṭār warns everyone about the lower self which can force humans to fall into degradation. It is this self which produces distinct demarcations between the subject and that which is unfamiliar. It is this self that needs to be de- and reconstructed before it can embrace the other. It is only through cutting across barriers that this self has created in the mind of the individual that the individual will be able to unmake and make his or her subjectivity. Once again, writing about sinners as individuals who have violated the limit, ʿAṭṭār shows that he embraces members of all classes of society.

ʿAṭṭār depicts different ways of living by portraying sexual minorities, social outcasts, religious sinners, and the like in his poetry. In *Manṭiq al-ṭayr* (line 1850), ʿAṭṭār writes about a sinner who had committed numerous sins but was ashamed, had repented, and returned to the divine path. However, despite his repentance, the desires and temptations of the flesh had not left him. He fell prey to earthly lust and seduction. For the second time, he went astray and indulged in all kinds of wickedness. After a while, he felt ashamed again and wanted to repent. However, this time he had no courage, so he kept quiet and suffered. One day, at dawn, he heard a voice telling him that since he had repented, he has been given an opportunity. The voice tells him that if the desire to commit sins comes back to him and he falls, he can go back to God again.

> Poor fool—would you repent once more? My gate
> Stands open always; patiently I wait.

باز آی آخر که در بگشاده ایم
توغرامت کرده ما ایستاده ایم.

In this narrative, ʿAṭṭār suggests that if the door to God's grace is always open, his creatures' hearts should be equally open to those different from themselves.

ʿAṭṭār's affirmative approach towards the other transpires yet again in another story in *Ilāhī-nāma*, discourse 18, part 10. ʿAṭṭār writes about a gambler whom libertines carry on their shoulders when the shaykh of Mihna catches sight of him. The shaykh asks him to what deeds he owes such rank and glory. The libertine gambler replies that he owes it to losing everything. The shaykh cries out and announces that the gambler transcends the world because he has lost all. ʿAṭṭār, again, is suggesting that if you want to be sincere on the divine path, you should be ready for the possibility of losing everything. If you cannot risk all, then you are not sincere:

> All those lions that were men of the Road
> were foxes in the world of love.
> Walk carefully; look well; be wise.
> Calamities rain down upon thee here. Beware!
> If thou be willing to lay down thy head,
> to yield up thy body to destruction,
> Then shalt thou in this manner have lost all thou hast;
> otherwise thou art deficient and unclean.
> If thou wilt be like those who stake all,
> do not keep even a needle, as Jesus did.
> If thou hast only a needle,
> that needle will be a screen in front of thee, neither more nor less.'

همه شیران که مرد راه بودند
جهان عشق را روباه بودند
بهش رو، نیک بنگر، باخبر باش
بلا می بارد اینجا، بر حذر باش
اگر داری سر گردن نهادن
برای جان فشانی تن نهادن
مسلم باشدت این پاک بازی

وگر نه ناقصی و نانمازی
اگر چون پاک بازان می کنی کار
چو عیسی سوزنی با خود بمگذار
اگر جز سوزنی با تو بهم نیست
جز آن سوزن حجابت بیش و کم نیست

ʿAṭṭār uses the libertine gambler as a model to teach a lesson of Sufism to believers. He warns wayfarers against their worldly concerns and advises them to be prepared for difficulties of all kinds and for losing all earthly wealth and connections. For ʿAṭṭār, even a libertine gambler is respectable. Losing all worldly concerns and materials is similar to losing one's logic and moving forward trusting one's heart, which both Foucault and ʿAṭṭār advocate. It is only after one loses concern for earthly constructed paradigms that one is able to break through all barriers, reshape one's own subjectivity, and accept what was rejected previously.

Associating human identity with the perception of the other, ʿAṭṭār, in *Muṣībat-nāma*, writes about a burglar who breaks into a house at midnight. Feeling hungry, he eats a loaf of bread. After that, he finds himself unable to go through with his plan of burglary. He realizes that it is because he has eaten in that house that his conscience will not allow him to steal anything. ʿAṭṭār advises readers to learn from the burglar (discourse 34, part 2). This narrative refers to a very popular belief in Muslim culture. According to this belief, if a person shares their bread and salt (*nūn* o *namak*) with you, you become forever indebted to them and should always show them gratitude. ʿAṭṭār is referring to this belief and is speaking about the supplier of all things, the Creator. If all human beings, like the burglar in the story, remember at all times who provides them with everything they have, they will become God's true followers and be forever grateful to him. Repeatedly, ʿAṭṭār presents members of marginalized populations with the opportunity to teach lessons of sincerity and piety to the followers of the divine. In this narrative, a burglar shows more gratitude and sincerity than a pious person might have.

In another narrative in *Muṣībat-nāma*, ʿAṭṭār tells the story of Abū Saʿīd Abū al-Khayr Mihna, who meets a crying and complaining drunkard in a *khāniqāh*. Abū Sāʿīd Mihna asks him what has happened and offers his help. The drunken man answers that the shaykh cannot help him; he advises the shaykh not to lose his dignity by helping a wretch like him. Feeling the man's pain, the shaykh becomes ashamed of his offer. He falls down and asks the drunkard to help him stand up. ʿAṭṭār writes that if a desperate man comes to you asking for help, do not decline, as the Creator never sends you away hopeless from his kingdom (epilogue 17). In this narrative, ʿAṭṭār demonstrates his explicit affirmation of the other once again, presenting a discourse of equality and inclusiveness.

Although otherness attracts oppression and exclusion, ʿAṭṭār acknowledges different voices by inviting them into his stories. In *Manṭiq al-ṭayr* (lines 1899–1901), there is a story of a corrupt man whose coffin people are carrying to the cemetery. To avoid praying for the corrupt man, an ascetic distances himself from the crowd. However, in his dream that night, he sees the corrupt man in paradise. He asks him how a sinner like him could attain such an exalted status. The corrupt man tells him that because the ascetic did not extend compassion to him, the Creator did. Then the man speaks to the ascetic about God's wisdom and explains how God chides his creatures for not extending kindness when necessary,

If all were pure of all iniquity,
God could not show His generosity;
The end of wisdom is for God to show—
Perpetually—His love to those below.
One drop of God's great wisdom will be yours,
A sea of mercy with uncharted shores.

گر همه کس جز نمازی نیستی
حکمتش را عشقبازی نیستی
کار حکمت جز چنین نبود تمام
لاجرم خود این چنین آمد مدام
در ره او صد هزاران حکمت است
قطره ای را حصه بحری رحمت است.

The corrupt man tells the ascetic that if everyone were prayerful, there would be no need for seeking God's wisdom. However, since people are not compassionate toward one another, God's wisdom finds numerous ways to display itself, and the compassion that God shows is only a small part of his wisdom. As in previous narratives, ʿAṭṭār questions people's ways of treating others and contrasts it with the way the Creator treats them. If only people could set aside their differences and accept one another, the world would be a more peaceful and forgiving place. ʿAṭṭār did this; and it is his appeal to spirituality and the love of all which makes his openness toward human diversity distinct.

Looking at these narratives, we see that ʿAṭṭār's position in Sufism allows him to experience a great degree of openness to embrace the other; and his vision of otherness takes concrete form in his works. Through his writings, he shows the possibilities of various human identities. His language and content are inclusive, incorporating issues related to sexual, religious, gender, and social diversity. ʿAṭṭār's works are a powerful cry for the inclusion of all members of society. He strives to remove the barriers that uphold exclusion, and recognizes people's equality and interdependence in the face of their differences. He does so through advancing the necessity to break away from the barriers that our minds have constructed and to reshape our subjectivities.

Through a contrapuntal reading of medieval literature and modern theory, I observe that in order to be able to cope with diversity and strive towards inclusion, we need to be aware of systematic marginalization, structured silences, and imposed invisibility. Although subjectivity in the medieval period was very different from subjectivity as we know it in our modern world, we need to acknowledge the interdependence of the concept of subjectivity and human experience in the face of all differences. We have to admit that by excluding and demeaning those who are different from us, we trample the rights of a great number of people; this is true in any period. In our modern world, we should not forget Sufi poets such as ʿAṭṭār's invitation to accept the coexistence of diverse voices, regardless of whether they are contesting or cohering. These are the voices that deserve attention. As we can see in ʿAṭṭār's works, literature—medieval or modern—can fulfill this demand to pay attention to the marginalized members of society by making us aware of alternative possibilities of human forms. Literature has the potential to defamiliarize the familiar. It is the place for asking questions and taking action. It is where we can give birth to new modes of thinking. In this book, through reading medieval literature alongside modern theory, I tried to shed light on voices which are still being silenced, on subjectivities which are still being discriminated against, and human rights which are still being violated. I conjecture that medieval works such as ʿAṭṭār's are not antiquated historical pieces, but are very much living texts which can teach us as much about the present as the past. Through this reading, I hope to have opened up new venues for medieval as well as modern scholars to think about the interdependence of medieval and modern, and Western and Middle Eastern subjectivities as complementary rather than independent of or against each other.

Works Cited

Abbott, H. Porter. "Humanists, Scientists, and the Cultural Surplus." Special issue, *On the Origin of Fictions: Interdisciplinary Perspectives. Substance*, 94/95, edited by H. Porter Abbott, *Substance* vol. 30, nos. 1–2, 2001, pp. 203–19.

Abdul Sabour, Salah. *Leila and the Madman* (*Laila wal-Majnoun*). Translated by M. Anani, Cairo: Ministry of Culture, Egypt, Foreign Cultural Relations in collaboration with the Supreme Council for Culture, 1999.

Abou-El-Hai, Barbara. "The Audiences for the Medieval Cult of Saints." *Gesta*, vol. 30, no. 1, 1991, pp. 3–15.

Adams Helminski, Camille. *Women of Sufism: A Hidden Treasure: Writings and Stories of Mystic Poets, Scholars and Saints*. Boston: Shambhala, 2003.

Adang, Camilla. *Muslim Writers on Judaism and the Hebrew Bible: From Ibn Rabban to Ibn Hazm*. Leiden: Brill, 1996.

Afary, Janet. *Sexual Politics in Modern Iran*. Cambridge: Cambridge UP, 2009.

Aflakī, Shams al-Dīn Aḥmad. *Manāqib al-ʿārifīn* [*The Feats of the Knowers of God*]. MS India Office 1670, translated by K. John O'Kane, Leiden: Brill, 2002.

Ahmed, Leila. "Early Islam and the Position of Women: The Problem of Interpretation." *Women in Middle Eastern History: Shifting Boundaries in Sex and Gender*. Edited by Nikki R. Keddie and Beth Baron, New Haven: Yale UP, 1991, 58–73.

———. *Women and Gender in Islam*. New Haven: Yale UP, 1992.

Alcalay, Ammiel. *After Jews and Arabs: Remaking Levantine Culture*. Minneapolis: U of Minnesota P, 1993.

Alford, John A. "Biblical Imitatio in the Writings of Richard Rolle." *ELH*, vol. 40, no. 1, Spring 1973, pp. 1–23.

Allen, Prudence. *The Concept of Woman*. Cambridge: Eerdmans Publishing, 2002.

Almond, Ian. *Sufism and Deconstruction: A Comparative Study of Derrida and Ibn ʿArabī*. London: Routledge, 2004.

Andrae, Tor. *In the Gardens of Myrtles: Studies in Early Islamic Mysticism*. Translated by Birgitta Sharpe, Albany: State U of New York P, 1987.

Andrews, Walter G., and Mehmet Kalpakh. *The Age of Beloveds: Love and the Beloved in Early Modern Ottoman and European Culture and Society*. Durham: Duke UP, 2005.

Anidjar, Gil. *The Jew, the Arab: A History of the Enemy*. Palo Alto: Stanford UP, 2003.

Antonopoulos, Anna. "Writing the Mystic Body: Sexuality and Textuality in the ecriture-feminine of Saint Catherine of Genoa." Special issue, *Feminism and the Body*, edited by Elizabeth Grosz, *Hypatia*, vol. 6, no. 3, Autumn 1991, pp. 185–207.

Arberry, Arthur John. *Discourses of Rumi*. Surrey: Curzon, 1961.

———, translator. *Mystical Poems of Rumi: First Selection: Poems 1–200*. Chicago: U of Chicago P, 1968.

———. *Sufism: An Account of the Mystics of Islam*. New York: Harper and Row, 1970.

———. *Tales from the Masnavi*. Surrey: Curzon, 1961.

Arthur, Karen. "Equivocal Subjectivity in Chaucer's 'Second Nun's Prologue and Tale.'" *Chaucer Review*, vol. 32, no. 3, 1998, pp. 217–31.

Atkinson, Clarissa W. *Mystic and Pilgrim: The Book and the World of Margery Kempe*. Ithaca: Cornell UP, 1989.

ʿAṭṭār, Farīd al-Dīn. *Conference of the Birds*. Translated by Afkham Darbandi and Dick Davis, London: Penguin Classics, 1984.

———. *Conference of the Birds*. Edited by Muhammad Rezā Shafī Kadkanī, Tehran: Sukhan, 2007.

———. *The Ilāhī-nāma or Book of God*. Translated by John Andrew Boyle, 1976. Edited by Muhammad Rezā Shafī Kadkanī. Tehran: Sukan, 2009.

———. *Muṣībat-nāma* [*The Book of Suffering*]. Edited by Muhammad Rezā Shafī Kadkanī, Tehran: Sukhan, 2008.

———. *Muslim Saints and Mystics*. [Original title: *Tadhkirat al-awlīyā* {*Memoirs of the Saints*}]. 1905. Translated by A. J. Arberry, London: Routledge and Kegan Paul, 1966.

———. *The Speech of the Birds: Concerning the Migration to the Real (the Manṭiq al-ṭayr)*. Translated by P. W. Avery, Cambridge: Islamic Texts Society, 1998.

ʿAttarpour, Ardalan. *Pizhūhishī Dar Dāstān-i Shaykh Ṣanʿān: Iqtidā Bih Kufr* [*A Study of Shaykh Ṣanʿān's Story: Blasphemous Sanity*]. Tehran: An and Hameh, 2003.

Augustine. *City of God*. Translated by Henry Bettenson, Harmondsworth: Penguin, 1972.

ʿAwfī, Muḥammad. *Lubāb al-albāb* [*Quintessence of Intellectuals*]. Edited by E. G. Browne and Mirza Muhammad-i Ghazwini, London: Leiden, 1903.

Awn, Peter J. "The Ethical Concerns of Classical Sufism." *Journal of Religious Ethics*, vol. 11, no. 2, Fall 1983, pp. 240–63.

———. *Satan's Tragedy and Redemption: Iblis in Sufi Psychology*. Leiden: Brill, 1983.

Bailey, Derrick Sherwin. *Homosexuality and the Western Christian Tradition*. London: Longmans, Green, 1955.

Bakhtiar, Laleh. *Sufi Expression of the Mystic Quest*. London: Thames and Hudson, 1976.

Baldick, Julian. *Mystical Islam: An Introduction to Sufism*. New York: New York UP, 1989.

Banani, Amin, Richard Hovannisian, and Georges Sabbagh, editors. *Poetry and Mysticism in Islam: The Heritage of Rumi*. Cambridge: Cambridge UP, 1994.

Barks, Coleman. *Rumi, We are Three: New Rumi Translations*. Athens, GA: Maypop Books, 1987.

Barks, Coleman, and John Moyne. *The Essential Rumi*. San Francisco: HarperSanFrancisco, 1995.

Barthold, W. *Turkestan: Down to the Mongol Invasion*. London: Luzac, 1977.

Bartlett, Anne Clark. *Male Authors, Female Readers: Representation and Subjectivity in Middle English Devotional Literature*. Ithaca: Cornell UP, 1995.

Barzi, Asgar. *The Complete Description of the Conference of the Birds: Manṭeqot ṭayr ʿAṭṭār-e Nayshabūrī*. Bonab: Azam, 1995.

Bashir, Shahzad. *Fazlallah Astarabadi and the Hurufis*. Oxford: Oneworld, 2005.

———. *Messianic Hopes and Mystical Visions*. Columbia: U South Carolina P, 2003.

Bataille, Georges. *Erotism: Death and Sensuality*. Translated by Mary Dalwood, San Francisco: City Lights, 1986.

———. *Inner Experience*. Translated by Leslie A. Boldt, New York: SUNY Press, 1988.

———. *The Story of the Eye*. Translated by Joachim Neugroschal, New York: Penguin, 1982.

Bayat, Mojdeh, and Mohammad Ali Jamnia. *Tales from the Land of the Sufis*. Boston: Shambhala, 1994.

de Beauvoir, Simone. *The Second Sex*. Translated by Constance Borde and Sheila Malovany-Chevallier, New York: Alfred A. Knopf, 2010.

Beckwith, Sarah. *Christ's Body: Identity, Culture and Society in Late Medieval Writings*. London: Routledge, 1996.

———. "Passionate Regulation: Enclosure, Ascesis, and the Feminist Imaginary." *South Atlantic Quarterly*, vol. 93, 1994, pp. 811–12.

Bell, Joseph Norment. *Love Theory in Hanbalite Islam*. New York: State U of New York P, 1979.

Biernoff, Suzannah. *Sight and Embodiment in the Middle Ages*. New York: Palgrave Macmillan, 2002.

Blamires, Alcuin. *Chaucer, Ethics, and Gender*. Oxford: Oxford UP, 2006.

Bloch, Ernst. *Atheism in Christianity: The Religion of the Exodus and the Kingdom*. Translated by J. T. Swann, New York: Herder and Herder, 1972.

Bloom, Harold. *King Arthur*. Broomall, PA: Chelsea House, 2004.

Blumenthal, David R. *Facing the Abusing God: A Theology of Protest.* Louisville: Westminister/John Knox, 1993.

Boon, Jessica A. "Trinitarian Love Mysticism: Ruusbroec, Hadewijch, and the Gendered Experience of the Divine." *Church History*, vol. 72, no. 3, Sept. 2003, pp. 484–503.

Boswell, John. *Christianity, Social Tolerance, and Homosexuality: Gay People in Western Europe from the Beginning of the Christian Era to the Fourteenth Century*. Chicago: U of Chicago P, 1980.

———. *Same-Sex Unions in Premodern Europe*. New York: Villard, 1994.

Bosworth, C. E. "The Development of Persian Culture under the Early Ghaznavids." *Iran*, vol. 6, 1968, pp. 33–44.

———. "Maḥmūd of Ghazna in Contemporary Eyes and in Later Persian Literature." *Iran*, vol. 4, 1966, pp. 85–92.

Boteach, Samuel. *Wrestling with the Divine: A Jewish Response to Suffering*. Northvale: J. Aronson, 1995.

Bouhdiba, Abdelwahab. *Sexuality in Islam*. Translated by Alan Sheridan, London: Saqi, 2004.

Bourdieu, Pierre. *Outline of a Theory of Practice*. Translated by Richard Nice, Cambridge: Cambridge UP, 1977.

Bowering, Gerhard. "Ideas of Time in Persian Sufism." *Iran*, vol. 30, 1992, pp. 77–89.

Bowker, John. *Problems of Suffering in Religions of the World*. Cambridge: Cambridge UP, 1975.

Boyarin, Daniel. *Border Lines: The Partition of Judaeo-Christianity*. Philadelphia: U of Pennsylvania P, 2004.

Boyle, John Andrew, editor. *The Cambridge History of Iran: The Saljuq and Mongol Periods*. Vol. 5, Cambridge: Cambridge UP, 1968.

———. "The Religious 'Mathnavīs' of Farīd al-Dīn ʿAṭṭār." *Iran*, vol. 17, 1979, pp. 9–14.

Brison, Susan J. *Aftermath: Violence and the Remaking of the Self*. Princeton: Princeton UP, 2002.

———. "Surviving Sexual Violence: A Philosophical Perspective." *Violence Against Women: Philosophical Perspectives*. Edited by Stanley G. French, Wanda Teays, and Laura M. Purdy, Ithaca: Cornell UP, 1998. 11–26.

Browne, Edward Granville. *A Literary History of Persia*. London: Unwin, 1906–08.

Bruijn, J. T. P. "Comparative Notes on Sana'i and ʿAttar." *Sufi*, vol. 16, Winter 1992–93, pp. 13–19.

———. *Persian Sufi Poetry: An Introduction to the Mystical Uses of Classical Persian Poems*. Richmond: Curzon, 1997.

———. "The Preaching Poet: Three Homiletic Poems by Farid al-Din ʿAttar." *Edebiyat: Journal of Middle Eastern Literatures*, vol. 9, no. 1, 1998, pp. 85–100.

Bulliet, Richard W. "Local Politics in Eastern Iran under the Ghaznavids and Seljuks." Special issue, *State and Society in Iran*, *Iranian Studies*, vol. 11, nos. 1–4, 1978, pp. 35–56.

———. *The Patricians of Nishapur: A Study in Medieval Islamic Social History*. Cambridge: Harvard UP, 1972.

Butler, Judith. "Performative Acts and Gender Constitution." *The Twentieth-Century Performance Reader*. Edited by Michael Huxley and Noel Witts, 2nd ed., London: Routledge, 1996.

———. "Sex and Gender in Simone de Beauvoir's Second Sex." *Yale French Studies*, vol. 72, 1986, pp. 35– 49.

Bynum, Caroline Walker. "The Blood of Christ in the Later Middle Ages." *Church History*, vol. 71, no. 4, Dec. 2002, pp. 685–714.

———. "The Cistercian Conception of Community: An Aspect of Twelfth-Century Spirituality." *Harvard Theological Review*, vol. 68, nos. 3–4, July–Oct. 1975, pp. 273–86.

———. "Death and Resurrection in the Middle Ages: Some Modern Implications." *Proceedings of the American Philosophical Society*, vol. 142, no. 4, Dec. 1998, pp. 589–96.

———. *Fragmentation and Redemption: Essays on Gender and the Human Body in Medieval Religion*. New York: Zone, 1994.

———. *Holy Feast and Holy Fast: The Religious Significance of Food to Medieval Women*. Berkeley: U of California P, 1988.

Cahill, Susan N. *Wise Women*. New York: Norton, 1996.

Campbell, Emma. "Sexual Poetics and the Politics of Translation in the Tale of Griselda." *Comparative Literature*, vol. 55, no. 3, Summer 2003, pp. 191–216.

Campbell, Joseph. *The Masks of God: Creative Mythology*. Vol. 4, Harmondsworth: Penguin, 1987.

Capellanus, Andreas. *Andreas Capellanus On Love*. Edited by and translated by P. G. Walsh, London: Duckworth, 1982.

Chelkowski, Peter J., editor. *The Scholar and the Saint*. New York: New York UP, 1975.

Chewning, Susannah Mary. "Mysticism and the Anchoritic Community: 'A Time . . . of Veiled Infinity.'" *Medieval Women in Their Communities*. Edited by Diane Watt, Toronto: U of Toronto P, 1997.

Chittick, William C. *Me and Rumi: The Autobiography of Shams-i Tabrizi*. Louisville: Fons Vitae, 2004.

———. *The Sufi Doctrine of Rumi*. Bloomington: World Wisdom, 2005.

———. *The Sufi Path of Love*. Albany: State U of New York P, 1983.

———. *Sufism, A Short Introduction*. Boston, Oneworld, 2000.

Chittick, William C., and Peter Lamborn Wilson. *Fakhruddin 'Iraqi: Divine Flashes*. New York: Paulist Press, 1982.

Clanchy, Michael T. *From Memory to Written Record: English, 1066–1307*. Cambridge: Harvard UP, 1986.

Coakley, John W. *Women, Men, and Spiritual Power: Female Saints and Their Male Collaborators*. New York: Columbia UP, 2006.

Cohen, Mark R. *Under Crescent and Cross: The Jews in the Middle Ages*. Princeton: Princeton UP, 1994.

Coleman, Janet. *A History of Political Thought: From the Middle Ages to the Renaissance*. Oxford: Blackwell, 2000.

———. *Medieval Readers and Writers, 1350–1400*. New York: Columbia UP, 1981.

Cook, Michael. *The Koran: A Very Short Introduction*. Oxford: Oxford UP, 2000.

Cooney, Helen, editor. *Writings on Love in the English Middle Ages*. New York: Palgrave Macmillan, 2006.

Cooper, Christine F. "Miraculous Translation in *The Book of Margery Kempe*." *Studies in Philology*, vol. 101, no. 3, Summer 2004, pp. 270–98.

Cowan, James. *Rumi's Divan of Shems of Tabriz*. Rockport: Element, 1997.

Dabashi, Hamid. *Truth and Narrative: The Untimely Thoughts of 'Ayn al-Qudat al-Hamadhani*. Richmond: Curzon, 1999.

Darling, Linda T. "Circle of Justice." *Encyclopedia of Islam, Three*. 2012.

———. "'Do Justice, Do Justice, For That is Paradise': Middle Eastern Advice for Indian Muslim Rulers." *Comparative Studies of South Asia, Africa and the Middle East*, vol. 22, nos. 1–2, 2002, pp. 3–19.

———. "Medieval Egyptian Society and the Concept of the Circle of Justice." *Mamluk Studies Review*, vol. 10, no. 2, 2006, pp. 1–17.

Daulatshāh, Samarqandī. *Tadhkirat al-shuarā* [*Biographies of the Poets*]. Ed E. G. Browne, London, 1901.

Davis, Dick. "The Journey as Paradigm: Literal and Metaphorical Travel in ʿAttar's *Mantiq al- Tayr*." *Edebiyat: Journal of Middle Eastern Literatures*, vol. 4, no. 2, 1993, pp. 173–83.

Dehqani, Muhammad. *Vasvasehāy-i 'Ashiqān-i Barrisī-i Taḥavvul-i ʿIshq dar Adab-i Pārsī*. [*Romantic Temptations: A Study of the Development of Love in Persian Literature*]. Tehran: Barnameh Publications, 1999.

Delcambre, Anne-Marie. *Inside Islam*. Milwaukee: Marquette UP, 2005.

Deleuze, Gilles, and Felix Guattari. "Of the Refrain." *A Thousand Plateaus*. Translated by Brian Massumi, Minneapolis: U of Minnesota P, 1987. 310–350.

Dickinson, J. C. *Monastic Life in Medieval England*. Westport: Greenwood, 1979.

Dinshaw, Caroline. *Chaucer's Sexual Poetics*. Madison: U of Wisconsin P, 1989.

Dols, Michael W. *Majnun: The Madman in Medieval Islamic Society*. Edited by Diana E. Immisch, Oxford: Clarendon Press, 1992.

East, W. G. "*This Body of Death*: Abelard, Heloise and the Religious Life." *Medieval Theology and The Natural Body*. Edited by Peter Biller and A. J. Minnis, Woodbridge: York Medieval Press, 1997. 43–60.

Eckhart, Meister. *The Essential Sermons, Commentaries, Treatises and Defense*. Translated by Edmund College and Bernard McGinn, New York: Paulist, 1981.

Eliade, Mircea. *The Sacred and the Profane: The Nature of Religion*. Orlando: Harcourt, 1959.

Elias, Jamal J. "Sufism." Special issue, *A Review of the* Encyclopedia Iranica, edited by Abbas Amanat and William L. Hanaway, *Iranian Studies*, vol. 31, nos. 3–4, Summer–Autumn 1998, pp. 595–613.

Elliott, Dyan. *Proving Women: Female Spirituality and Inquisitional Culture in the Later Middle Ages*. Princeton: Princeton UP, 2004.

———. *Spiritual Marriage: Sexual Abstinence in Medieval Wedlock*. Princeton: Princeton UP, 1993.

Engen, John Van. "The Future of Medieval Church History." *Church History*, vol. 71, no. 3, Sept. 2002, pp. 492–522.

Ernst, Carl W. *Eternal Garden: Mysticism, History, and Politics at a South Asian Sufi Center*. Albany: State U of New York P, 1992.

———. *Following Muhammad: Rethinking Islam in the Contemporary World*. Chapel Hill: U of North Carolina P, 2003.

———. *Ruzbihan Baqli: Mysticism and the Rhetoric of Sainthood in Persian Sufism*. Richmond: Curzon, 1996.

———, translator. *Ruzbihan Baqli, The Unveiling of Secrets: Diary of a Sufi Master*. Chapel Hill: Parvardigar, 1997.

———. *The Shambhala Guide to Sufism*. Boston: Shambhala, 1997.

———. *Sufism: An Essential Introduction*. Boston: Shambhala, 1997.

———, translator. *Teachings of Sufism*. Boston: Shambhala, 1999.

———. *Words of Ecstasy in Sufism*. Albany: State U of New York P, 1985.

Evans, Dylan. *An Introductory Dictionary of Lacanian Psychoanalysis*. London: Routledge, 1996.

Everett, Dorothy. "The Middle English Prose Psalter of Richard Rolle of Hampole II: The Connexion between Rolle's Version of the Psalter and Earlier English Versions." *Modern Language Review*, vol. 17, no. 4, Oct. 1922, pp. 337–50.

Fackenheim, Emil. "A Treatise on Love by Ibn Sina." *Medieval Studies*, vol. 7, 1945, pp. 208–28.

Fakhry, Majid. *A Short Introduction to Islamic Philosophy, Theology and Mysticism*. Oxford: Oneworld, 1998.

———. "Three Varieties of Mysticism in Islam." *International Journal for Philosophy of Religion*, vol. 2, no. 4, Winter 1971, pp. 193–207.

Farhadi, A. G. Ravan. *Abdullah Ansari of Herat: An Early Sufi Master*. Richmond: Curzon, 1996.

Farina, William. "Arabic Roots." *Chretien de Troyes and the Dawn of Arthurian Romance*. Jefferson: McFarland, 2010. 19–27.

Farmer, Sharon, and Barbara Rosenwein, editors. *Monks and Nuns, Saints and Outcasts*. Ithaca: Cornell University Press, 2000.

Fayzizadah, Taha. *Dar Bārah-i Dāstān-i ʿArifān-i Shaykh Ṣanʿān: Gustardagī-i Dāmanah-i Nufuz-i ān dār Adabīyāt-i Jahān beh Vīzhih dar Adabīyāt-i Fārsī, Turkī va Kurdī Dar Hamiy-i Lahji-hā* [*On the Mystical Story of Shaykh Ṣanʿān: The Extent of its Influence on World Literature, Particularly on Persian, Turkish, and Kurdish Literatures in All Dialects*]. Tabriz: Tabesh, 1986.

Fazeli, Qader. *Farhang-i mużʿī-i adab-i pārsī: Muṣibatnāma va Maẓhar al-ʿajāyib* [*Thematic Dictionary of Persian Literature: Muṣibatnāma* {*The Book of Suffering*} *and Maẓhar al-ʿajāyib* {*The Symbols of Wonder*}]. Tehran, 1374 Sh./1982.

Fienberg, Nona. "Thematics of Value in *The Book of Margery Kempe*." *Modern Philology*, vol. 87, no. 2, Nov. 1989, pp. 132–41.

Ford, Heidi A. "Hierarchical Inversions, Divine Subversions: The Miracles of Rabi'a al- 'Adawiyya." *Journal of Feminist Studies in Religion*, vol. 15, no. 2, Fall 1999, pp. 5–24.

Foucault, Michel. "The Concern for Truth: An Interview with Francois Ewald." *Michel Foucault: Politics, Philosophy, Culture. Interviews and Other Writings*. Edited by Lawrence D. Kritzman, New York, Routledge, 1988. 293–308.

———. *Discipline and Punish: The Birth of the Prison*. Translated by Allan Sheridan, 2nd ed., New York: Vintage, 1995.

———. *The History of Sexuality: The Use of Pleasure*. Translated by Robert Hurley, New York: Vintage, 1990.

———. "Preface to Transgression." *Language, Counter-Memory, Practice*. Edited by Donald F. Bouchard, Ithaca: Cornell UP, 1977. 29–52.

———. "Space, Knowledge, Power." *Power*. Edited by James D. Faubion and translated by Robert Hurley. New York: New Press, 1994. 349–64.

Fradenburg, Aranye L. O. *Sacrifice Your Love: Psychoanalysis, Historicism, Chaucer*. Minneapolis: U of Minnesota P, 2002.

———. "Sovereign Love." *City, Marriage, Tournament: Arts of Rule in Late Medieval Scotland*. Madison: U of Wisconsin P, 1991, pp. 67–83.

Fradenburg, Louise, and Carla Freccero, editors. Introduction. *Premodern Sexualities*. New York: Routledge, 1996, pp. xiii–xiv.

France, Marie de. *Lais*. Edited by A. Ewert, Oxford: Blackwell, 1944.

Friedlander, Shams. *The Whirling Dervishes: Being an Account of the Sufi Order, Known as the Mevlevis, and Its Founder, the Poet and Mystic, Mevlana Jalalu'ddin Rumi*. New York: Macmillan, 1975.

Fries, Maureen. "Female Heroes, Heroines, and Counter-Heroes: Images of Women in Arthurian Tradition." *Arthurian Women: A Casebook*. Edited by Thelma S. Fenster, New York: Garland, 1996. 59–76.

Frye, Richard N. *The Golden Age of Persia: The Arabs in the East*. London: Weidenfeld and Nicholson, 1988.

Fulton, Rachel. *From Judgment to Passion: Devotion to Christ and the Virgin Mary, 800–1200*. New York: Columbia UP, 2002.

Furūzānfar, Badi' al-Zamān. *Aḥādīs-i Masnavī* [*The Traditions of Masnavī*]. Tehran, 1361 Sh./1982.

———. *Sharḥ-i Aḥvāl va Naqd va Taḥlīl-i āsār-i Shaykh Farīd al-Dīn Muḥammad 'Aṭṭār Nishāpūrī*. [*The Biography, Crticism, and Analysis of the Works of Shaykh Farīd al-Dīn Muhammad 'Aṭṭār Nishāpūrī*]. Tehran: Tehran U Publications, 1961–62.

Gage, John. *Color and Culture: Practice and Meaning from Antiquity to Abstraction*. New York: Bulfinch Press, Little Brown, 1993.

al-Ghazzālī, Abu Ḥāmid Muḥammad. *The Alchemy of Happiness*. Armonk: Sharpe, 1991.

———. *The Book of Knowledge: The Revival of Religious Sciences, Book 1*. Translated by Kenneth Honerkamp. Amsterdam: The Fons Vitae al-Ghazali Series, 2016.

———. *Risāla fī taḥqīq ru'yat Allah fī'l-manā'm wa- ru'yat al-nabī.* [*Treatise on Seeing God and the Prophet in the Visible Form*]. Litho. Mecca, n.d.

al-Ghazzālī, Aḥmad ibn Muḥammad. *Sawānih: Inspirations from the World of Pure Spirits. The Oldest Persian Sufi Treatise on Love.* London: KPI; distributed by Routledge and Kegan Paul, 1986.

Gibb, E. J. W. *History of Ottoman Poetry.* London: Gibb Memorial Trust, 1900.

Gilman, Sander L. *Difference and Pathology: The Stereotypes of Sexuality, Race, and Madness.* New York: Cornell UP, 1985.

Gilson, Étienne. *Heloise and Abelard.* U of Michigan P, 1992.

———. *History of Christian Philosophy in the Middle Ages.* New York: Random House, 1955.

Glenn, Cheryl. "Author, Audience, and Autobiography: Rhetorical Technique in *The Book of Margery Kempe.*" *College English*, vol. 54, no. 5, Sept. 1992, pp. 540–53.

Goddard, Hugh. *Christians and Muslims: From Double Standard to Mutual Understanding.* Richmond: Curzon, 1995.

———. *Muslim Perceptions of Christianity.* London: Grey Seal, 1996.

Goitein, Shlomo D. *Jews and Arabs: A Concise History of their Social and Cultural Relations.* Mineola: Dover, 2005

Golb, Norman, editor. *Judaeo-Arabic Studies: Proceedings of the Founding Conference of the Society for Judaeo-Arabic Studies.* London: Routledge, 1997.

Griffith, Sidney H. *The Church in the Shadow of the Mosque: Christians and Muslims in the World of Islam.* Princeton: Princeton UP, 2008.

Hakim, Khalifa Abdul. *The Metaphysics of Rumi.* 1933. Lahore: Ashraf, 1948.

al-Ḥallāj, Manṣūr. *Al-Ḥusayn ibn Manṣūr: Kitāb al-ṭāwasīn* [*Al-Ḥusayn ibn Manṣūr: The Book of T and S* (in reference to the Quran)]. Edited by Louis Massignon, Paris, 1913.

Hamidi, Mehdi. *'Aṭṭār dar Masnavīha-yi guzīdi-yi ū va guzīdi-yi Masnavīha-yi ū* [*'Aṭṭar in his Selected Works and his Selected Works*]. Tehran, 1347 Sh./1968.

Hanaway, William L. "Classical Persian Literature." Special issue, *A Review of the* Encyclopedia Iranica, edited by Abbas Amanat and William L. Hanaway, *Iranian Studies*, vol. 31, nos. 3–4, Summer–Autumn 1998, pp. 543–59.

———. "The Concept of the Hunt in Persian Literature." Special issue, *Persian Carpet Symposium, Boston Museum Bulletin*, vol. 69, nos. 355–56, 1971, pp. 21–69.

Hary, Benjamin, John L. Hayes, and Fred Astren, editors. *Judaism and Islam: Boundaries, Communication and Interaction. Essays in Honor of William M. Brinner.* Leiden: Brill, 2000.

Haskins, Charles Homer. *The Renaissance of the Twelfth Century.* Cambridge: Harvard UP, 1973.

Hastie, William. *The Festival of Spring from the Divan of Jalal ed-Din.* Glasgow: MacLehose, 1903.

Heath, Jennifer. *The Scimitar and the Veil: Extraordinary Women of Islam.* Mahwah: Hidden Spring, 2004.

Hegel, G. W. F. *Phenomenology of Spirit*. Translated by A. V. Miller, Oxford: Oxford UP, 1979.

Hellwarth, Jennifer Wynne. *The Reproductive Unconscious in Medieval and Early Modern England*. Edited by Francis G. Gentry, New York: Routledge, 2002.

Helminski, Camille, and Kabir Helminski. *Rumi: Daylight. A Daybook of Spiritual Guidance*. Boston: Shambhala, 1999.

Herman, Arthur L. *The Problem of Evil and Indian Thought*. Delhi: Motilal Banarsidass, 1976.

Hillenbrand, Carole. *The Crusades: Islamic Perspectives*. Edinburgh: Edinburgh UP, 1999.

Hilton, Walter. *The Scale of Perfection*. Edited by Thomas H. Bestul, Kalamazoo: West Michigan U, 2001.

Hodgson, Phyllis. "Walter Hilton and *The Cloud of Unknowing*: A Problem of Authorship Reconsidered." *Modern Language Review*, vol. 50, no. 4, Oct. 1955, pp. 395–406.

Hoffman, Valerie J. "Oral Traditions as a Source of the Study of Muslim Women: Women in the Sufi Orders." *Beyond the Exotic: Women's Histories in Islamic Societies*. Edited by Amira El-Azhary Sonbol, Syracuse: Syracuse UP, 2005.

Hollywood, Amy. *Sensible Ecstasy: Mysticism, Sexual Difference, and the Demands of History*. Chicago: U of Chicago P, 2002.

———. *The Soul as Virgin Wife*. Notre Dame: U of Notre Dame P, 2001.

Hollywood, Amy, and Patricia Z. Beckman. *The Cambridge Companion to Christian Mysticism*. Cambridge: Cambridge UP, 2012.

Howes, Laura L. "On the Birth of Margery Kempe's Last Child." *Modern Philology*, vol. 90, no. 2, Nov. 1992, pp. 220–25.

Hoyland, Robert G. *Seeing Islam as Others Saw it: A Survey and Evaluation of Christian, Jewish and Zoroastrian Writings on Early Islam*. Princeton: Darwin, 1997.

Hudson, Ann, editor. *The Works of a Lollard Preacher*. Oxford: Oxford UP, 2001.

al-Hujwīrī, ʿAlī ibn ʿUthmān al-Jullābī. *Kashf al-maḥjūb: The Oldest Persian Treatise on Sufism* [*The Revelation of the Veiled: The Oldest Persian Treatise on Sufism*]. Translated by Reynold A. Nicholson, Leiden, 1911.

Hume, David. *Dialogues Concerning Natural Religion*. Cambridge: Cambridge UP, 2007.

Hussey, S. S. "Langland, Hilton, and the Three Lives." *Review of English Studies*, vol. 7, no. 26, April 1956, pp. 132–50.

Huxley, Aldous. *The Perennial Philosophy*. New York: Harper and Row, 1970.

Hyman, Arthur, and James J. Walsh, editors. *Philosophy in the Middle Ages: The Christian, Islamic and Jewish Traditions*. Indianapolis: Hackett, 1983.

Ibn 'Abbad. *Letters on the Sufi Path*. Translated by John Renard, New York: Paulist Press, 1986.

Ibn Iskandar, and Kai Kā'ūs. *A Mirror for Princes: The Qabūs-nāma*. Translated by Reuben Levy, London: Cresset, 1951.

———. *A Mirror for Princes: The Qabūs-nāma*. Edited by Reuben Levy. London: Luzac, 1951.

———. *A Mirror for Princes: The Qabūs-nāma*. Edited by Saeed Nafisi. Tehran: Foroughi, 1963.

Ibn Maymun. *The Guide for the Perplexed*. Charleston: Forgotten Books, 1925.

Ibn Sīnā. *Risāla fi al-'Ishq* [*Treatise on Love*]. Edited by M. A. F. Mehren, Traitres mystiques d'Abou Ali al-Hosain b. Abdallah b. Sina ou d'Avicenne, Fascicule III, Leiden: E. J. Brill, 1899, pp. 1–27.

Ilahi-Ghomshei, Husayn. "Of Scent and Sweetness: 'Aṭṭār's Legacy in Rumi, Shabistari and Hafiz." *'Aṭṭār and the Persian Sufi Tradition: The Art of Spiritual of Flight*. Edited by Leonard Lewisohn and Christopher Shackle, London: I. B. Tauris, 2006, pp. 27–56.

Iqbal, Afzal. *The Life and Work of Jalaluddin Rumi*. London: Octagon, 1956.

Irigaray, Luce. *Speculum of the Other Woman*. Translated by Gillian C. Gill. Ithaca: Cornell UP, 1974.

Izutsu, Toshihiko. *Creation and the Timeless Order of Things: Essays in Islamic Mystical Philosophy*. Ashland: White Cloud, 1994.

Jackson, A. V. W. "The Allegory of the Moths and the Flame, Translated from the *Mantiq at-tayr* of Farid ad-Din 'Attar." *Journal of the American Oriental Society*, vol. 36, 1916, pp. 345–47.

al-Jāhiz, Abū 'Uthmān 'Amr ibn Baḥr ibn Maḥbūb al-Kinā'nī al-Basrī. *Kitāb al-Ḥayawān* [*Book of Animals*]. Edited by A. M. Hārūn, Cairo: n.p., 1938. 7 vols.

Jāmī, Maulānā 'Abd al-Raḥmān. *Nafaḥāt al-uns* [*Breaths of Intimacy*]. Edited by Mahdi Tauhidipur. Tehran: n.p., 1957.

Jansen, Katherine L. "Like a Virgin: The Meaning of the Magdalen for Female Penitents of Later Medieval Italy." *Memoirs of the American Academy in Rome*, vol. 45, 2000, pp. 131–52.

Jantzen, Grace M. "Feminists, Philosophers, and Mystics." *Feminist Philosophy of Religion*. Special issue, edited by Nancy Frankenberry and Marylin Thie, *Hypatia*, vol. 9, no. 4, Autumn 1994, pp. 186–206.

al-Jawzī, Abū al-Faraj. *Talbīs Iblīs* [*The Devil's Delusion*]. 1926. Translated by D. S. Margoliouth. *Islamic Culture*, vol. 12, 1938.

Johnson, Lynn Staley. "The Trope of the Scribe and the Question of Literary Authority in the Works of Julian of Norwich and Margery Kempe." *Speculum*, vol. 66, no. 4, Oct. 1991, pp. 820–38.

Jones, Alan, translator. *The Qur'an*. Cambridge: Gibb Memorial Trust, 2007.

De Jong, Frederick and Bernd Radtke, editors. *Islamic Mysticism Contested: Thirteen Centuries of Controversies and Polemics*. Leiden: Brill, 1996.

Jung, Leo. *Fallen Angels in Jewish, Christian and Mohammedan Literature*. Eugene: Wipf and Stock, 2007.

Kane, Paula M. "'She Offered Herself Up': The Victim Soul and Victim Spirituality in Catholicism." *Church History*, vol. 71, no. 1, March 2002, pp. 80–119.

Kant, Immanuel. *Religion and Rational Theology*. Translated by Allen W. Wood and George di Giovanni, Cambridge: Cambridge UP, 2011.

Karamustafa, Ahmet T. *God's Unruly Friends: Dervish Groups in the Islamic Later Middle Period, 1200–1550*. Salt Lake City: U of Utah P, 1994.

———. *Sufism. The Formative Period*. Berkeley: U of California P, 2007.

Karras, Ruth Mazo, and David Lorenzo Boyd. "'*Ut cum Muliere*': A Male Transvestite Prostitute in Fourteenth-Century London." *Premodern Sexualities*. Edited by Louise Fradenburg and Carla Freccero, pp. 101–16, New York: Routledge, 1996.

Keddie, Nikki R. "Introduction: Deciphering Middle Eastern Women's History." *Women in Middle Eastern History: Shifting Boundaries in Sex and Gender*. Edited by Nikki R. Keddie and Beth Baron, New Haven: Yale UP, 1991, pp. 1–22.

———. *Women in the Middle East: Past and Present*. Princeton: Princeton UP, 2007.

Keiser, George R. "The Mystics and the Early English Printers: The Economics of Devotionalism." *The Medieval Mystical Tradition in England*: *Exeter Symposium IV. Darlington 1987*. Edited by Marion Glasscoe, pp. 9–26, London: Brewer, 1987.

Kelly-Gadol, Joan. *Did Women Have a Renaissance?* Boston: Houghton Mifflin, 1977.

Kermani, Navid. *The Terror of God: ʿAṭṭār, Job and the Metaphysical Revolt*. Cambridge: Polity, 2011.

Keroes, Jo. "Heloise and Abelard: The Lure of the Sexy Mind." *Tales Out of School: Gender, Longing, and the Teacher in Fiction and Film*. Carbondale: Southern Illinois UP, 1999, 17–32.

Keshavarz, Fatemeh. "Flight of the Birds: The Poetic Animating the Spiritual in ʿAṭṭār's *Manṭiq al-ṭayr*." In *ʿAṭṭār and the Persian Sufi Tradition: The Art of Spiritual Flight*. Edited by Leonard Lewisohn and Christopher Shackle, London: I. B. Tauris, 2006, pp. 112–34.

———. *Reading Mystical Lyric: The Case of Jalāl al-Dīn Rumi*. Colombia: U of South Carolina P, 1998.

Khairallah, Asʿad E. *Love, Madness, and Poetry: An Interpretation of the Magnūn Legend*. Beirut: Steiner, Wiesbaden, 1980.

Khanbaghi, Aptin. *The Fire, the Star, and the Cross: Minority Religions in Medieval and Early Modern Iran*. London: I. B. Tauris, 2006.

Khuri, Fuad I. *The Body in Islamic Culture*. London: Saqi, 2001.

Kieckhefer, Richard. *Unquiet Souls: Fourteenth-Century Saints and their Religious Milieu*. Chicago: U of Chicago P, 1987.

Koslowski, Peter, editor. *The Origin and the Overcoming of Evil and Suffering in the World Religions*. Dordrecht: Kluwer, 2001.

Kraemer, David Charles. *Humanism in the Renaissance of Islam: The Cultural Revival during the Buyid Age*. Leiden: Brill, 1992.

Kristeva, Julia. *Desire in Language: A Semiotic Approach to Literature and Art.* Edited by Leon S. Roudiez, New York: Columbia UP, 1980.

———. *New Maladies of the Soul.* Translated by Ross Guberman, New York: Columbia UP, 1995.

———. *Tales of Love.* Translated by Leon S. Roudiez, New York: Columbia UP, 1987.

Lacan, Jacques. *Ecrits: A Selection.* Translated by Alan Sheridan, New York: Norton, 1977.

———. *The Four Fundamental Concepts of Psychoanalysis.* Translated by Alan Sheridan, New York: Norton, 1978.

———. *The Seminar of Jacques Lacan, Book VII: The Ethics of Psychoanalysis 1959–1960.* Edited by Jacques-Alain Miller and translated by Dennis Porter, New York: Norton, 1986.

———. *The Seminar of Jacques Lacan, Book XX: On Feminine Sexuality. The Limits of Love and Knowledge, 1972–1973.* Edited by Jacques-Alain Miller and translated by Bruce Fink, New York: Norton, 1999.

Lakoff, George, and Mark Johnson. *Metaphors We Live By.* 2nd ed., Chicago: U of Chicago P, 2003.

Lala, Chhanganlal. *The Immortal Sufi Triumvirate: Sana'i, 'Attar, Rumi.* Translated by Bankey Behari, Delhi: B. R. Publishing, 1998.

Lambton, Ann K. S. *Continuity and Change in Medieval Persia: Aspects of Administrative, Economic and Social History, 11th–14th Century.* New York: State U of New York P, 1988.

———. "Justice in the Medieval Persian Theory of Kingship." *Studia Islamica*, vol. 17, 1962, pp. 91–119.

Landolt, Hermann. "ʿAṭṭār, Sufism and Ismailism." *ʿAṭṭār and the Persian Sufi Tradition: The Art of Spiritual Flight.* Edited by Leonard Lewisohn and Christopher Shackle, London: I. B. Tauris, 2006. pp. 3–26.

Lawlor, John. "A Note on the Revelations of Julian of Norwich." *Review of English Studies*, vol. 2, no. 7, July 1951, pp. 255–58.

Lawrence, Bruce. *The Qur'an: A Biography.* New York: Atlantic, 2006.

Lazarus-Yafeh, Hava. *Intertwined Worlds: Medieval Islam and Bible Criticism.* Princeton: Princeton UP, 1992.

Lerner, Robert E. "The Image of Mixed Liquids in Late Medieval Mystical Thought." *Church History*, vol. 40, no. 4, Dec. 1971, pp. 397–411.

Lévinas, Emmanuel. *Emmanuel Levinas: Basic Philosophical Writings.* Edited by Adriaan Peperzak, Simon Critchley, and Robert Bernasconi. Bloomington: Indiana UP, 1996.

———. *Totality and Infinity: An Essay on Exteriority.* Translated by Alphonso Lingis. Pittsburgh: Duquesne UP, 1969.

Levy-Rubin, Milka. *Non-Muslims in the Early Islamic Empire: From Surrender to Coexistence.* Cambridge: Cambridge UP, 2011.

Lewis, Franklin D. *Rumi: Past and Present, East and West. The Life, Teaching and Poetry of Jalal al-Din Rumi*. Oxford: Oneworld, 2000.

———. "Sexual Occidentation: The Politics of Conversion, Christian-Love and Boy-Love in ʿAṭṭar." *Iranian Studies*, vol. 42, no. 5, 2009, pp. 693–723.

Lewisohn, Leonard, editor. *Classical Persian Sufism: From its Origins to Rumi*. London: Khaniqanhi Nimatullahi, 1993.

———, editor. *Hafiz and the Religion of Love in Classical Persian Poetry*. New York: I. B. Tauris, 2010.

———, editor. *The Heritage of Sufism: The Legacy of Medieval Persian Sufism*. Oxford: Oneworld, 1999. 2 vols.

———. "Sufi Symbolism in the Persian Hermeneutic Tradition: Reconstructing the Pagoda of ʿAṭṭār's Esoteric Poetics." *ʿAṭṭār and the Persian Sufi Tradition: The Art of Spiritual Flight*. Edited by Leonard Lewisohn and Christopher Shackle, London: I. B. Tauris, 2006, pp. 255–308.

Lings, Martin. *What is Sufism?* Berkeley: U of California P, 1975.

Lochrie, Karma. *Margery Kempe and Translations of the Flesh*. Philadelphia: U of Pennsylvania P, 1994.

Losensky, Paul, translator. *Farid ad-Din ʿAttar's Memorial of God's Friends: Lives and Sayings of Sufis*. [Original title: *Tadhkirat al-awlīyā* {*Memoirs of the Saints*}]. New York: Paulist Press, 2009.

Lubis, H. M. B. "Farid al-Din ʿAttar and Scholarly-Literary Works in Malaysia: Brief Remarks." *Gombak Review: A Biannual Publication of Creative Writing and Critical Comment*, vol. 1, no. 2, 1996, pp. 133–42.

Makdisi, George. *The Rise of Humanism in Classical Islam and the Christian West: With Special Reference to Scholasticism*. Edinburgh: Edinburgh UP, 1990.

al-Makkī, Abū Ṭālib Muḥammad ibn ʿAlī. *Qūt al-qulūb fi muʾamalāt al-Maḥbūb wa waṣf tarīq al-murīd ila maqām al-tawḥīd* [*The Nourishment of Hearts in Dealing with the Beloved and the Description of the Seeker's Way to the Station of Declaring Oneness*]. Cairo: n.p., 1892.

Malamud, Margaret. "Gender and Spiritual Self-Fashioning: The Master-Disciple Relationship in Classical Sufism." *Journal of the American Academy of Religion*, vol. 6, no. 1, Spring 1996, pp. 89– 117.

———. "The Politics of Heresy in Medieval Khurasan: The Karramiyya in Nishapur." *Religion and Society in Islamic Iran during the Pre-Modern Era*. Special issue, edited by Abbas Amanat, *Iranian Studies*, vol. 27, nos. 1–4, 1994, pp. 37–51.

———. "Sufi Organizations and Structures of Authority in Medieval Nishapur." *International Journal of Middle East Studies*, vol. 26, no. 3, Aug. 1994, pp. 427–42.

Maleki, Hurmuz. *Rāz-i Darūn-i Pard-i: Hermeneutic-i Dāstānī-yi Shaykh Ṣanʿān* [*The Hidden Secret: The Hermeneutics of the Shaykh Ṣanʿān Story*]. Tehran: Intishar, 2000.

Marmon, Shaun E., editor. "Domestic Slavery in the Mamluk Empire: A Preliminary Sketch." *Slavery in The Islamic Middle East*. Princeton: Markus Wiener, 1999, pp. 1–23.

Massignon, Louis. *Hallaj: Mystic and Martyr of Islam*. Translated by and edited by Herbert Mason, Princeton: Princeton UP, 1994.

Matter, E. Ann. "My Sister, My Spouse: Woman-Identified Women in Medieval Christianity." *Journal of Feminist Studies in Religion*, vol. 2, no. 2, Fall 1986, pp. 81–93.

McAvoy, Liz H. *Authority and the Female Body in the Writings of Julian of Norwich and Margery Kempe*. Cambridge: Brewer, 2004.

Mechthild of Magdeburg. *The Flowing Light of the Godhead*. Translated by Frank J. Tobin, New York: Paulist, 1998.

Meech, Stanford B., and Hope Emily Allen, editors. *The Book of Margery Kempe*. London: Oxford UP, 1940.

Meier, Fritz. *Baha-i Walad. Acta Iranica* 27. Leiden: Brill, 1989.

———. *Essays on Islamic Piety and Mysticism*. Translated by John O'Kane, with the editorial assistance of Bernd Radtke, Leiden: Brill, 1999.

Meisami, Julie Scott. "Arabic Culture and Medieval European Literature." *Journal of the American Oriental Society*, vol. 111, 1991, pp. 343–51.

———. *Medieval Persian Court Poetry*. New Jersey: Princeton UP, 1987.

———. *Persian Historiography to the End of the Twelfth Century*. Edinburgh: Edinburgh UP, 1999.

———. *Structure and Meaning in Medieval Arabic and Persian Poetry*. London: Routledge, 2003.

Melchert, Christopher. "The Hanabila and the Early Sufis." *Arabica*, vol. 48, no. 3, 2001, pp. 352–67.

———. "Sufis and Competing Movements in Nishapur." *Iran*, vol. 39, 2001, pp. 237–47.

———. "The Transition from Asceticism to Mysticism at the Middle of the Ninth-Century C.E." *Studia Islamica*, vol. 83, 1996, pp. 51–70.

Melville, Charles. "Earthquakes in the History of Nishapur." *Journal of Persian Studies*, vol. 18, 1980, pp. 103–20.

Menocal, María Rosa. *The Arabic Role in Medieval Literary Theory: A Forgotten Heritage*. Philadelphia: U of Pennsylvania P, 2003.

———. *Shards of Love: Exile and the Origins of the Lyric*. Durham: Duke UP, 1994.

Meyvaert, Paul. "The Medieval Monastic Claustrum." *Gesta*, vol. 12, nos. 1–2, 1973, pp. 53–59.

Mile, Margaret. "Vision: The Eye of the Body and the Eye of the Mind in Saint Augustines *De trinitate* and *Confessions*." *Journal of Religion*, vol. 63, no. 2, 1983, pp. 125–42.

Mir, Mustansir. *Understanding the Islamic Scripture: A Study of Selected Passages from the Quran*. New York: Pearson, 2008.

Mir Ansari, Ali. *Kitābshināsī-yi Shaykh Farīd al-Dīn ʿAṭṭār-i Nishāpūrī* [*Bibliography of the Works of Shaykh Farīd-al-Dīn ʿAṭṭār-i Nishāpūrī*]. Tehran: Society for the Appreciation of Cultural Works and Dignitaries, 2004.

Moayyad, Heshmat, and Franklin Lewis, translators. *The Colossal Elephant and His Spiritual Feats: Shaykh Ahmad-e Jam. The Life and Legend of a Popular Sufi Saint of 12th-Century Iran*. Costa Mesa: Mazda, 2004.

Mojaddedi, Jawid A. *Beyond Dogma: Rumi's Teachings on Friendship with God and Early Sufi Theories*. Oxford: Oxford UP, 2011.

———. *The Biographical Tradition in Sufism: The Tabaqāt Genre from al-Sulami to Jami*. Richmond: Curzon, 2001.

Mooney, Catherine M., editor. *Gendered Voices: Medieval Saints and Their Interpreters*. Philadelphia: U of Pennsylvania P, 1999.

Morgan, David O. *Medieval Persia 1040–1797*. London: Longman, 1988.

Muir, Laurence. "The Influence of the Rolle and Wyclifite Psalters upon the Psalter of the Authorized Version." *Modern Language Review*, vol. 30, no. 3, July 1935, pp. 302–10.

Murata, Sachiko, and William C. Chittick. *The Vision of Islam*. New York: Paragon, 1994.

Myers, Michael D. "A Fictional-True Self: Margery Kempe and the Social Reality of the Merchant Elite of King's Lynn." *Albion: A Quarterly Journal Concerned with British Studies*, vol. 31, no. 3, Autumn 1999, pp. 377–94.

Nafisi, Saeed. *Zindigīnāma Shaykh Farīd-al-Dīn ʿAṭṭār-i Nishāpūrī* [*The Biography of Shaykh Farīd-al-Dīn ʿAṭṭār -i Nishāpūrī*]. Tehran: Eqbal, 2002.

Najmabadi, Afsaneh. *Women with Mustaches and Men without Beards: Gender and Sexual Anxiety of Iranian Modernity*. Berkeley: U of California P, 2005.

Nashat, Guity, and Judith E. Tucker, editors. *The Middle East and North Africa: Restoring Women to History*. Bloomington: Indiana UP, 1999.

Nasr, Seyyed Hossein. "Self-Awareness and Ultimate Selfhood." *Religious Studies*, vol. 13, no. 3, Sept. 1977, pp. 319–25.

———. "Shi'ism and Sufism: Their Relationship in Essence and in History." *Religious Studies*, vol. 6, no. 3, Sept. 1970, pp. 229–42.

———. "The Sufi Master as Exemplified in Persian Sufi Literature." *Iran*, vol. 5, 1967, pp. 35–40.

Neale, Harry S. "The Zoroastrian in ʿAttar's *Tadkiratu'l-awliya'*." *Middle Eastern Literatures*, vol. 12, no. 2, 2009, pp. 137–56.

Newman, Barbara. *God and the Goddesses: Vision, Poetry, and Belief in the Middle Ages*. Philadelphia: U of Pennsylvania P, 2003.

———. "'What Did it Mean to Say I Saw?' The Clash between Theory and Practice in Medieval Visionary Culture." *Speculum*, vol. 80, no. 1, 2005, pp. 1–43.

Nicholson, Reynold A. *The Mathnawi of Jalalu'ddin Rumi*. Cambridge: Gibb Memorial Trust, 1926. Books 1–6.

———. *The Mystics of Islam*. London: Bell, 1914.

———. *Rumi: Poet and Mystic*. Cambridge: Gibb Memorial Trust, 1926.

———, translator. *Tadhkirat al-awlīyā* [*Memoirs of the Saints*]. By Farīd al-Dīn ʿAttar, London, 1905.

Nietzsche, Friedrich. *The Birth of Tragedy*. 1876. Edited by Michael Tanner and translated Shaun Whiteside, London: Penguin, 1993.

———. *Daybreak: Thoughts on the Prejudices of Morality*. Translated by R. J. Hollingdale, Cambridge: Cambridge UP, 1997.

———. *Thus Spoke Zarathustra: A Book for Everyone and No One*. Translated by R. J. Hollingdale, London: Penguin, 1961.

Nizāmī Ganjavī. *Haft Peykar: A Medieval Persian Romance*. Translated by Julie Scott Meisami, Oxford: Oxford UP, 1995.

———. *The Story of Layla and Majnun*. Translated and edited by R. Gelpke, Boulder: Shambhala; distributed by Random House, 1978.

Norwich, Julian. *The Showings of Julian of Norwich*. Edited by Denise N. Baker, New York: Norton, 2005.

Nuth, Joan M. *God's Lovers in an Age of Anxiety*. New York: Orbis, 2001.

Olney, James, editor. *Autobiography: Essays Theoretical and Critical*. Princeton: Princeton UP, 1980.

Ormsby, Eric L. *Theodicy in Islamic Thought: The Dispute over al-Ghazali's "Best of All Possible Worlds."* Princeton: Princeton UP, 1984.

Owen, H. P. "Christian Mysticism: A Study in Walter Hilton's *The Ladder of Perfection*." *Religious Studies*, vol. 7, no. 1, Mar. 1971, pp. 31–42.

Ozmont, Steven. *The Age of Reformation 1250–1500: An Intellectual and Religious History of Late Medieval and Reformation Europe*. New Haven: Yale UP, 1980.

Petroff, Elizabeth. *Body and Soul: Essays on Medieval Women and Mysticism*. New York: New York UP, 1994.

———, editor. *Medieval Women's Visionary Literature*. New York: Oxford UP, 1986.

Pizan, Christine. *The Book of the City of Ladies*. Translated by Earl Jeffrey Richards, New York: Persea, 1982.

Plato. *Phaedrus*. Translated by Benjamin Jowett, Boston: Forgotten Books, 2008.

Powell, Raymon A. "Margery Kempe: An Exemplar of Late Medieval English Piety." *Catholic Historical Review*, vol. 89, no. 1, Jan. 2003, pp. 1–23.

Purnamdarian, Taqi. *The Vision of Sīmurgh: ʿAṭṭār's Poetry, Mysticism and Thought*. Tehran: Institute for Humanities and Cultural Studies, 2007.

Pyle, Howard. *The Story of Sir Launcelot and his Companions*. New York: Scribner, 1907.

al-Qushayrī, Abū al-Qāsim ʿAbd al-Karīm ibn al-Hawazin. *al-Risalā al-qushayriyya* [*Qushayrī's Epistle on Sufism*]. Edited by Abd al-Halīm Maḥmūd and Maḥmūd b. al-Sharif, Cairo: Dar al-Kutub al-Hadītha, 1966.

———. *al-Risalā fī ʿilm al-Taṣawwuf* [*Qushayrī's Epistle on Sufism*]. Cairo: n.p., 1951.

Radice, Betty, translator. *The Letters of Abelard and Heloise*. Baltimore: Penguin, 1974.

Rashdall, Hastings. *The Universities of Europe in the Middle Ages*. Edited by F. M. Powicke and A. B. Emden, 2nd ed., Oxford: Oxford UP, 1895.

Reinert, B. "ʿAṭṭār, Sheikh Farīd-al-Dīn." *Encyclopedia Iranica*, vol. 3, no. 1, 1987, pp. 20–25.

Richards, Jeffrey. *Sex, Dissidence and Damnation*. New York: Routledge, 1990.

Rippin, Andrew. "Desiring the Face of God: The Qu'ranic Symbolism of Personal Responsibility." *Literary Structures of Religious Meaning in the Qur'ān*. Edited by Issa J. Boullata, Richmond: Curzon, 2000, pp. 117–24.

Ritter, Hellmut. *The Ocean of the Soul: Man, The World, and God in the Stories of Farid-al-Din ʿAṭṭār*. Translated by John O'Kane and edited by Bernd Radtke, Leidenn: Brill, 2003.

Roded, Ruth. *Women in Islamic Biographical Collections: From Ibn Saʿd to* Who's Who. Boulder: Rienner, 1994.

Rolle, Richard. *The English Writings*. Translated by Rosamund S. Allen, Mahwah, NJ: Paulist, 1988.

Rolle, Richard, and M. Deanesly. "The 'Incendium Amoris' of Richard Rolle and St. Bonaventura." *English Historical Review*, vol. 29, no. 113, Jan. 1914, pp. 98–101.

Ross, Ellen M. "Spiritual Experience and Women's Autobiography: The Rhetoric of Selfhood in *The Book of Margery Kempe*." *Journal of the American Academy of Religion*, vol. 59, no. 3, Autumn 1991, pp. 527–46.

Ross, Robert C. "Oral Life, Written Text: The Genesis of *The Book of Margery Kempe*." *Medieval Narrative Special Number*. Special issue, edited by Andrew Gurr and Phillipa Hardman, *Yearbook of English Studies*, vol. 22, 1992, pp. 226–37.

El-Rouayheb, Khaled. *Before Homosexuality in the Arab-Islamic World: 1500–1800*. Chicago: U of Chicago P, 2005.

Rouhi, Layla. "The Medieval Near-Eastern Go-Between." *Meditation and Love: A Study of the Medieval Go-Between in Key Romance and Near-Eastern Texts*. Leiden: Brill, 1999.

Rubin, Miri. "A Decade of Studying Medieval Women, 1987–1997." *History Workshop Journal*, vol. 46, Autumn 1998, pp. 213–39.

Rypka, Jan. *History of Iranian Literature*. Dordrecht, Reidel, 1968.

Sade, Marquis de. *Philosophy in the Bedroom*. Translated by Richard Seaver and Austryn Wainhouse, New York: Grove, 1971.

Said, Edward. *Reflections on Exile and Other Essays*. Harvard UP, 2000.

Samir, Samir Khalil, and Jorgen S. Nielsen. *Christian Arabic Apologetics during the Abbasid Period (750–1258)*. Leiden: Brill, 1994.

Saremi, Sohelia. *Musṭalaḥāt-i ʿirfānī wa mafāhīm-i barjista dar zabān-i ʿAṭṭār* [*Mystical Terminology and Important Concepts in ʿAṭṭār's Language*]. Tehran: n.p., 1373 Sh./1994.

Sattari, Jalal. *Pizhūhishī dar qiṣa-i shaykh-i Ṣanʿān va dukhtar-i tarsā* [*A Study of the Story of Sheikh Ṣanʿān and the Christian Girl*]. Tehran: Markaz, 1999.

Saunders, Corinne. "Love and Loyalty in Middle English Romance." *Writings on Love in the English Middle Ages*. Edited by Helen Cooney, New York: Palgrave Macmillan, 2006, pp. 45–62.

Scala, Elizabeth. "Desire in the Canterbury Tales: Sovereignty and Mastery between the Wife and Clerk." *Studies in the Age of Chaucer*, vol. 31, 2009, pp. 81–108.

Scarry, Elaine. *The Body in Pain: The Making and Unmaking of the World*. Oxford: Oxford UP, 1987.

Scattergood, John. *Occasions for Writing: Essays on Medieval and Renaissance Literature, Politics and Society*. Dublin: Four Courts, 2010.

———. "The Unequal Scales of Love: Love and Social Class in Andreas Capellanus's *De Amore* and Some Later Texts." *Writings on Love in the English Middle Ages*. Edited by Helen Cooney, New York: Palgrave Macmillan, 2006, pp. 63–80.

Schimmel, Annemarie. *As Through a Veil: Mystical Poetry in Islam*. New York: Columbia UP, 1982.

———. *Mystical Dimensions of Islam*. Chapel Hill: U of North Carolina P, 1975.

———. "Some Aspects of Mystical Prayer in Islam." *Die Welt des Islams*, new ser., vol. 2, no. 2, 1952, pp. 112–25.

———. *The Triumphal Sun: A Study of the Works of Jalāloddin Rumi*. London: East-West, 1980.

Sells, Michael, editor and translator. *Early Islamic Mysticism: Sufi, Qur'an, Mi'raj, Poetic and Theological Writings*. New York: Paulist, 1996.

Sells, Michael, and James Webb. "Lacan and Bion: Psychoanalysis and the Mystical Language of Unsaying." *Theory and Psychology*, vol. 5, no. 2, 1995, pp. 195–215.

Seyed-Gohrab, Ali Asghar. *Laylī and Majnūn: Love, Madness and Mystic Longing in Nizāmī's Epic Romance*. Leiden: Brill, 2003.

Shabistarī, Maḥmūd. *Gulshan-i rāz* [*The Garden of Mystery*]. Edited by Samad Muvahhid, n.p.: Sirang, 1990.

Shafii Kadkani, Mohammad Reza. *Zabūr-i Pārsī: Nigāhī be Zindigī va Ghazalhāy-i 'Aṭṭār* [*Persian Scriptures: A Study of the Life and Lyrics of 'Aṭṭār*]. Tehran: n.p., 1387 Sh./1999.

Shah, Indries. *The Sufis*. New York: Doubleday, 1964.

Shamisa, Sirus. *Shāhidbāzī dar adabīyāt-i Fārsī* [*Pederasty or the Philosophy of Gazing at the Beauty of Young Men in Persian Literature*]. Tehran: Rāmīn, 2002.

Sharma, Sunil. *Amir Khusraw: The Poet of Sultans and Sufis*. Oxford: Oneworld, 2005.

———. "The Sufi-Poet-Lover as Martyr: Aṭṭār and Hāfiz in Persian Poetic Traditions." *Martyrdom in Literature: Visions of Death and Meaningful Suffering in Europe and the Middle East from Antiquity to Modernity*. Edited by Friederike Pannewick, Wiesbaden: Reichert, 2004. pp. 237–43.

Sipahsalar, Faridun. *Risāla dar Aḥvāl-i Mulānā Jalāl al-Dīn Rūmī* [*A Treatise on The Biography of Maulānā Jalāl al-Dīn Rūmī*]. Edited by Badi' al-Zamān Furūzānfar, Tehran 1325 Sh./1946.

Sirvatian, Bihruz. *Ṭanz va Ramz dar Ilāhī-nāma* [*Irony and Sarcasm in Ilāhī-nāma*]. Tehran: Sureh Mehr, 2006.

Smith, Margaret . *The Persian Mystic: ʿAṭṭār*. London: Murray, 1932.

———. *Rābiʿa the Mystic and Her Fellow-Saints in Islam*. Cambridge: Cambridge UP, 1984.

———. *Studies in Early Mysticism in the Near and Middle East*. Amsterdam: Philo, 1973.

———. *The Way of the Mystics: The Early Christian Mystics and the Rise of the Sufi*. London: Sheldon, 1976.

Spivak, Gayatri Chakravorty. "Can the Subaltern Speak?" *Marxism and the Interpretation of Culture*. Edited by Cary Nelson and Lawrence Grossberg, Chicago: U of Illinois P, 1988. 271–313.

Staines, David, translator and editor. *The Complete Works of Chretien de Troyes*. Bloomington: Indiana UP, 1993.

Staley, Lynn, editor and translator. *The Book of Margery Kempe*. New York: Norton, 2001.

Stallybrass, Peter, and Allon White. *The Politics and Poetics of Transgression*. Ithaca: Cornell UP, 1986.

Star, Jonathan. *Rumī: In the Arms of the Beloved*. New York: Penguin, 1997.

Stark, Rodney. "Upper Class Asceticism: Social Origins of Ascetic Movements and Medieval Saints." *Review of Religious Research*, vol. 45, no. 1, Sept. 2003, pp. 5–19.

Stehling, Thomas. translator and editor. *Medieval Latin Poems of Male Love and Friendship*. New York: Garland, 1984.

Steiner, Emily. *Documentary Culture and the Making of Medieval English Literature*. Cambridge: Cambridge UP, 2003.

Stiefel, Tina. *The Intellectual Revolution in Twelfth-Century Europe*. London: Croom Helm, 1985.

Stroumsa, Sarah. *Freethinkers of Medieval Islam: Ibn al-Rawandi, Abu Bakr al-Razi, and their Impact on Islamic Thought*. Leiden: Brill, 1999.

al-Sulamī, Abū ʿAbd al-Raḥmān. *Early Sufi Women: Dhikr an-Niswa al- Mutaʿ abbidāt as-Sūfiyyāt*. Edited and translated by Rkia Elaroui Cornell. Louisville: Fons Vitae, 1999.

Sultan Walad. *Waladnāma*. Edited by Jalal Huma'i. Tehran, 1315 Sh./1936.

Thackston, W. M. *Signs of the Unseen: The Discourses of Jalaluddin Rumi*. Boston: Shambhala, 1999.

Thompson, Augustine. "Hildegard of Bingen on Gender and the Priesthood." *Church History*, vol. 63, no. 3, Sept. 1994, pp. 349–64.

Totosy de Zepetnek, Steven. "Comparative Cultural Studies and the Study of Central European Culture: Theory and Application." *Comparative Central European Culture*. Edited by Steven Totosy de Zepetnek, West Lafayette: Purdue UP, 2002. pp. 1–32.

Touraj, Mahdi. *Rumi and the Hermeneutics of Eroticism*. Leiden: Brill, 2007.

Triggs, Tony D., translator. *The Book of Margery Kempe: The Autobiography of the Madwoman of God*. Liguori: Triumph, 1995.

Trimingham, J. Spencer. *The Sufi Orders of Islam*. Oxford: Oxford UP, 1971.

Tritton, A. S. *The Caliphs and their Non-Muslim Subjects: A Critical Study of the Covenant of 'Umar*. London: Cass, 1970.

Uhlman, Diana R. "The Comfort of Voice, the Solace of Script: Orality and Literacy in *The Book of Margery Kempe*." *Studies in Philology*, vol. 91, no. 1, Winter 1994, pp. 50–69.

Vahdat, Salih. *Khaudshinākhtigī: rivāyatī dīgar az dāstān-i ʿārifānīy-i Shaykh Ṣanʿān* [*Know Thyself: Another Interpretation of the Story of Shaykh Ṣanʿān*]. Tehran: Ketab-i Zaman, 1999.

Varisco, Daniel Martin. "Metaphors and Sacred History: The Genealogy of Muhammad and the Arab Tribe." *Anthropological Analysis and Islamic Texts*. Special issue, edited by Daniel Martin Marisco, *Anthropological Quarterly*, vol. 68, no. 3, July 1995, pp. 139–56.

de Vitray-Meyerovitch, Eva. *Rumi and Sufism*. Sausalito: Post-Apollo, 1987.

Voaden, Rosalynn. *God's Words, Women's Voices: The Discernment of Spirits in the Writing of Late-Medieval Women Visionaries*. Woodbridge: York Medieval Press, 1999.

Waardenburg, Jacques, editor. *Muslim Perceptions of Other Religions: A Historical Survey*. New York: Oxford UP, 1999.

Wach, Joachim. "Spiritual Teachings in Islam: A Study." *Journal of Religion*, vol. 28, no. 4, Oct. 1948, pp. 263–80.

Wallace, John R. "Romantic Entreaty in *The Kagero Diary* and *The Letters of Abelard and Heloise*." *Crossing the Bridge: Comparative Essays on Medieval European and Heian Japanese Women Writers*. Edited by Barbara Stevenson and Cynthia Ho, New York: Palgrave, 2000, pp. 117–32.

———. *Muslims and Others: Relations in Context*. Berlin: de Gruyter, 2003.

Warren, Nancy Bradley. *Women of God and Arms: Female Spirituality and Political Conflict, 1380–1600*. Philadelphia: U of Pennsylvania P, 2005.

Wasserstrom, Steven. *Between Muslim and Jew: The Problem of Symbiosis under Early Islam*. Princeton: Princeton UP, 1995.

Watkins, Renée Neu. "Two Women Visionaries and Death: Catherine of Siena and Julian of Norwich." *Numen*, vol. 30, no. 2, Dec. 1983, pp. 174–98.

Watson, Nicholas. "The Composition of Julian of Norwich's Revelation of Love." *Speculum*, vol. 68, no. 3 1993, pp. 637–83.

———. "Visions of Inclusion: Universal Salvation and Vernacular Theology in Pre-Reformation England." *Journal of Medieval and Early Modern Studies*, vol. 27, no. 2, 1997, pp. 145–87.

Weigand, Hermann J. *Three Chapters on Courtly Love in Arthurian France and Germany: Lancelot—Andreas Capellanus—Wolfram von Eschenbach's Parzival*. New York: AMS, 1966.

Wensinck, A. J. *The Muslim Creed: Its Genesis and Historical Development*. London: Cass, 1965.

Wiethaus, Ulrike. "Sexuality, Gender, and the Body in Late Medieval Women's Spirituality: Cases from Germany and the Netherlands." *Journal of Feminist Studies in Religion*, vol. 7, no. 1, Spring 1991, pp. 35–52.

Williams, Tara. *Inventing Womanhood: Gender and Language in Later Middle English Writing*. Columbus: Ohio State UP, 2011.

Windeatt, Barry, editor. *The Book of Margery Kempe*. Cambridge: Brewer, 2004.

———. "Julian of Norwich and Her Audience." *Review of English Studies*, vol. 28, no. 109, Feb. 1977, pp. 1–17.

Wolcott Robbins, Harry. "An English Version of St. Edmund's *Speculum*, Ascribed to Richard Rolle." *PMLA*, vol. 40, no. 2, June 1925, pp. 240–51.

Yaghoobi, Claudia. "Against the Current: Farīd-al-Dīn ʿAṭṭār's Diverse Voices." *Persian Literary Studies Journal*, vol. 1, no. 1, 2012, pp. 87–109.

———. "Sexual Trauma and Spiritual Experiences: Rābiʿa al-A'dawiyya and Margery Kempe." *Persian Literary Studies Journal*, vol. 3, no. 4, 2014, pp. 73–92.

———. "Subjectivity in ʿAṭṭār's Shaykh Ṣan'ān Story in *The Conference of the Birds*." *Comparative Literature and Culture*, vol. 16, no. 1, 2014, https://doi .org/10.7771/1481-4374.2425.

Yarshater, Ehsan. "The Theme of Wine-Drinking and the Concept of the Beloved in Early Persian Poetry." *Studia Islamica*, vol. 13, 1960, pp. 43–53.

Ye'or, Bat. *The Decline of Eastern Christianity under Islam: From Jihad to Dhimmitude*. Translated by Miriam Kochan and David Littman, Madison: Fairleigh Dickinson UP, 1996.

Zaehner, R. C. "Mysticism without Love." *Religious Studies*, vol. 10, no. 3, Sept. 1974, pp. 257–64.

Zargar, Cyrus. *Sufi Aesthetics: Beauty, Love, and the Human Form in the Writings of Ibn 'Arabi and 'Iraqi*. Columbia: U of South Carolina P, 2011.

Zarrinkub, ʿAbd al- Husayn. *Arzish-i Mīrās-i Ṣūfīya* [*The Value of the Sufi Heritage*]. Tehran: Amir Kabir, 2007.

———. *Daftar-i Ayyām: Majmūah-i Guftār'hā, andīshah'hā va Justijū'hā* [*A Book of the Days: A Collection of Sayings, Thoughts, and Researches*]. Tehran: Ilmi and Moin, 1989.

———. *Ḥikāyat-i Hamchinān Bāqī* [*The Forever Story*]. Tehran: Sukhan, 2000–01.

———. *Justijū dar Taṣawwuf-i Irān* [*A Study of Mysticism in Iran*]. Tehran: Amir Kabir, 1984–85.

———. "Persian Sufism in its Historical Perspective." *Persian Sufism in Its Historical Perspective*. Special issue, edited by Ali Banuazizi, *Iranian Studies*, vol. 3, nos. 3–4, Summer–Autumn 1970, pp. 139–220.

———. *Rūzigārān* [*Those Days and Times*]. Tehran: Sukhan, 1997. 2 vols.

———. *Ṣidā-yi Bāl-i Sīmurgh: Darbār-i Zindigī vā Andīshi-yi ʿAṭṭār* [*The Voice of Simurgh's Wings: On the Life and Thought of ʿAṭṭār*]. Tehran: Sukhan, 2008.

———. *Tārīkh-i Irān bad az Islām* [*The History of Iran after Islam*]. Tehran: Idarah-i Kull-i Nigarish-i Vizarat-i Amusish va Parvarish, 1964–65.

Ze'evi, Dror. *Producing Desire: Changing Sexual Discourse in the Ottoman Middle East, 1500– 1900*. Berkeley: U of California P, 2006.

Žižek, Slavoj. *For They Know Not What They Do: Enjoyment as a Political Factor*. 2nd ed., London: Verso, 2002.

Zwanzig, Rebekah. "Why Must God Show Himself in Disguise? A Look at the Role of the Mirror in 'Aṭṭar's *The Conference of the Birds*." *Disguise, Deception, Trompe-L'oeil: Interdisciplinary Perspectives*. Edited by Leslie Boldt-Irons, Corrado Federici, and Ernesto Virgulti, New York: Peter Lang, 2009, pp. 273–99.

Author's Profile

Claudia Yaghoobi is a Roshan Institute Assistant Professor in Persian Studies in the Department of Asian Studies at the University of North Carolina, Chapel Hill. She teaches courses on Middle Eastern and Persian literature. Yaghoobi's recent publications include "Yusuf's Queer Beauty in Persian Cultural Productions," *Comparatist* (2016); "Socially Peripheral, Symbolically Central: Sima in Behrouz Afkhami's *Showkaran*," *Journal of Asian Cinema* (2016); "Subjectivity in ʿAṭṭār's Shaykh Ṣan'ān Story in *The Conference of the Birds*," *CLCWeb: Comparative Literature and Culture* (2014); and "Sexual Trauma and Spiritual Experience: Rābiʿa al-ʿAdawiyya and Margery Kempe," *Persian Literary Studies Journal* (2014).

Index

Ābādān, 18
Abbasid caliphate and empire, 19–20, 48, 55–56, 96, 127; Sufism and, 20, 27
Abbott, H. Porter, on reductionism, 3–4
ʿAbd al-Malik, al-Walīd ibn, 17, 18, 19
ʿAbd al-Wāḥid ibn Zayd, 18, 61
Abelard, Peter, 142–44, 146, 147–48; life and career of, 125; students of, 80; *The Story of His Misfortunes*, 125, 135, 136, 147
Abelard and Heloise story, 12, 13, 125, 126, 135–36, 142–44, 147–48, 149; compared to Shaykh Ṣanʿān and the Christian Girl story, 125, 135–36
abject feelings, 131, 135, 139; fascination with other and, 144; of Margery Kempe, 10, 46, 57, 59
Abū Bakr, 16
Abū Ḥamza, Muḥammad ibn Ibrāhīm, 73
Abū Yaḥyā of Merv, 20
Adam, 87, 152; creation of, 15, 26, 103; transgression of, 1
al-ʿAdawiyya, Rābiʿa, 151; as ascetic, 49; celibacy of, 50, 60, 62; compared to Margery Kempe, 10, 45, 46–47, 55, 60, 64, 65–66, 68–70; as convert, 45; crosses gender boundaries, 60–64; as female Sufi, 23, 48, 152; al-Ḥasan al-Baṣrī and, 51–52, 60, 61; mysticism of, 10, 46, 47, 57, 62; religiosity of, 56; sexual trauma of, 55–57, 62; spirituality of, 48–52; in *Tadhkirat al-awlīyā*, 45–47, 50–52, 55, 56–57, 60–64, 66–67; unites with divine, 61, 66–67
adultery, 12, 97, 99, 101
aesthetics, 38, 75, 99
Afary, Janet, 55–56, 74–75
Afghanistan, 71
affect, affection, 11, 79, 82, 90, 111, 135, 143; affective piety and, 53
Aflakī, Shams al-Dīn Aḥmad, 49
Ahmed, Leila, 52, 62
ʿAʿisha, 50, 51
Alastu, 15
Alcibiades, 79
Alcuin, 80
Alexandria, 17
ʿAlī ibn Abī Ṭālib, 154
ʿAlīd, 154
allegory, 97, 129; in ʿAṭṭār's works, 5, 24, 25, 112, 124, 151
Almond, Ian, *Sufism and Deconstruction*, 4
anchoresses, 46, 53, 65
anthropology, 5
Antioch, 17
Aphraates, 62
apocalypse: as Christian literary genre, 19
Apollo, 38–39

apostasy, 127
Arabian Peninsula, 99; Christians in, 127
Arabic language and literature, 5, 11, 17, 19–20
Arab tribes, 16, 45, 96, 97; conquests by, 47, 48
Aristotle, 20, 58
art, 3, 7: duality of, 38–39; medieval European, 78
Arthurian legend, 97. *See also* Chrétien de Troyes; Guinevere; King Arthur; Lancelot
Arundel, Thomas, 55, 65
asceticism, ascetics, 12, 61, 99; Christians and, 16, 79; early Sufis and, 15, 18–19, 26; in *Manṭiq al-ṭayr*, 158–59; mysticism vs., 27, 79, 129–38, 145, 147; Prophet Muḥammad and, 15; Rābiʿa al-ʿAdawiyya and, 45; Shaykh Ṣanʿān and, 124, 129, 130
Asrār-nāma (*The Book of Secrets*) (by ʿAṭṭār), 30
ʿAṭṭār Nishāpūrī, Farīd al-Dīn: characters of, 3, 5, 6, 9, 23, 124; in dialogue with Foucault, 5, 11, 13, 42–43,, 72, 140, 148–49, 151; gender and, 47, 49, 52, 69; homoerotic narratives of, 71–72, 81–92; hunting metaphor and, 80; ideology of, 5; ʿishq and, 22; life of, 9; living texts of works of, 160; love and, 2, 28–29, 103, 118, 126, 129–30, 145, 148, 159; love narratives of, 95, 123, 151; master of, 26; as medieval Persian Sufi poet, 1, 8; nonconformity of, 13, 72, 153; pilgrimage to Mecca of, 26; poetry of, 5, 9, 10–11, 22, 23–25, 72, 92, 96, 99, 103, 104–5, 113, 120, 128; puns of, 24, 25; queering of, 154; scholarship on, 4, 5, 7; spirituality of, 3, 8, 9, 21–22, 26, 30; spiritual stories of, 24; Sufism and, 9, 25–26; tolerance of, 155–56; as transgressor, 13, 70, 153; *Vīs and Rāmīn,* references of, 77; works of, 15–30. *See also titles of ʿAṭṭār's works*
Avicenna. *See* Ibn (Abū Alī) Sīnā
Ayāz, Malik: career of, 71; as character type in Persian literature, 5; Sultan Maḥmūd of Ghazna's same-sex relationship with, 10–11, 71, 72, 81–92, 93

bachchabāzī, 76
Baghdad, 20, 26, 101, 123
Balkh, 30
Baqlī, Rūzbihān, 73
Basra, 45, 55, 61, 97
Bataille, Georges, 1, 31, 39, 40; *Eroticism: Death and Sensuality*, 36–37, 39; on law, 38; *L'Histoire de l'oeil* (*The Story of the Eye*), 33–36; transgression and limit and, 5, 10, 33
Bayat, Mojdeh, on *Ilāhī-nāma*, 24
beatific vision, 9, 21
beauty: ancient ideal of, 78; contemplation of beautiful objects and, 73; divine, 2, 3, 9, 21, 22, 62, 73, 76, 99, 103, 115, 129, 130, 151; feminine, 101, 103, 134; moral, 104; *shāhidbāzī* and, 11, 71, 72–81
beloved, 86, 111, 116; ʿAṭṭār and, 126; beholding, 85; divine, 105, 112, 138; humility and, 84; lover and, 90, 104, 112–13, 114; as metaphorical divine, 97; other as, 92; in Persian literature, 80, 104; sacrifice for, 138–39; scent of, 104–5; ultimate, 93; union with heavenly, 118–20; young boy as symbol for, 81
Beckman, Patricia, 62
Bernard of Clairvaux, 58, 79
Bible: commentary on, 19; Latin, 65; Margery Kempe and, 54, 65; Old Testament, 21, 140; Song of Songs, 129; in vernacular, 53, 65

birds, in *Manṭiq al-ṭayr*, 24–25, 123
blasphemy, 124, 146
body, bodies, 62, 81, 123; Bataille and, 37; of beloved, 83–85, 89–90; boys', 75, 80; fallen, 40; Lacan and, 68; metaphor and, 129; reality and, 153; *tan*, 91; transcending, 47; women's, 47, 49, 56, 57–58, 59, 64, 68, 70
Bokht, Isho, 20
boundaries: Apollonian perspective of, 38; artificial, 2; in ʿAṭṭār's works, 42; Bataille on, 33–34; social, 12; transgression of, 1, 29, 92
boundary crossing: in ʿAṭṭār's works, 25, 85, 87, 92, 106; Foucault and, 5, 41, 92; by Rābiʿa al-ʿAdawiyya, 47, 60–64; by Margery Kempe, 47, 54, 60, 64–66. *See also* transgression of boundaries
Bourdieu, Pierre, on groups, 65–66
Boyd, David, 81
Boyle, John Andrew, 23
Bridget of Sweden, 54
Brison, Susan, 57
Brunham, John, 53
bullfights, 35
Burger, Glenn, *Queering the Middle Ages*, 154
Buthayna, 97
Butler, Judith, 5, 43, 153
Byzantine Empire, 16–17, 127

Caister, Richard, 55
Campbell, Joseph, 143
Canterbury, 65
Capellanus, Andreas, 116; *Andreas Capellanus On Love* (*De Amore*), 100, 101, 104
catamite, catamites (*mukhannas̲*), 64, 154–55
celibacy, 45; of European clergy, 81, 125; female, 47; of Margery Kempe, 60, 64; of Rābiʿa al-ʿAdawiyya, 50, 60, 62
chastity, 53, 55, 64, 97, 100–101, 104
Chewning, Susannah, 70
childbirth, Margery Kempe and, 10, 46, 57, 58
Chrétien de Troyes: *Cheavalier de la charrete* (*Knight of the Cart*), 98; *The Romance of Lancelot and Guinevere*, 95, 97, 100, 104, 110–11, 114, 117; plot of, 97–98
Christian Child, trope of (*tarsā-bachcha*), 12, 127, 128–29, 132
Christian girl, Shaykh Ṣanʿān's, 12, 124; conversion of, 126, 136–37; death of, 136, 137; requests of, 139–41; love of, 131–32; as symbol of heavenly love, 124, 130–31
Christianity, Christians, 20; asceticism in, 16; conversion to, 124, 125, 127, 128, 139; cross and, 17, 18, 127; God appearing as human in, 21–22; Holy Communion in, 21, 22, 36; Islam and, 9, 11, 15–21, 81, 126–27; monks and monasticism in, 20, 101, 125; mysticism in, 39, 40, 41; Neoplatonists and, 100; nuns and convents in, 53, 62, 125; orthodoxy of, 79; as People of the Book, 17–18, 127; priests in, 65; same-sex desire and, 79–81; taboos and, 37; Trinitarians, 128; women and, 47–48; *zunnār* and, 124, 128, 139, 145, 146. *See also* Church, Catholic
Church, Catholic: clerics of, 53–55, 125; same-sex desire and, 78; women and, 53. *See also* Christianity, Christians
Circle of Justice, 29
Clanchy, Michael T., 54
class. *See* society
comparative studies, 4, 7–8; of culture, 9; of transgressive love, 12
concubinage, 48, 78
contrapuntal reading, 2, 43, 46; of ʿAṭṭār and Foucault, 92, 126, 148–49; of ʿAṭṭār and medieval European

literature and modern theory, 4–6, 11, 13, 159
conversion, 12; to Christianity, 124, 125, 126, 128, 139; to Islam, 17, 20, 45, 124, 126, 127, 136–37, 146; politics of, 4
courtship, 75, 76, 80, 101. *See also* love, courtly
Covenant of ʿUmar, 17–18
Creator, God as, 15, 27, 67, 138, 158; creatures and creations of, 2, 6, 24, 27, 28, 83, 106
Crusades, 17
cultural theory, 5, 42. *See also* theory, modern; *and names of cultural theorists*
Cupid, 89

Damascus, 18, 19, 20
Daulatshāh Samarqandī, 25, 30
de Beauvoir, Simone, 68
Derrida, Jacques, 4
dervishes, 25, 27, 155; adolescent boys and, 71, 73–74, 77
desire: Foucault and, 39; nature and, 33; non-normative, 154; of Rābiʿa al-ʿAdawiyya for divine, 50; redefinition of, 71–81; sexual, 73, 101; *ṭamaʿ*, 60–61
dhimmī (non-Muslims), 17–18; Christian, 19
Dihkhudā, *Lughat-nāma* (Dihkhudā's dictionary), 51, 55, 57, 73, 83, 90, 91, 128
dīn al-ḥaqq (religion of Truth), Islam as, 16
Dionysus, 38–39
diversity in: ʿAṭṭār's works, 8, 30, 72; embracing of, 3, 6; human, 1, 2, 6, 151–60; nonuniversality of, 8; sexual, 72
divine, the, 25; ʿarsh (throne of), 24; breath of, 103; contemplation of, 76; erotic and, 40; holy fools and, 102; light of, 134; other, 6, 46, 100; path to, 24, 29, 112, 157; praise of, 106; proximity of, 137; selfless love for, 26, 50, 61, 82; Sufi lover of, 119; surrender to, 6, 140; (re)union with, 10, 15, 21, 26, 29, 49, 61, 66–67, 70, 84, 85, 91, 126, 128, 129, 133; unveiling of, 83–84, 85, 105
divorce, 48, 62
dīwāna (madman), 102. *See also* madness
Dīwān (*Collection of Poetry*) (book of poetry by ʿAṭṭār), 23
Dols, Michael, 96–97
domestic sphere, 54, 55
dreams, 73; Nietzsche on, 38

ecstasy, 68
ego, 59; annihilation of, 9, 25, 29, 61, 100, 145, 147; breaking of Majnūn's, 110; egoism and, 129–30, 141; God's grace and, 156. *See also* identity; self
Egypt, 17, 20
Enlightenment, 42, 145
ephebe (beautiful human being), 9, 21
equality: for all Muslims, 17; gender, 49–50; of individuals, 6
Ernst, Carl W., *Teachings of Sufism*, 52
erotic, eroticism, 36; in ʿAṭṭār's Sufi lyrics, 99; divine and, 40; eros and, 99; language of, 29, 108; poetry of, 101
Europe, medieval, 8; celibacy and marriage in, 64; chivalric codes in, 101; courtly love in, 12, 99; culture of, 1, 2, 3; England in, 46, 53; Middle East and, 81; religious oppression in, 125; same-sex desire and relationships in, 11, 71–94
European literature, 2, 3, 5, 8, 78–81, 125; Ganymede topoi in, 80
Eve, 59; as tainted, 53, 58
excess, Bataille and, 33
exclusion, 1, 6, 7. *See also* inclusion, inclusiveness

excrement, Bataille and, 33

Fakhry, Majid, 27
al-Fārābī, Abū Naṣr Muḥammad, 73
Farina, William, 98
femininity: Margery Kempe and, 10, 46, 55, 57, 58, 59, 68; in medieval England, 53; of Rābiʿa al-ʿAdawiyya, 51–52, 55
fiqh (Islamic jurisprudence), 19
Firdawsī, 128
al-Fīrūzābādī, Majd al-Dīn, 73
flame, as metaphor, 84–85, 111–12, 131
Foucault, Michel, 1, 3, 46, 84, 92, 103, 158; antihumanist tendencies of, 145; in dialogue with ʿAṭṭār, 5, 11, 13, 42–43, 72, 90, 113, 126, 140, 148–49, 151; *Discipline and Punish*, 6; on genealogy, 6; *The History of Sexuality*, 74–76; on homosexuality, 74; influences on, 10, 37; modern theory and, 39–41; "Preface to Transgression," 39–41; sexual transgression and, 37; on spiral movement of boundary crossing, 5, 39–41, 117; taboo breaking and, 70, 72; transgression and boundary crossing and, 5, 10, 62, 86, 100, 105, 110, 129, 131, 140, 152
Fradenburg, Aranye: *Sacrifice Your Love*, 6; Louise Fradenburg and Carla Freccero, 81; on sovereign love, 126
French Revolution, 31
Freud, Sigmund, 39, 40, 59, 105
Furūzānfar, Badiʿ al-Zamān, 25–26, 30, 115

Ganymede topoi in medieval European literature, 80
gender, 5; in ʿAṭṭār's works, 7, 49; binary of, 50; boundaries and norms of, 10, 11, 21, 46–47, 62–63, 48, 82, 85, 93; medieval demarcations of, 47–48, 51, 55, 69, 74; nonuniversality of, 8; Rābiʿa al-ʿAdawiyya and, 49–50; relations between, 99; roles of, 74; unity of, 51. *See also* male, males; woman, women
genealogy: Foucault on, 6; of literary theory, 9–10
Ghānim al-Maqdisī, 50
ghazals, 28, 30
Ghaznavid Empire, 71, 76
al-Ghazzālī, Aḥmad (1061–1123), 9, 21, 28
al-Ghazzālī, Muḥammad (1058–1111), 50, 73; *Tuḥfat al-mulūk* (*Masterpieces of the Saints*), 123
God: Adam and, 152; appearing as human, 21, 73; communicating with, 65–66; creates man, 26; creations of, 2, 6, 9, 21, 22, 83; death of, 38, 40, 41, 140; disregards forms, 50; as embodiment of infinite, 40, 43; faith in one, 17; in form of beardless youth, 73; friends of, 102; generosity of, 159; grace of, 156, 157; love as essence of, 28–29; love of, 9, 11; mercy of, 136; path toward, 113; praise of, 23, 24; presence and absence and, 118; pursuit of Eternal Presence of, 24; in Quran, 15; Rābiʿa al-ʿAdawiyya's communication with, 56–57; rights of (*ḥaqq Allah*), 74; Sade on, 33; seeing, 115; union with, 120; will of, 29. *See also* Creator, God the; divine, the
Greece, ancient: gods of, 38; homosexuality in, 74–75; language of, 19–20; logic of, 49; philosophers of, 100; *shāhidbāzī* originates in, 72
Griffith, Sidney, 17–18
Guinevere, Lancelot and, 97–98, 104, 110, 117, 120
Gurgānī, Fakhr al-Dīn, *Vīs and Rāmīn*, 77

al-Ḥallāj, Manṣūr, 20, 29, 112; ʿAṭṭār's biography of, 23; execution of, 27–28; followers of, 28; influences ʿAṭṭār, 9, 26
al-Hamadānī, ʿAyn al-Quḍāt (967–1007), 21, 28, 50; works of, 9
Hārūn al-Rashīd, 20, 127
al-Ḥasan al-Baṣrī, 18; Rābiʿa al-ʿAdawiyya and, 51–52, 55, 60, 61
al-Hāshimī, Muḥammad ibn, 61–62
Ḥaylān, Yuḥannā ibn, 20
Heath, Jennifer, 56
Hellwarth, Jennifer, 58
Heloise: Abelard and, 12, 13, 125, 135–36, 142–44; intelligence of, 125, 135
heresy, heretics, 53, 65
Hoffman, Valerie, 60–61
Hollywood, Amy, 62; *Sensible Ecstasy*, 70
Homer, 20
homoeroticism, homoerotic relationships: Sufism and, 71–94; of Sultan Maḥmūd and Ayāz, 81–92
homosexuality, homosexuals, 42; as inadequate term, 74; as marginalized, 13; queering malehood and, 86, 93; sodomy and, 81
Hrabanus Maurus, 80
al-Hujwīrī, ʿAlī ibn ʿUthmān al-Jullābī, 73
hulūl (incarnation), 73
humanism, 42, 79
humanity: in ʿAṭṭār's works, 5; love of, 8; source of, 62
humility, 84, 92, 109, 111, 114, 116
Ḥunayn ibn Isḥāq, as translator, 20
hunting and game metaphors, 80–81; in *Ilāhī-nāma*, 87, 89–90
hypocrisy, hypocrites, 23, 24, 65, 102, 117

Iblīs (Satan), in *Ilāhī-nāma*, 87
Ibn (Abū Alī) Sīnā (Avicenna), *Risāla fi'l ʿishq* (*Treatise on Love*), 73; *Qānūn* (*The Canon of Medicine*), 101
Ibn al-ʿArabī, 4, 28
Ibn Dāwūd, 96
Ibn Ḥazm, *The Neck-Ring of the Dove*, 98
Ibn Qutayba, 96
Ibn-Saghā, 123
Ibn-Saqā, 123
identity: de- and reconstruction of, 9, 12, 21, 25, 41, 46, 82, 91, 120, 135; reshaping of, 10. *See also* self
Ilahi-Ghomshei, Husayn, 128–29
Ilāhī-nāma (*The Book of God*) (lyrical poem by ʿAṭṭār), 9, 22, 25, 152, 155–56; catamite in, 154–55; gambler in, 157–58; holy fools in, 102; Majnūn and Lailā's love story in, 95; quotations from, 82–83, 84, 85, 86, 87, 88, 89–90, 115, 116, 117, 119, 154, 156, 157–58; repentance in, 156; review of, 23–24; romantic language in, 87, 90; "Story of Fakhr al-Dīn Gurgānī and the Sultan's Slave" in, 77; Sultan Maḥmūd in, 71; Sultan Maḥmūd and Ayāz's homoerotic relationship in, 82–90
ʿilm al-ḥadīth (sayings of Muḥammad), 19
imaginary, sociocultural, 7
incest, 32, 37
inclusion, inclusiveness, 1, 7; in ʿAṭṭār's works, 8, 29, 151; human diversity and, 151–60; in medieval period, 13; of minorities, 2; nonuniversality of, 8. *See also* exclusion
India, 23, 71
indiscretion and discretion, 11, 74, 75, 77, 82, 90, 95, 101
intention, 50, 51
Iran, 8, 28, 30, 73; medieval, 121, 125; modern, 13, 71
Iraq, 17, 18, 45, 48

Irigaray, Luce, 69
al-Iṣfahānī, Abū Faraj, 96
al-Iṣfahānī, Abū Nuʿaym, 50
ʿishq (profane love), 9, 22, 25, 28. *See also* love, profane
Islam, 8, 16, 17, 19; Christianity' interaction with, 11, 15–21, 47–48, 81, 124, 126–27; conversion to, 17, 20, 45, 124, 127, 136–37, 146; expansion of, 9, 126; literary tradition of, 98; marriage in, 11–12, 48, 95, 99; orthodoxy in, 21, 22, 73; patriarchy in, 11, 52, 99; pork and, 140; sins in, 74; as universal religion, 16, 17; wine forbidden in, 12, 22, 124, 128, 139, 148; women and, 10, 11, 45–46, 47–48. *See also* Muslims; Sufis; Sufism
Islamic Empire, 18, 19, 55
Israel of Kashgār, 20

Jafar Sādiq, 23
al-Jāhiz of Basra, 50; on Rābiʿa al-ʿAdawiyya, 49
Jāmī, Maulānā ʿAbd al-Raḥmān, 26, 27, 30; *Nafaḥāt al-uns* (*Breaths of Intimacy*), 25, 49–50
Jamīl al-ʿUdhrī, 97
Jamnia, Mohammad Ali, on *Ilāhī-nāma*, 24
al-Jawālīqī, Hishām ibn Sālim, 73
al-Jawzī, Abū al-Faraj ibn, 73, 101; *Dhamm al-hawā* (*Vilifying Love*), 101; *Talbīs Iblīs* (*The Devil's Delusion*), 73–74
Jerusalem, 16, 17
Jesus Christ, 157; Abelard and, 147; as 'Isa, 51; as Logos, 21; Margery Kempe and, 46, 67–68; in medieval paintings, 78
al-jizyah (poll tax), 17–18, 127
jouissance (Lacan), 41–42, 86, 126; Margery Kempe and, 59
Judaism, Jews, 16, 47; Islam and, 127; as People of the Book, 17–18, 127; pork and, 140
Judgment Day, 15, 18, 155–56
Julian of Norwich, 20–21, 46
al-Junayd, Abū al-Qāsim, 73
justice, 29, 55

Kai Kā'ūs Iskandar, *Qabūs-nāma*, 29
al-Kalābādhī, Abū Bakr, 49
kalām (Islamic theology), 19
Karras, Ruth, 81
Kasāʾī, 128
Keddie, Nikki, 56
Kempe, John, 46, 53–54
Kempe, Margery: *The Book of Margery Kempe*, 10, 46, 54–55, 57, 58, 65, 67, 68, 70; celibacy of, 60, 64; compared to Rābiʿa al-ʿAdawiyya, 10, 46, 55, 57, 60, 64, 65–66, 68–70; life of, 46; thyng of, 58–59; as transgressor, 53, 54; unites with Jesus Christ, 67–68; visions of, 57
Keroes, Jo, 135
Keshavarz, Fatemeh, 134–35; "Flight of the Birds," 4
Khurāsān, 22, 30, 49, 50
King Arthur, 97, 98
kings and leaders, 29: hypocrisy of, 23; in *Ilāhī-nāma*, 23–24; mirror for princes genre and, 72
knowledge: construction of, 1; production of, 8, 93; spiritual, 26
Kristeva, Julia, 5, 43, 91, 135; on impossible couple, 142, 143; *Tales of Love*, 21; zenith of subjectivity and, 29, 91
Kruger, Steven, *Queering the Middle Ages*, 154
Kubrawīyya order, 26
Kufa, 97

Lacan, Jacques, 4, 5, 43, 46, 66, 70, 142; on courtly love, 105; on *das Ding*, 58–59, 105; on idea, 7; on jouissance, 41–42, 86; on women's

lack of signifier, 68–69; *The Ethics of Psychoanalysis*, 58–59
Lahore, 71, 82
Lailā (Leylā), 11–12; as character type in Persian literature, 5; death of, 96, 105; family of, 95–96, 99, 106; idealized beauty of, 102–6, 115; marriage of, 96; Majnūn's love for, 102, 118; name of, 95, 117; scent of, 104–5, 106, 107. *See also* Majnūn and Lailā love story
Lailā and Majnūn, 77
Lancelot: Guinevere and, 97–98, 104, 110, 117, 120; suffering of, 114
Landolt, Hermann, "ʿAṭṭār, Sufism and Ismailism," 26
Latin, 54, 65
law, laws, 7, 41; ʿAṭṭār and, 120; Bataille on, 36–37, 38; breaking of, 2, 3, 4, 5; Islamic, 19; Lacan on, 42; moralists and, 32; religious, 12; superego and, 42, 142; violation and transgression of, 11, 31, 42, 62, 72, 106–14, 129, 138–44. *See also* taboo, taboos
Letters of Abelard and Heloise, The, 125
Lévinas, Emmanuel, 5, 43, 132, 133
Lévi-Strauss, Claude, 37
Lewis, Franklin, 128; "Sexual Occidentation," 4
Lewisohn, Leonard, 1–2, 4, 99, 129
libertinage, libertines: Bataille on, 34; in *Ilāhī-nāma*, 157–58; Sade on, 31–33
liminality, 5; in ʿAṭṭār's works, 29, 43; construction of, 3
limit, the: ʿAṭṭār's use of, 3, 43, 118, 132–33, 140; Foucault and, 40–41, 92, 100, 110, 152; genealogy of, 6, 9–10; Lacan on, 105; transgression and, 1, 2, 6, 10, 41, 62, 86, 93, 100, 110, 129, 140, 151, 152
literacy, women and, 54
literature, 5; European, 2, 3, 5, 8, 78–81, 125; image of real in, 7; interpretation of, 4; Islamic, 98; textual transmission and literary production and, 123–24; theory and, 2; topoi in, 80. *See also* Persian literature
logic, 36, 43, 86; ʿAṭṭār and, 4, 120, 158; freedom from, 131, 142; Greek, 49; as limit, 40, 41, 92, 103, 140; loss of, 119. *See also* reason
Logos, Christ as, 21
Lollardy, 46, 53, 65
love: alternative ways of loving and, 93; Aṭṭār and, 2, 28–29, 42, 43, 82, 103, 118, 126, 129–30, 145, 148, 159; Capellanus on, 100; Christian, 4; ego annihilated by, 129–30; eros and, 99; al-Ḥallāj on, 27; heart and, 86, 87, 90; idealized, 98; internalization of, 119; *maḥabba*, 22; reason and, 145; sovereign, 126; subversive, 138–44; in Sufism, 9, 26–28, 103; transformative power of, 8, 11, 21, 77, 79, 87, 92, 93, 109, 113–18, 129, 136, 148
love, chaste, 97, 100–101, 104
love, courtly: Arab tradition of, 97; Lacan on, 105; lover and beloved in, 104, 114; in medieval Europe, 12, 95, 98, 99, 101, 104, 110, 114
love, divine or sacred, 2, 3, 28–29, 71, 103, 139; in ʿAṭṭār's works, 151; Christian Child trope and, 128–29; earthly love and, 9, 21, 25, 27; Margery Kempe's turn to, 10, 46; as pure, 124; spiritual love as, 97; Sufis and, 9, 21, 105; thresholds for, 12, 100
love, passionate, 84–85, 96, 98; ʿAṭṭār's positive view of, 100; madness and, 101; Majnūn's, 102, 103, 113; in Muslim mysticism, 99; reason vs., 110; of Shaykh Ṣanʿān, 131
love, profane or earthly, 9, 25, 27, 62, 97, 101, 151; narratives of, 3; Sufis and, 21, 22, 29. See also ʿishq

love, transgressive: passionate love as, 98; as Sufi ideal, 99; as theme in ʿAṭṭār's works, 2, 8, 89
love, unconventional: ʿAṭṭār and, 2, 3, 89; narratives of, 3, 95, 123, 151
love madness: condemnation of, 100–102; of Lancelot, 111; of Majnūn, 11–12, 95, 96, 99, 113, 120
love mysticism, 26–28, 146
love of God, 93; love of God's creations and, 2, 6, 9; ʿAṭṭār's, 72
Llull, Ramon, as Christian mystic, 20
lust, 60, 101, 113, 119, 143, 157

madness, 33; art and, 38–39; of Majnūn, 95, 96, 99, 120. See also *dīwāna*; love madness
al-Mahdī, 19–20
Maḥmūd of Ghazna, 23, 24; as character type in Persian literature, 5; Malik Ayāz's same-sex relationship with, 10–11, 71, 72, 81–92, 93, 151, 152
Majd al-Dīn of Baghdad, 26
Majnūn and Lailā love story, 151; in ʿAṭṭār's works, 95–121; compared to Lancelot and Guinevere story, 95, 97, 98, 120; history of, 96–97; narrative lines of, 95–97
Majnūn (Qays): as character type in Persian literature, 5; death of, 96; as epitome of mystical lover, 97, 152; madness of, 95, 96, 99, 120; name change of, 106; renounces society, 106, 110; self-annihilation of, 116–17; spiritual transformation of, 118–19; story of, 11–12, 95–96; as Sufi lover, 119–20; traits of holy fools possessed by, 102
Makkī, Abū Ṭālib Muḥammad ibn ʿAlī, 49, 61
male, males, 46–47; acknowledgment of, 70; beauty of adolescent, 71, 71, 75–76; Christian, 57; desire for adolescent, 74–77, 80; as ideal in Sufism, 52, 63; passivity of, 75; pride and, 101; as prostitutes, 78, 81; queering malehood and, 86, 93; as slave masters, 48, 56; stereotypes of, 103; view Rābiʿa al-ʿAdawiyya's spirituality, 48–52, 69
Maleki, Hurmuz, 145
Malikshāh of Seljuk, 22
Mallory, Thomas, *Morte d'Arthur* (*The Death of Arthur*), 98
Manṭiq al-ṭayr (*Conference of the Birds*) (lyrical poem by ʿAṭṭār), 4, 9, 22, 23, 152; Majnūn and Lailā's love story in, 95, 106–19; quotations from, 91, 106–8, 109, 111, 112, 113, 130, 133, 134–35, 137, 138–39, 139–40, 141, 144–45, 146, 155, 157, 159; review of, 24–25; Shaykh Ṣanʿān and the Christian Girl story in, 123, 130–35; sinner in, 156–57; Sultan Maḥmūd and Ayāz's homoerotic relationship in, 88; transvestite in, 155
Marbod of Rennes, 80
marginalized, socially, 2, 160; as ʿAṭṭār's characters, 3, 8, 12, 13, 25, 30, 133, 152, 158; Majnūn as, 11–12, 106–14
Marie de Champagne, 97
marriage, 100; of Abelard and Heloise, 125, 135–36, 142–43; in Islam, 11–12, 48, 95, 99; Rābiʿa al-ʿAdawiyya and, 45, 60–62; medieval European women and, 53
Mary of Oignies, 54
master-slave relationship: fluidity of, 93; reversal of, 85, 86, 92
Mecca, 15, 145; ʿAṭṭār's pilgrimage to, 26; Shaykh Ṣanʿān and, 124, 146
medieval era, 8; concepts of, 6; egalitarianism in, 1; gender hierarchies and paradigms in, 50, 52, 53; queering of, 154; religious paradigms of, 126–27; studies of, 4, 6; subjectivity in, 4, 7, 11, 43, 90, 124, 151; tolerance in, 152

Medina, 16, 18, 96
Mesopotamia, 127
metaphor: in ʿAṭṭār's works, 133–34; body and, 129; erotic language as, 29; for pain, 111–12
Middle East: Christian environment of, 15–16; Europe and, 81, 98; Islam and, 9, 15, 47; justice in, 29; medieval culture of, 1, 2–3, 4, 8; religious oppression in, 125; urban, 48
millet system, 18
minorities, 1, 5, 156; integration of, 4; modern treatment of, 2; tolerance for, 79
mirror, mirrors: art as, 7; Foucault and, 110; heart and, 130; Lailā as, 105; man as, 27; Shaykh Ṣanʿān's Christian girl as, 134
Mirror for Princes genre, 29
misogyny, 47–48
modernism, 39
modesty, 32
monotheism, 16, 87
moon, 49, 50
morality: in ʿAṭṭār's works, 5; Sade on, 32–33
Morris, William, 98
moth, as metaphor for pain, 111–12
motherhood, mothers, 10, 46; Margery Kempe and, 54, 55, 57, 58, 67, 68
Mukhtār-nāma (*The Book of the Empowered*), (book of poetry by ʿAṭṭār), 23
al-Mulawwaḥ, Qays ibn (Majnūn), 97
Musāḥiq, Nawfal ibn, 96
Muṣībat-nāma (*The Book of Suffering*) (lyrical poem by ʿAṭṭār), 9, 22, 23, 25, 26, 152; Abū Saʿīd Abū al-Khayr Mihna in, 159; Majnūn and Lailā's love story in, 95, 103–4, 118; review of, 24; Sultan Maḥmūd and Ayāz's homoerotic relationship in, 82, 90–91, 92; Sultan Maḥmūd in, 71–72
Muslims: conquests of, 17; early, 9; equality of, 127; hospitality and, 158; slavery and, 55–56; social status of, 106; women as, 10, 45–46. *See also* Islam
mystical literature, 8
mysticism: animals and, 106; asceticism and, 129–38, 145, 147; Christian, 9, 20–21, 39, 79, 103; definition of, 27; erotic language and, 29; in Islam, 19, 20–21; love, 26; of Margery Kempe, 47; nature of, 70; Persian tradition of, 28; of Rābiʿa al-ʿAdawiyya, 10, 46, 47, 57, 62; women's, 69. *See also* mystics; Sufis; Sufism
mystics: Christian, 9, 40, 41, 62; ecstatic experiences of, 37; female, 10; rapture of, 139–40; Sufi, 12, 15, 140, 147

Najmabadi, Afsaneh, 74, 76
Najm al-Dīn Kubrā, as ʿAṭṭār's master, 26
narratives: ʿAṭṭār's, 5; binary, 1; homoerotic, 71; of Majnūn and Lailā's love, 95–100; of profane love, 3; of same-sex love, 10–11; of unconventional love, 3, 95
Nāṣir Khusraw, *Jāmiʿal-ḥikmatayn* (*The Reconciliation of Philosophy and Religion*), 128
nature: crimes against, 32; culture and, 39; sex and, 33
naẓar (gaze, glance), 85, 89, 101
naẓarbāzī (gazing at beardless adolescent boys), 10–11, 71, 72, 76, 85
Near East, 9, 15–16
Nebenmensch (neighbor), 59
Neoplatonists, 9, 21, 100, 101
Nestorians, 20
Nicholson, Reynold A., 23
Nietzsche, Friedrich, 1, 31; Foucault influenced by, 37–39; transgression and limit and, 5, 10
Nizāmī Ganjavī, 97

North Africa, 17
nuns, 53, 62, 125. *See also* Heloise

obscenity, 33
Oghūz Turks, 22
other, the: absolute, 59, 105; acceptance of, 89, 155–56; Christian, 129, 131, 133; desire for, 144; divine, 6, 46, 67, 100, 118, 119, 129; embracing of, 92, 118, 156; face of, 132, 135; self and, 2, 5, 7, 37, 41, 67, 92, 129, 147, 151; societal, 6, 30, 31, 100, 118, 119
otherness, 83, 86, 158; disappearance of, 91, 92, 118; embracing of, 93
Ottomans, 17, 18
outcasts, in ʿAṭṭār's works, 6, 31, 156
Ovid, 101; *Art of Love*, 79

Pakistan, 71
Palestine, 17
Pand-nāma (*The Book of Counsel*) (book of poetry by ʿAṭṭār), 23
paradise, 27, 96, 115, 145, 159
passion. *See* love, passionate
patriarchy: in Islam, 11, 52, 99; in medieval Europe, 64
pederasty, pederasts (*mukhannas̱*), 63, 64
performativity: Butler on, 153; subversion of, 144–47
Persia, medieval: army of, 76; in ʿAṭṭār's time, 21; conquered by Muslims, 17; culture of, 3, 8; poets of, 1; popular national leaders of, 24; Seljuk Empire and, 9
Persian Gulf, 18
Persian (language), 51, 84; Middle, 20; in Muslim world, 2; puns in, 24. *See also* Dihkhudā, *Lughat-nāma*
Persian literature, 5, 8, 28–29, 97; *adab* (literary canon) and, 102; character types in, 3, 5; contemplation of divine in, 103; idol in, 132; love stories in, 77; Majnūn narrative lines in, 11, 96; poetry of, 104, 111, 128, 132; puns in, 25; *shāhid* in, 76; of Sufis, 22, 30, 76–77; *Tadhkirat al-awlīyā* and, 23; *tarsā-bachcha* in, 128
pilgrimages, 26, 46; by Margery Kempe, 54; by pious women, 53. *See also* Mecca
pīr (Sufi master), 24, 25; Shaykh Ṣanʿān as, 12
Plato, 9, 100; on art, 7; on beauty, 21; erotics of, 75–76; *Phaedrus*, 21; Truth and, 76
pleasure, 34; Freud's principle of, 59; Lacan on, 41–42; sex and, 33, 58; Sade on, 33; transgression and, 31–32
poetry, poems, 128; of ʿAṭṭār, 5, 9, 10–11, 22, 23–25, 92, 96, 99, 103, 104–5, 113, 120; Bataille and, 33; early medieval European, 80; eroticism and sexuality in, 77, 101; exilic, 2; Majnūn's, 95, 99; Persian, 28–29, 76, 96, 104, 132; slaves in, 76; Sufi, 30; ʿudhrī, 97
polygamy, 48
polytheism, polytheists, 16
post-Enlightenment movement, 31
postmodernism, 1, 39
power: construction of, 1; Foucault and, 39; of love, 8, 11, 21, 77, 79, 87, 92, 93, 109, 113–18, 129, 136, 148
priests, 35–36
profane: ʿAṭṭār on, 138; Bataille and, 33
prophecy, in Quran, 15
Prophet Muḥammad, 17, 19, 127, 134, 156; asceticism of, 15; death of, 16, 47; as foremost mystical master, 24; *Ḥadīth al ruʾyā* of, 73; on intention, 50; praise of, 23; prayers answered by, 146; Quran and, 9; sayings of, 73; Shaykh Ṣanʿān and, 124; son-in-law of, 154; in *Tadhkirat al-awlīyā*, 50, 51; tribe of, 45; wife of, 51
prostitutes, male, 78, 81
Ptolemy, *Almagest*, 20
public sphere, women and, 53

Qādisiyyah, battle of, 17
al-Qārī, Sarrāj, 50; *Maṣāri' al-'ushshāq (The Gates of Lovers)*, 96
queering, of medieval literature, 154
Quran, 9, 19; burning of, 12, 124, 125, 127, 139; on Jews and Christians, 127; Sūra 5:59, 26; Sūra 7:172, 15; Zulaikhā's love for Yūsuf in, 103–4
al-Qushayrī, Abū al-Qāsim, *al-Risāla fī 'ilm al-Taṣawwuf (Epistle on Sufism)*, 49, 50, 73

real, reality, 7, 38, 133, 137, 153
reason, 42, 86, 145; passionate love vs., 101, 107, 110. *See also* logic
reciprocity, self-transformation and, 123–26
reductionism, 3–4
religion, 7, 8, 12, 40; Bataille on, 36–37; orthodoxy in, 46; paradigms of medieval, 126–27; Sade on, 32–33. *See also* Christianity, Christians; Church, Catholic; Islam; taboo, taboos
repentance, 156; of Rābi'a al-'Adawiyya, 57; of Shaykh Ṣan'ān's Christian girl, 136–37
riqbat (long for), 60
Ritter, Hellmut, 86, 111, 113–14; *The Ocean of the Soul*, 4
Roded, Ruth, 64
Romance of Lancelot and Guinevere, The, 12
Roman Empire, 20; decline of, 79; same-sex relations in, 78–79
Rossetti, Dante Gabriel, 98
el-Rouayheb, Khaled, 74
Rukn al-Dīn, 26
Rūm, 124, 145, 146, 154
Rūmī, Jalāl al-Dīn, 21, 22, 28, 154; 'Aṭṭār meets, 30; *Masnavī*, 30; writings of, 4, 9
Rykener, John, 81

sacred: 'Aṭṭār on, 138; Bataille and, 33; Foucault and, 41. *See also* divine, the
Sade, Donatien Alphonse François, Marquis de, 1, 31; Bataille and, 33, 37; *Philosophy in the Bedroom*, 31–33, 34; transgression and limit and, 5, 10
sadism, 37
Sahl ibn Rabn of Ṭabaristān, 20
Said, Edward, 2
St. Aelred of Rievaulx, 80
St. Anne, 46, 57, 67, 68
St. Augustine, 57; *City of God*, 58
St. Bernard, 58, 79
St. Catherine of Genoa, 20
St. John of Damascus, *Pege Gnoseos (The Fount of Knowledge)*, 19
St. John of the Cross, 20
St. Paul, 57
saints, Christian, 9, 21
same-sex desire, 77, 78–81
same-sex relationships, 64, 71–94; Ganymede topoi and, 80; in Iran, 76; love narratives of, 10–11, 77; passive and active members of, 74, 78–79, 89, 91, 93; in Persian literature, 76–77
Sanā'ī Ghaznavī, 30, 48
al-Sarrāj, Abū Naṣr, 50
Sassanian Empire, 16–17, 48
Satan, 87, 152–53
Sattari, Jalal, 129, 136
Saunders, Corinne, 111
Schimmel, Annemarie, 102, 103, 106; on 'Aṭṭār's works, 23, 25, 28; on love in Sufism, 27, 130
Schopenhauer, Arthur, 38
scribes: as male, 10, 69; of Margery Kempe, 46, 47, 54, 69, 70
self: annihilation of, 6, 25, 28, 46, 82, 84, 90, 92, 109, 119, 156; divine other and, 15, 67; individuation and, 38; losing, 89, 90; lower (*nafs*), 28, 141; medieval, 93; negation of, 118; new, 10; other and, 2, 5,

7, 37, 41, 90, 91, 93, 147, 151; reconstruction of, 95, 105, 110, 140. *See also* ego; identity
self-transformation, reciprocity and, 123–26
Seljuk Empire, 9, 22
Sells, Michael, 4, 51
sexuality, 5, 8, 42, 52; in ʿAṭṭār's works, 7, 91, 93; Bataille on, 33, 34–35; bi-, 32; boundaries of, 11, 21; Foucault and, 39–41, 43, 140, 145; hetero-, 42, 78; Kinsey Reports and, 37; Margery Kempe's, 68; mystical, 62, 69; pleasure and, 33, 58; Sade on, 32–33; sexual identity and, 81; sexual intercourse and, 125; as site for power and knowledge construction, 1, 10; of slaves, 56; transgressive, 39–40; trauma and, 55–60; women's, 10, 47, 49–50, 99
Seyed-Gohrab, Ali Asghar, 29, 104
Shabistarī, Maḥmūd, *Gulshan-i rāz* (*Garden of Mystery*), 128
shahadah, 17
shāhidbāzī (gazing at beardless adolescent boys), 10–11, 71, 73, 76, 77, 82, 85, 90; ʿAṭṭār breaks from, 72, 93; condemnation of, 73–74; courtship ritual of, 80
shāhid (eyewitness or testimony; witness to divine beauty), 22, 73, 76, 80, 128, 137; Lailā as Majnūn's, 95, 103, 105, 108; Shaykh Ṣanʿān's Christian girl as, 124, 130–31, 133
shame, 109, 133, 146, 155–58; Lancelot's, 98; Majnūn causes, 11, 95, 99; women and, 47, 48, 49, 137
Shamisa, Sirus, 76
sharʿ (divine law), 24. *See also* law, laws
sharīʿa (Islamic law), 19
Shaykh Ṣanʿān and the Christian Girl story, 12, 123–24, 125–26, 127–42, 144–46, 147, 148–49, 151, 152; compared to Abelard and Heloise's story, 125, 135–36; plot of, 124
Shaykh Ṣanʿān (Ṣamʿān): as ascetic, 124; converts to Christianity, 124, 125, 126, 127; disciples of, 144–47; empowered by Christian girl's love, 129; identity of, 123; as transgressor, 128
Shi'ism, 23
shiʿr (poetry), 24. *See also* poetry, poems
sīmurgh (ultimate goal), 25
sin, 40, 76; *liwāṭ*, 74, 76
Sirvatian, Bihruz, 117
slave, slaves, 10; al-ʿAdawiyya, Rābiʿa as, 45–46, 55–57, 64; *gholam* (male), 55, 56; *kaniz* (female), 47–48, 55, 56, 62; love and desire for, 77; Turkish, 76. *See also* Ayāz, Malik
Smith, Margaret, 26, 52, 61–62
society, 8; class and, 5, 7, 62, 86; class boundaries and, 11, 21, 82, 86, 88, 92, 93, 109; non-Muslims in, 17–18; norms of, 21, 81, 87, 109; social marginalization and, 106–14, 133–34; women and, 48
sociology, 5
Socrates, 79
sodomy (*liwāṭ*), sodomites, 32, 33, 73, 78, 79, 81
soul: longing of, 28; purification of, 112, 118; wayfarer's, 130
Spain, 17, 20, 98
spiral movement of boundary crossing (Foucault), 5, 39–41, 92, 117
spirituality: ʿAṭṭār's, 3, 8, 30, 43; in ʿAṭṭār's poetry, 104; crying and, 65; female, 49; growth of, 136; of al-Ḥallāj, 27; of Margery Kempe, 10, 46; public, 53; radical, 2; redefines subjectivity, 68; sexuality and, 37
subject, subjects: destabilized, 42; exiled, 2; modern, 33, 93, 94; new, 46, 68, 89, 92, 136, 145; object and, 37
subjectivity, construction of, 2, 3, 4, 5, 11, 13, 82, 98, 100, 151; Abelard and Heloise's, 126; in ʿAṭṭār's

works, 7, 8, 31, 72, 93, 95, 119, 124, 135, 153; comparative study of, 12; Foucault and, 105; genealogy of, 9–10; Majnūn's, 102; Shaykh Ṣanʿān's, 126, 129
subjectivity, subjectivities, 8; in ʿAṭṭār's poems, 120; deconstruction and reshaping of, 12, 84, 89, 105–6, 126, 148–49; jouissance and, 41–42; medieval, 4, 7, 11, 43, 90, 124, 151; modern, 11, 43, 90, 124, 149, 159–60; redefined by spirituality, 68; renewed, 60; zenith of, 21, 29, 91, 112, 140
submission: to divine, 6, 30, 47, 70; to will of God, 29, 91; of women, 10, 45, 53
subversion: in ʿAṭṭār's works, 88, 92, 93, 141; of master-disciple relationship, 145; of performativity, 144–47; of Shaykh Ṣanʿān, 124, 127, 138, 140; subversive love and, 95, 100, 131, 138–44
suffering and pain: jouissance and, 42; of love and lovers, 97, 114; of neediness (*mustamand*), 85; purgation and, 63; on Sufis' path to divine love, 28, 67, 77, 91, 108, 112, 113; symbols of, 111; of wayfarers seeking Truth, 24
Sufis: in ʿAṭṭār's *Tadhkirat al-awlīyā*, 23; beauty of young boys and, 76; disciples of, 144–47; God seen by some, 73; early, 15; female, 10; *Ḥulūlīs* as, 73; indulgences of, 101; as masters, 12; mystical longing of, 93; as Neoplatonists, 101; as poets, 1, 29, 30; quest for divine by, 24; on path to divine, 133; pride and, 155; rapture of, 12, 85, 96; *shāhidbāzī* and, 72–81; Shaykh Ṣanʿān as, 130; surrender to divine by, 6, 109, 118; view Rābiʿa al-ʿAdawiyya's spirituality, 48–52
Sufism, 3, 4, 26, 48, 158; asceticism in, 26, 129; ʿAṭṭār and, 9, 25–26, 159; background to, 9; becomes public, 28; Christian-Arabic literature of resistance and, 19; divine beauty in, 103; early writers on, 50; holy fools in, 102; homoeroticism and, 71–94; literature of, 128; love in, 5, 8, 9, 21, 99, 103, 113, 120, 126; male as ideal in, 52; modern theoretical perspectives on, 4; order of (*silsila*), 26, 76; origins of, 15, 20–21; perception of divine in, 105; Rābiʿa al-ʿAdawiyya and, 46, 49, 62; sacred and profane in, 102; Satan and, 87; scholarship on, 7, 13; sexual desire and, 60; *shāhidbāzī* in, 10–11, 71, 72–81; as transgressive, 93; Umayyads and, 18–19, 20; woolen coat (*khirqih*) of, 108
Suhrawardī, Shahāb al-Dīn, 73
al-Sulamī, Muḥammad ibn al-Ḥusain, 73
Sultan Sanjar, 22
summa theologiae, as Christian literary genre, 19
sun, 49, 50; as metaphor, 134–35
surplus, Bataille on, 33
surrender: to divine, 6, 70, 140; humility and, 84
swine: herding, 140; inner, 141
symbolism, symbols: in ʿAṭṭār's works, 5; literature and, 7
Syria, 17, 18, 19, 127
Syriac language, 19–20

taboo, taboos (*ḥarām*): in Aṭṭār's works, 42, 106, 126, 140; Bataille and, 36–37; breaking of, 2, 10, 70, 16, 126, 129; Foucault and, 10, 70; religious, 126, 140; sexual, 78–79
Tadhkirat al-awlīyā (*Memoirs of the Saints*) (ʿAṭṭār's only prose work), 9, 22; compared to *The Book of Margery Kempe*, 10; al-Ḥallāj in, 27, 28; quotations from, 49, 50–51,

55, 56–57, 60, 61, 63, 66–67; Rābiʿa al-ʿAdawiyya in, 45–47, 49, 50–52, 55–57, 60–63, 66–67, 152; review of, 23
tarsā-bachcha (Christian Child) trope, 12, 127, 128–29, 132
taverns: in Seljuk Empire, 9, 22–23; visiting, 124
temporality, 6
temptation, 74
Tennyson, Alfred Tennyson, First Baron, 98
Theodore bar Koni, *Scholion*, 19
Theophile b. Toma (Theophilus of Edessa), 20
theory, literary, 9–10
theory and theorists, modern, 2, 4–5, 42, 120–21; in dialogue with ʿAṭṭār, 3, 151; Foucault and, 31–43; literature and, 2–3, 8
thing, the: Lacan on, 59, 105; of Margery Kempe, 58
Timothy (catholicos), 20
Tirmidhī, 73
Tötösy de Zepetnek, Steven, 9
Touraje, Mahdi, *Rumi and the Hermeneutics of Eroticism*, 4
transcendence, 8, 15, 83, 91, 133; transgressive sexuality and, 40, 41
transgression of boundaries, 1, 5, 13, 21, 29, 93; ʿAṭṭār's use of, 3, 5–6, 7, 9, 23, 42–43, 92, 119, 120, 125; Bataille on, 36–37; Foucault on, 5, 10, 62, 86, 100, 105, 110; of gender, 46; genealogy of, 6, 9–10; in Islam, 124, 125; limit and, 1, 2, 6, 10, 41, 62, 86, 93, 100, 110, 129, 140, 151, 152; Nietzsche and, 38–39; sexual, 37; *shāhidbāzī* and, 74; social, 106; spectrum of, 31; Sufis and, 91
transgressor, transgressors: in ʿAṭṭār's works, 25, 31, 82, 124; Margery Kempe as, 53, 54; sexual, 155; Shaykh Ṣanʿān as, 124, 125, 138, 140
transvestites, 155
trauma, sexuality and, 55–60
Tristan and Isolde, 77
Truth, 7, 137; al-Ḥallāj and, 27; Platonic, 76; seeking of, 24–25
Turks, as slaves, 76
Ṭūs, 50

ʿUmar ibn ʿAbd al-ʿAzīz, 17, 18
ʿUmar ibn al-Khaṭṭāb, 16, 18
Umayyad caliphate, 17, 18, 19, 20, 45, 96
Uways al-Qaranī, 26

veil and unveiling, 83; divine and, 114–15; of ignorance, 131–32, 137; looking beyond, 7, 142; Sufism and, 27, 105, 112
veiling of women, 47, 50, 131–32
Virgin Mary (Maryam, mother of 'Isa), 21; Rābiʿa al-ʿAdawiyya and, 50, 51; Margery Kempe's mystical conversations with, 46, 57, 67–68; as sacred, 53
virtue, Sade on, 32–33
visions, of Margery Kempe, 55

Waardenburg, Jacques: on Islam, 16
Walad, Bahā al-Dīn, 30, 73
Walafrid, 80
Wallace, John R., 142
waraʿ (abstinence), 60
al-Warrāq, Abū Isā, 73
waste, Bataille on, 33
wayfarer (*sālik*): ego of, 141; feeble, 145; finds peace and love in divine, 26; path of, 29, 50, 130; as seeker of Truth, 24
Webb, James, 4
West: culture of, 2–3, 39; inclusiveness in, 13; literature of, 98; medieval Islam and, 8
wine, 36; Islam and, 12, 22, 124, 128, 139, 148. *See also* taverns
womanhood, Margery Kempe and, 54–55, 65

woman, women: bodies of, 47, 49, 56, 57–58, 59, 64, 68, 70; cults of, 54; in Islam, 10, 11, 45–46; commodification of, 47–48; desexualized, 55; free, 62; illiteracy of, 54; love madness and, 102; as marginalized, 13; marital status of, 53; nonconformity of, 55; religious, 53; sexuality of, 47, 49–50, 99; as slaves, 47–48, 55–56; as spiritual leaders, 48; as victims of sexual assault, 57; as weak, 49

Wycliffe, John, 53

Yarmūk, battle of, 17

Yemen, 123

ẓālim (oppressor, tyrant), 55

Zarrinkub, ʿAbd al-Husayn, 26, 76

Ze'evi, Dror, 74

Zoroastrians, 47, 124, 129

zunnār (belt worn by non-Muslim tribute payers), 124, 128, 139, 145, 146